BRINDLEY GENEALOGY

Including
The James Brindley Clan of Leek
Francis Brinley and New England
'Southern' Brindleys

Gordon Brindley BA

ACKNOWLEDGEMENTS

I am especially grateful to my sister Yvonne Elizabeth Long for her early interest and sustained support. She has contributed a great deal of information to the quest and her research efforts have been invaluable in turning up much of the information which appears to have gone unnoticed by previous Brindley researchers. Chapters 7-10, and 12-13 are substantially her work. She was also my internet mentor and encouraged me to get 'online' which was very good advice.

Many people have contributed their own research data freely and without preconditions. I am particularly grateful to Betty Jane Brindley Chalfont of Tennessee, USA, President of the Brindley International Historic Foundation; Nick Barratt, mediaeval historian, London; Gordon Pooley of Barnsley, Yorkshire; John R. Brinley, Morristown, New Jersey; Pauline Tebbs of North-east England; Alice Haskins of Wales; Barbara Longley of Berkshire; Ivy Mary Brunt of Tean, Staffs; William (Bill) Brindley of Woking; David Brindley, photographer, of Marple and Anglesey; Kathleen M. Evans; Amy Tatlow of Hollington, Staffs; Les Ashton of Stafford; Sheila Clare; Erica Ford: Peter Brindley of Bangor: Norman Brindley of Bedfordshire; Janet Oliver of Worcester; Jane Palmer; David Salt of BMSGH ; Beryl Thompson of Buxton; Kay Stonier of Surrey; Mike Harrison of Generac, France; Dr B. Kiernan; Joyce Hill of Buxton; Ann Sent of Manchester; Liz Brindley of London; Kay Wiss of Macclesfield; Gordon Lomas of Leek; Bob Kapsh; and many others too numerous to mention, who have all contributed information for the benefit of current and future researchers.

George Kieran Brindley

CHURNET VALLEY BOOKS

6 Stanley Street, Leek, Staffordshire. ST13 5HG 01538 399033

www.thebookshopleek.co.uk

© Gordon Brindley and Churnet Valley Books 2002

ISBN 1 897949 88 X

SOURCES ACKNOWLEDGED

Documents, books, parish registers, newspaper articles, census returns, etc, viewed:

American Philosophical Society, Philadelphia, Pennsylvania; Archives of American Art, Smithsonian Institute, Washington, D.C.; Archives of King's College, Cambridge, Cambridge, England; Archives of St John's College, Cambridge, Cambridge, England; Birmingham and Midland Society for Genealogy and Heraldry; Boston Historical Society, Boston, Massachussetts; Boyd's London Citizens; British Library; Buckinghamshire County Council. England; Burke's General Armory, 1884; Burlington Court Court Book of West New Jersey; Cambridge University Archives, Cambridge, England.
Cheshire County Archives, Chester, Cheshire.
Cheshire Family History Society Library, Alderley Edge, Cheshire.
Christ Church, Philadelphia.
Church of the Latter Day Saints, Atlanta, Georgia.
Church of the Latter Day Saints, Salt Lake City, Utah.
College of Arms, London.
Derbyshire Record Office, Matlock, Derbyshire.
Ellis Island Records, New York, New York.
Encyclopedia of American Quaker Genealogy by William Wade Hinshaw.
English Adventures, Vol 521.
Eton College, Eton, Bucks. England.
Fairburn's Book of Crests (1906)
Family History Library, Salt Lake City, Utah.
Friends Historical Society of Swarthmore College, Swarthmore, Pennsylvania.
Genealogical Dictionary of Rhode Island by Austin.
Genealogical Gleanings in England, by Henry F. Waters.
Haberdasher's Company of London
Harpers Ferry Historical Association, Harpers Ferry, West Virginia.
Harvard University Archives, Boston, Massachussetts.
Historical and Genealogical Miscellany by John E. Stillwell.
Historical Society, Newport, Rhode Island.
Historical Society of Pennsylvania, King's Chapel and Burying Ground, Boston, Massachussetts.
History of Bucks County Pennsylvania, Edited by J.H. Battle.
History of the County Palatine of Chester, by George Ormerod, Cheshire.
House of Lords Archives, London.
James Brindley, Engineer, 1716-1772, by Dr Cyril T. Boucher.
James Brindley (Shire books) by Harold Bode.
James Brindley, Canal Engineer. A New Perspective, by Kathleen M. Evans
Latter Day Saints Research Facility, Atlanta, Georgia.
Leek Library, Leek, Staffs, England.
Library of Congress, Washington, D.C.
Lichfield Joint Record Office, Lichfield, Staffs.
Lipscombe's History of the County of Buckingham.
Lives of the Engineers, by Samuel Smiles
Long Island Genealogy.
Macclesfield Library, Macclesfield, Cheshire.
Manchester Central Library, Manchester, England.
Matlock Library, Matlock, Derbyshire, England.
Memorial Biographies of New England.
Memorials of the Dead in Boston, by Robert J. Dunkle and Ann S. Lainhart.
Metropolitan Museum of Art, New York, New York.
Miller's Olde Leeke.
National Society Daughters of the American Revolution.
New York Historical Society, New York.
New England Historic genealogical Society, Boston, Massachussetts.
Oxford University Archives, Oxford, England.
Oxford Ancestors, Oxford, England.
Office of the Mayor, Boston, Massachussetts.
Passenger and Immigration Index.
Passengers and Ships Prior to 1684 by The Welcome Society of Pennsylvania.
Patents and Deeds of New Jersey, edited by William Nelson.

Pennsylvania Land Records, by Donna Bingham Munger.
Pennsylvania State Archives, Harrisburg, Pennsylvania.
Public Record Office, Kew, England.
Randall Holme's Heraldic Collections for Cheshire.
Redwood Library and Atheneum, Newport, Rhode Island
Rhode Island Historic Society, Providence, Rhode Island.
Rocester Parish Church, Rocester, Staffs. England.
Royal College of Surgeons, London, England.
Servants to Foreign Plantations by Gordon Ireland, J.S.D. Cambridge, Massachusetts.
Shirley Eustis House, Roxbury, Massachusetts.
Shelter Island and its Prestbyterian Church, by Rev. Jacob Mallman.
Shelter Island Organisation, Shelter Island, New York.
Sleigh's History of Leek, Staffordshire.
Society of Apothecaries, London.
Society of Genealogists, London.
Stafford Record Office, Stafford, Staffs, England.
Staffordshire Morris Men.
Stockport Central Library
St. Edward's Church, Leek, Staffs.
St. Mary the Virgin, Datchet, Bucks, England.
St. John the Divine, Hollington, Staffs.
St. James's Church, Clerkenwell, London.
St. Thomas's Church, Morgantown, Pennsylvania.
Sylvestor Manor Project, Mac Griswold, University of Massachusetts, Boston. Mass.
The Ancient and Honorable Artillery Company, Boston, Massachussetts.
The History of Burlington County by Major M. Woodward & Mr. Joseph Richards,
The History of Morris Dancing 1458–1750, by John Forrest.
New York, New York.
The Bostonian Society, Boston, Massachussetts.
The Brindleys of Brindley, Leek and London, by Charles A. Hoppin.
The Detroit Institute of Art, Detroit, Michigan.
The Story of the Old Friends Meeting House by Mrs. William P. Buffam
The Town of Roxbury, by Francis S. Drake.
Trinity Episcopal Church, Newport, Rhode Island.
Trinity Church and King's Burying Ground, Boston, Mass.
Uttoxeter Parish Church, St Mary of the Virgins, Uttoxeter, Staffs.
William Salt Library, Stafford, Staffs, England.
Windsor College of Heralds.
Wolverhampton Record Office, Wolverhampton, England.

In uncovering the story of James Brindley, the son of Joseph of Alton, much gratitude goes to Robert Kapsch PhD, ASCE, Hon. AlA, Scholar in Historic Architecture and Historic Engineering with the US National Parks Service, and Ray Nichols, Archivist with Holy Trinity (Old Swedes) Church Foundation. Their sources are as follows:

Holy Trinity (Old Swedes) Church Foundation, Wilmington, Delaware
Wilmington Public Library, Wilmington, Delaware
The Papers of George Washington, Confederation Series 3, 4, 5, years 1786-1787
Science and Technology in the Eighteenth Century by Lawrence Henry Gipson
George Washington, The Potomac Canal and the Beginning of American Civil
Engineering by Robert Kapsch, Ph.D., ASCE, Hon. AlA
Delaware Genealogical Society, Wilmington, Delaware
Lancaster County Historical Society, Lancaster, Pennsylvania
Chester County- Historical Society, West Chester, Pennsylvania
The Historical Society of Pennsylvania, Philadelphia, Pennsylvania
Pennsylvania Historical and Museum Commission, Harrisburg, Pennsylvannia
The Colonial Williamsburg Foundation, John D. Rockefeller Library, Williamsburg, Virginia
The History of York County edited by John Gibson
Maryland State Archives, Annapolis, Maryland
The Historical Society of Harford County, Bel Air, Maryland
Hall of Records Commission, Annapolis, Maryland

CONTENTS

INTRODUCTION

Starting to research your family history is like trying to sort out a thousand piece jigsaw puzzle with only a dozen or so known pieces. The remaining pieces have no detail on them. Not only that, but some pieces seem to fit in several places. You have to solve the mysteries and construct a recognisable picture. Slowly, a little at a time, you have to fill in the detail and painstakingly decide where all the pieces fit. Occasionally, you might have a flash of inspiration or a lucky guess. Eventually, you may have about 60% of the picture. That is how it is! Perspiration, dedication, frustration, consternation; and if you're very lucky - elation.

This book was inspired by the simple desire to know about my ancestors. As a child, I'd always been captivated by tales of the 'olden days'. So, when my grandfather George Edwin Brindley came to stay with us towards the end of his life, I interviewed him in an informal way. I was about nineteen at the time and he was approaching ninety. He was a reticent talker but I managed to draw him out a little and I made brief notes of what he told me for future use. He told of his upbringing at a country inn and riding in a stagecoach as a boy - I didn't know the truth of this but it sounded romantic and I liked to think it was a fact.

This was to be the only occasion I got close to him. He wasn't very communicative to me as a child. He was in the old-fashioned mould, shaped in the Victorian era, believing that children should be seen and not heard. Indeed, I remember Christmases in the 1940s when my cousins and I would gather at his house in the country, and he seemed a formidable, grouchy character in his brown striped suit with waistcoat. He would sit in the parlour, in his favourite armchair, walking stick at the side, pipe in mouth and occasionally taking his fob watch from his waistcoat pocket. He was a king on the throne and we his subjects!

"Ah dunna know wa tha's makin' such a din!" he would growl in his broad native Staffordshire accent, and we would be temporarily quiet as a mouse. The best thing about him then, as far as I was concerned, was the shiny half-crown piece he would shove dutifully in my little hand on my departure.

Although I had made a start, it was soon forgotten as life's distractions impinged on me. My notes festered at the back of a drawer; I was too wrapped up in my own life for more than the occasional foray. However, after a career, marriage, two children and the passage of nearly thirty years, I took the opportunity to take early retirement, and one day, idly wondering what I would do with the rest of my life, I remembered the long forgotten quest - there would never be a better time to get on with it.

My early feeble efforts were a struggle because I knew nothing of the resources available to family researchers. On advice, I joined a family history society and this proved to be an excellent move. The resources and help that then came my way were invaluable because I was on a steep learning curve.

My maternal family surrendered with relative ease (excuse the pun)! A couple of lucky breaks, the timely help of John Fielding of the Cheshire Family History Society at Alderley Edge, and they fell off the tree like apples in an autumn gale. In double quick time I found my maternal Irish links and had gone back two hundred years.

But my Brindleys were not about to be found so easily - though, as you will read later, they were actually there all the time....

As a Brindley whose family roots were well established in North Staffordshire, I had long been aware of the connection of Brindleys to Leek. Leek, one could say, was almost the capital city of Brindleydom. The earliest Brindley family in the area, circa 1450, appears to have been that of Christopher Brindley of Wyldegoose House, Bradnop, a descendent of the original Norman family from Brindley in Cheshire, near Brereton. Wyldgoose Farm still exists and although altered a little, it is still substantially the place it was in the 15th century.

By the early 16th century, a Brindley/Brundley family were occupying the mill at Mill Street, Leek, with their family and had a blacksmith's shop nearby. In 1619, a Lawrence Brindley was trading as a blacksmith in Milne (Mill) Street. Records of that time are sparse because many records were destroyed in the English Civil War or simply lost or decayed. This makes it difficult to prove the relationship between some of those early families. However, the fact that all known Brindleys up to that period were shown to be descended from the original Brundlegh de Brindley makes it hard to doubt that the 16th century Leek Brindleys were of that same origin. There were no other types of Brindleys known!

In 1682, a stonemason called Luke Brindley left Leek for Liverpool, where he boarded one of William Penn's ships, the Friends Adventure, bound for Philadelphia in the new colony of Pennsylvania. Luke was a Quaker, and there is evidence to show that Luke had been to America before, so he must have been reasonably affluent. On this occasion he remained in the new colony and made a new life. He might have been responsible for founding some of the Pennsylvanian and New Jersey Brindleys. Of course, other Brindleys were already in North America and more would continue to emigrate from the old country to America over the next several hundred years.

Over time, the Brindleys' presence increased in Leek. They have been in and near the town ever since. Today, most Leek Brindleys go about their daily lives unconcerned and unaware of their natural family history and heritage. I recently attended St Edward's churchyard intending to view some of the notable Brindley headstones. Sadly, it was impossible to readily identify them. Like graveyards everywhere, the depredations of weather, decay and neglect have obliterated the inscriptions. Fortunately, records still exist which help to identify the locations of the tombs and graves.

As I started searching Parish Records and looking at various census returns, many Brindleys unknown to me were discovered. I hadn't the heart to ignore them. Besides, one never knew if they might eventually prove to be connected to my own family! Soon, I had a growing database of them - almost by stealth, it grew to over twenty thousand entries! Contacts with other Brindleys were established, and I was able to help them find their Brindleys. In turn, they often supplied family trees and other Brindley data.

Early in the quest, I realised that there were many variations in the spelling of what is essentially the same name. Accepted variations include Brandley, Branley, Brainley, Breanley, Brendley, Brenley, Bramley, Bringley, Bringleye, Brinley, Brinaley, Brineley, Brinly, Brinsley, Brindsley, Brindsly, Brindly, Briendley, Brinelea, Brondley, Bronley, Brundelegh, Brundlea, Brundley, Brunlea, Brunley, Brunsley, Brunsleigh, Bruntlea, Bruntlegh, Brandeley, Brimley, Brindeley, Brindleye, Brindliy, Brinlee, Brindlee, Bringley, Brynley, and more.

I had to decide whether or not to include Brindle as a variant. I decided not to, on the grounds that there seemed to be an independently derived family of Brindles in Central Lancashire from early days. Therefore, unless there was indisputable evidence that a Brindle was a Brindley, they are not included. (I welcome any feedback if you know differently) The same thinking decided me not to include Bromley as a variation, except for proven cases. One has to draw the line somewhere!

A good example of the way clergy had trouble interpreting the name is to be seen in the register for Bradley in the Moors, near Alton. Thomas and his wife Zilph/Zilpha/Zilpah had several children baptised on consecutive years from 1797 to 1810. The surname was variously spelt Brinsley, Brunsley, Brindley and Brundley.

Surnames were adopted or came into being in the period from the 14th to 16th century. At first, in England it was only the aristocrats and gentry who had them but gradually the population at large had surnames too. The rule was that the man's surname was what mattered. His wife and children took his surname. The surname was handed on from father to son. Daughters obviously took the name of the man they married. Although this was the norm for hundreds of years, there has always been the possibility of surnames being 'lost', or adopted contrary to the general rule.

Most people who carry the Brindley soubriquet will be Brindleys genealogically but it is worth bearing in mind that occasionally circumstances arise where names are changed or incorrectly applied. The most common reason is aptly demonstrated by the current British Prime Minister, Tony Blair. He carries the name of the couple that adopted him. In his case, he knows the name of his biological parents but others may not.

I recently met a fellow Brindley at a research facility and he told a sad tale. He had been researching his line for many years believing he was a Brindley. Recently, he had arrived six generations back, only to discover that a maternal ancestor, a widow, must have acquired the Brindley name upon her second marriage. The two children she already had by her previous marriage (one from whom he was descended) were then re-designated the Brindley surname and the surname of his true paternal ancestor, her first husband, was not recorded. He did not know when or where the second marriage took place. Unfortunately, he had no means of finding out the identity of this previous male ancestor.

Another related case, this time of gaining the Brindley name contrary to the established tradition of taking one's father's surname, occurred with the illegitimate birth of a James Brindley on 4th January 1819, at Alstonefield. His mother was Sarah Brindley, and his father was named as George Smith. Sarah does not appear to have married George Smith. James kept his mother's surname, and did not take or claim the surname of his natural father. In the course of time, James moved to Birmingham where he became a painter and married Catherine Humber. He fathered several children, one of whom, Frederick James Brindley, went on to found a successful steel forge manufacturers in Sheffield. Obviously, all the subsequent 'Brindley' descendents derived from that original female Sarah Brindley, and therefore Brindley is not their true paternal ancestoral surname, in genealogical terms.

It also happens that on occasion a married woman has an affair with another man. Later, finding herself pregnant, she lets her husband believe that her offspring is the natural child of the marriage. The husband may well accept and love the child as his own, unaware of the subterfuge. Genealogically, of course, the child is not his even though it carries his surname.

As already mentioned, illegitimacy is a common circumstance for losing one's father's surname. Many women had their illegitimate offspring baptised using their own surname and did not mention who the father was. Most of these children retained that name. Few recaptured their paternal surname, though some did, particularly if their mother later married the true father of that child.

Some people just didn't like their names and called themselves something else. I remember two people of my acquaintance who took the trouble to change their names by deed pole. Though their surnames sounded fine to me, they obviously thought differently and formalised their change of name. Some don't bother to go that far but call themselves something other than their 'official' name. The register for Bradley in the Moors contains many examples of dual identity. One man is variously known as Mace or Mais alias Canwell/ Cambel/Camel.

Immigrants often adopted a new name or anglicised a foreign sounding one. Mountbatten (as in Lord Louis) was an Anglicised translation of the Germanic name Battenburg. Others retain their foreign name but spell it and perhaps pronounce it in a more British way. In the case of the Chinese Lees, there is no problem.

When surnames started to be generally adopted around the 13th to 14th centuries, they either reflected occupation, such as Smith, Cooper, Thatcher, Pinder, etc; or personal characteristics such as Brown, Grey, Bold, Black, Wild, Young, etc; or names associated with place, such as Moor, Hill, Field, or settlement names - Leek, Buxton, Stoke, and so on. For those already living in large places, many genealogically unrelated persons may have taken the same surname around the same time. That, of course, makes it harder for someone alive today to trace with any certainty the original ancestor.

We Brindleys are indeed fortunate that our founding father was from a place so small that no other family took that name. Brindley, in the Cheshire Parish of Acton, appears to have only one family noted in the 13th century - the Brundeleghs/Brunleys. Much later on, two other families were noted as being from Brindley; the Allens of Brindley and the Huxleys of Brindley. The Brindleys of Brindley - the family of the Norman landowner who assumed the name because he owned the land 'Brundelegh', were thus able to establish their line without others of the same name to complicate the genealogical jigsaw puzzle. From Brundelegh come all the Brindleys, with very few exceptions, as you will read later.

Researching and compiling the Brindley story has given me great pleasure. This book represents a beginning. The research will continue and, God willing, there will be revisions and more to reveal in the future.

What follows is the story of the quest and discovery of my own family's link to Leek and its famous son James Brindley of canal engineering fame. The wider Brindley story is covered also and you will read about many other Brindleys who achieved fame or notoriety - or simply had something interesting happen to them. Many have links traceable to Leek.

I hope you enjoy reading about them and will be encouraged to take up your own research.

Gordon Brindley.

The ancestral pub, Hollington.

Top: The James Brindley Memorial at Wormhill, Derbyshire
Middle: The commemorative mural at the Sentinel Newspapers' canteen
Bottom: The James Brindley Memorial at Tunstead

PART 1
OLD ENGLAND

" That noble race of proud, impatient, disagreeable beings."

John Scott   Rhode Island. 17th C.

Chapter 1
The Brindley Quest

I blame my mother, Margaret Mary Brindley (née Lynch) for arousing my interest in family ancestors. As a child she would tell me all manner of interesting stories about her relatives and friends. She, in turn, was passing on the stories her dad had told her.

William Lynch, her father, was clearly an inventive, entertaining father and much given to playing practical jokes. Among his many talents was the ability to 'magic' fruit or sweets from unlikely places around the house. He also had an ingenious way of warning the children from playing near millponds or canals; he told spine-chilling stories of a 'Ginny Green Teeth' who loitered by watery places and abducted children. Of course, my stating this baldly doesn't convey the thrill and terror he was able to impart to his children. The art is in the telling more than the facts of a story. My mother had clearly inherited her father's 'gift of the gab' (as she would say). However, the Lynches' story is worth a different book. This one is about my father's eccentric clan - the Brindleys.

From the outset I hoped to try and get to know each individual as a full person, to understand in context, as if from the inside. Merely noting names and bare statistics would not be enough. I would go to the places they knew and see the scenes they saw.

My quest probably began seriously around August 1987 when my father Richard (known as 'Dick') and I set off together from Didsbury, Manchester, on a day out to Hollington, Staffordshire. I had long intended the trip but reasons not to go seemed to have cropped up. Now we were on our way. It was a rare chance to have him to myself. My dad was a quiet, reserved kind of a man, and not particularly verbal, so being able to chat to him without the distraction of others present was a treat.

The journey there took about an hour and a half. Passing the James Brindley watermill in Leek, I asked whether we had any connection to the famous James. My dad didn't think so. *"All Brindleys want to claim him"*, he said, **"but I don't think we're related."**

Eventually, we went through Alton, famous for its proximity to the Alton Towers theme park. We passed by the Royal Oak pub, once run by my uncle George Brindley and made our way along the narrow road that lead to Great Gate, Croxden. About four miles along the road, we paused outside the cottage in Great Gate, next to Gents' farm where my grandparents and he had lived. It was slightly changed from the way he knew it. The house itself was more or less the same from the outside but the vegetable garden, of which my grandfather George Edwin was so proud, was now given over to flowers only. The front garden, which used to be planted with roses and pansies, was now mostly dug out to facilitate a garage in the raised ground. Happily, the village school next door looked much the same, although it was now used as a house rather than a school.

We drove on and through the little stream that crosses the road, and reached a spot a few hundred yards on, where my Dad recalled an incident from his boyhood. Apparently, soon after he had won a scholarship to Uttoxeter Grammar School, he was cycling home when a man appeared out of the bushes at the side of the road and addressed him. *"He seemed to know all about me"*, said Dad. *"He asked how I was getting along at school and advised me to be a good student. When I asked him who he was, the tramp-like man had responded - They call me Bob the devil."* After that incident, the man would appear from time to time, as if out of nowhere and he always knew what Dick had been doing and would ask him about his schoolwork. My Dad never found out who this man was. Strangely, nobody else ever seemed to see him and after about three years of these meetings 'Bob' took his leave and was never seen again! Suitably impressed by this tale, I pointed the car up the long steep hill towards Hollington.

Hollington is a small and pretty village of Staffordshire-stone houses built on a ridge of high ground running East-West. It overlooks Croxden with its ancient Abbey ruins to the North and affords lovely views southward towards Leigh. Today, it looks much as it always has - timeless.

Once on Main Road, Hollington, my dad pointed out the house where he was born at Ground Hollow. I had always thought he was born at Great Gate but now I learnt otherwise. After this pause while he recalled happy days there, we continued to the Star Inn where my grandfather George Edwin had been born to George Brindley. My Dad didn't remember George because he was already dead when my Dad was born and he couldn't remember his grandma's name. We enjoyed a quiet pint in the ancestoral pub before continuing our day out. It was a strange feeling to be in the very building my great grandfather had inhabited. I imagined him behind the bar, chatting with the locals in the evening after a hard day in the quarry. He must have felt proud to have achieved a respectable standing in the locality.

The church of St John the Divine lay only about 100 yards past the pub. Once in the churchyard, it was a matter of moments before I found a headstone to George and his wife Mary Ann. Would this prove to be my great-grandparents' grave? I had no doubts that it would. I also took the opportunity to look for other Brindleys there. Nearby, I found a headstone to a child called Edward and his sister Emily whose parents were William and Ellen Brindley. This couple looked promising as potential parents for George, I thought. At the southern end of the churchyard I came across a headstone to the memory of John Brindley, of Dove House, Stramshall, and I duly noted his details, wondering how he fitted in. No other Brindleys were apparent, so we left.

On the way home, I reflected on how much I had enjoyed the day and my father's company. I had also discovered my great-grandparents and possibly my great-great grandparents. I was looking forward to learning more about them.

Unfortunately, life has its ways of imposing itself, and apart from an occasional foray it was not to be until 1999 drew to a close that I would be able to continue the challenge of the Quest seriously. In the years in between my father was taken ill in 1988 and died in 1990 after a long illness. Other things seemed to crop up, not the least work commitments and my own health problems. However, I retired at Christmas 1999 and remembering the quest, determined to re-commence research with renewed enthusiasm and the intention this time to see the job through to the end.

January 2000

As a novice researcher I had much to learn. However, the staff of Stockport Central Library were friendly and gave me some useful pointers. They had records from the 1881 census of England and the International Genealogical Index, so I could sit down immediately and start looking. They also mentioned that it would be helpful to join a family history society. I determined to do this very soon - and it proved to be a very good idea indeed.

I started by looking for George and Mary Ann of The Star Inn in the 1881 census. This showed them as being in occupation with three children - George E., Clara A. and Prudence E. My great grandfather was a publican and quarryman. Later, my mother recalled having met both of George Edwin's sisters. She recalled them as being named Clara and Nellie. It soon became clear that 'Nellie' was synonymous with Prudence Ellen. Apparently, she was always called Ellen (probably after her paternal grand mother) and of course Ellens were often referred to as 'Nellie'.

Also present at the Star Inn, on the night of the census, were Joseph Brindley, age 10, a nephew and Eliza A. Smith, a niece aged 16. This obviously implied an unknown brother and sister. Finding Joseph's family was relatively easy, again using the 1881 census. There were a limited number of other Brindley families in the general area. By looking carefully at their ages and situations I homed in on a William Brindley, a widower and stonemason, living at 16 Churnet Row, Rocester, with his several children. He seemed a good prospect to be George's brother. There was a gap in the ages of his children that would allow Joseph to be a possible sibling. By sending for various certificates and patiently waiting the obligatory month for their return from Southport, I was eventually able to establish that the Joseph staying with George at the Star Inn was indeed the son of the William in Churnet Row. I had found the first brother of my great-grandfather and it gave me a sense of triumph. Unfortunately, by the time of the census, William, another stonemason, was a widower. I would have to track down his wife before too long.

Sunday 9th April 2000

My sister Yvonne was back from Altlanta, Georgia, on a short visit. She and her husband Mike Long had been living and working in America for the last five years. Early on in the quest she had caught my enthusiasm and today we were going together on an exploratory adventure in the Alton area. We arrived in Alton around 11.30 am. After a quick tour of the village area, we decided on an early lunch at the Royal Oak Inn, once leased by my uncle George, but first we went in and spoke to the licensee. After ordering a drink, we told him that we were seeking 'lost' relatives and wondered if he knew of any local Brindleys? He said he did and mentioned my cousin Edwin as one. I already knew of him. Then he mentioned a 'Tony' Brindley. This was likely to be a second cousin whom we had never met. The landlord explained how to find him and a few minutes later we were knocking on his door.

His wife Elaine opened the door and I asked for Tony. When he appeared at the door I told him I believed we were related and that I was trying to trace those relations with whom we had lost contact. Well, he was surprised but immediately welcomed us in. It was great. He and his wife Elaine made us feel at home straightaway. Tony was the son of my cousin George who had died some years earlier, and he had a young son himself, George Kieran, a handsome little boy of four.

After a cup of tea and some initial exchange of family news, Tony took us to the Alton Catholic graveyard and showed us relevant graves of his father and grandfather and that of my cousin Edwin's first wife, Kathleen Elizabeth. I asked Tony if he thought that there might be any Irish blood in the Brindley ancestors? (I had come across a Dougherty and wondered if she was from Ireland) Tony said he wouldn't be surprised because his family had always owned horses and greyhounds and hand in hand with this went investments in their performances. And whenever the family congregated in any of the local pubs, the liquid stock would be tested to the full.

All too soon, it was time to say goodbye. Of course, we exchanged our addresses and phone numbers and promised to keep in touch (which we have).

Yvonne and I really enjoyed our lunch. Finding 'new' family was a thrill. After, we paid a visit to the Hollington Churchyard of St John the Divine and we found a local farmer's wife, Amy Tatlow, who had the church keys and was kind enough to let us inside the church. A plaque at the back of the church honoured the local men who had served in the Second World War. My father Richard, his brother Frederick Arthur and my uncle George A. Belfield were all listed. I took a photograph. It was a good day and, to cap it off, I stopped on our way home at the James Brindley Water Mill in Leek and took a photograph of Yvonne with the Mill in the background.

16th April 2000

Today I went to Rocester hoping to catch the vicar in. A pint of milk still on the doorstep indicated that he wasn't and there was no answer to my knocking on the door so I pressed on to check out the churchyard. The church itself was locked up so I didn't get to see the inside. Many headstones had been removed from the grounds and were standing along the boundary wall, shoulder to shoulder, as if expecting a Sergeant Major to review them. I slowly scanned the inscriptions. Not a Brindley to be seen.

I turned my attention to the churchyard proper and systematically read every inscription. It was on the furthest row from the church that I abruptly ceased patrol. The inscription was to a William Burton Brindley and his wife Charlotte. I carefully noted the full details and felt a frisson of excitement. I just had that feeling that this one was mine. William had died on 8th April 1896 aged 58 and Charlotte on 3rd March 1880, aged 45 years. It didn't take me long to work out that this matched the approximate birth date of my great grandfather's older brother, of Churnet Row. When I checked later against the 1881 census return I was proved correct. This find alone had made my day out worthwhile. I had found his full name *and* his wife. Now, I could start checking further and assembling this William's family.

I returned home a happy man. All family history buffs know what it is to be frustrated and up against an apparent impasse. This is soon forgotten when one gets the "Yes" effect. This is the typical scene in a library or research room: There is almost total silence, even though the room is packed, except for the soft whirring noise of film reels being wound on. Suddenly, one lucky person finds what they have been seeking, perhaps for years. There is a long intake of breath through closed teeth and an explosive "Y-E-S!" rends the air. Those of us not yet so lucky smile a smile which is a mixture of pleasure on behalf of the fortunate one and deepening dismay that it wasn't our turn yet.

31st May 2000

I sallied forth to visit the birthplace of James Brindley, canal engineer. Tunstead, near Buxton, Derbyshire, was as small a place as you would be likely to find. It had two neglected-looking council houses and a telephone box. Within a matter of yards was the largest quarrying operation I had ever seen. There was a huge man-made cliff face and a yawning chasm.

I knew there was supposed to be a marker for where James' cottage once stood but I could not find it (happily, I have since). I moved on to Wormhill village itself, which looked as pretty as a picture in the sunshine. I found the memorial to James and it looked quite impressive. I took a photograph, and walked up the lane to St Margaret's Parish Church. A funeral was in progress, so I just walked around the churchyard. No Brindleys were in evidence.

Next stop was Alstonefield, a parish in the most northerly portion of Staffordshire. I had long known that Alstonefield was home to numerous Brindleys over hundreds of years. The Derbyshire boundary snakes close to the village and it was going to be useful to see how things shaped up on the ground. I approached the village from the A515 road, which leads from Ashbourne to Buxton. The scenery was wonderful. The road led through steep canyons and rose and fell like a roller coaster. After a few miles of this, it emerged into the spick and span stone houses of the village.

The village exceeded my expectation. The church was set picturesquely on slightly higher ground overlooking the village centre. There was a post office, a village store, and a pub that once had a Brindley landlord. I checked out the church and found a few Brindley graves. In the afternoon sun it looked like a piece of paradise. However, it must be a cold and windswept place in mid-winter.

After a final look round, I just had time to take a quick look at Hartington. This village appears to be undecided as to which county it is in. Not surprising, really, because it is split by a stream that marks the county boundary. I am sure the locals have no problem with that. It just makes outsiders like myself struggle when trying to pin down ancient residents!

Tired by now, but happy, I took the scenic route home through Buxton and along the Macclesfield Road. It had been another rewarding day.

10th June 2000

I woke up at 8am to a bright cheerful day, and set off early for Brindley country. By 11.15am I found myself in the churchyard of Ellastone church. This beautiful and ancient church is set on high ground commanding a magnificent view over the surrounding area. There was not another soul to be seen as I started reviewing the massed ranks of headstones.

Occasionally I failed to notice a dip in the ground and stumbled in the long grass. Eventually, among the Salts' and Phillips' graves I found a Brindley headstone. It said - Mary *"at rest 3rd March 1938 age 73"* and John, *"Beloved husband at rest 17th August 1941"*. Pleased to have found at least one Brindley, I headed to Mayfield. This proved to be another pretty church in a delightful bucolic setting. I didn't find any Brindleys but I was having a lovely day out so it didn't matter too much. Next stop was Norbury where I managed not to find the church - at least meaning I'd have an excuse to come back.

As usual, I stopped by at Rocester but with the expected negative result. However, this time I noticed an overflow graveyard for the church and in this I found Isaac Brindley who later proved to be one of William's sons (of Churnet Row).

Next stop was Church Leigh. The church was set next to the Admiral Nelson public house and stood on a prominence of ground affording magnificent country views. As luck would have it, a lady appeared from inside the church where she had been cleaning and tidying. She was kind enough to welcome me in. Within this pretty and ancient church I noticed a plaque that mentioned Thomas Howe and his wife Louisa (formerly Brindley). This couple had donated eight stained glass windows to the church and it gave me added pleasure, seeing them, to know of the Brindley connection.

Back on the outside I started checking the ranks of headstones. There was an extra sense of orderliness about this churchyard. The headstones stood close to each other, at attention in neat geometric lines. Immediately to the rear of the church stood a regimented row of Brindleys and I spent some considerable time writing down their details. I had never seen so many Brindleys, all together in one place, since my Grandparents' Golden Wedding Anniversary in 1952. Once I had finished, I retired to the Lord Nelson and had a satisfying pub lunch. What a wonderful day it was turning out to be.

After that, I retraced my steps, stopping at Alton Parish church. I could not gain access to the church but managed to find a Brindley headstone, now rooted out of its proper location and stashed against a wall pending disposal. I managed to move it and scrape away some vegetation. I could just make out that it was for Margaret (née Brindley) who was married to Joseph Salt. I would check the find against my database when I got home. The afternoon was giving way to evening as I started to make my way back to Cheshire. I had really enjoyed the peace and tranquillity. Staffordshire was getting into my blood!

My grandparents' golden wedding in 1952.

Chapter 2
Frustrations

Eliza A. Smith was not proving so easy or obvious to sort out. Finding her parents had been relatively easy. In the 1881 census there was a Smith family living nearby in Hollington (fortunately the only one) and I had thought it was just a matter of waiting a few weeks for Eliza A.'s birth certificate, followed by her mother's marriage certificate, to establish that her mother was another Brindley.

Regrettably, or so I thought at the time, her mother's maiden name on the birth certificate was shown as Horobin. This fact was a surprise and gave me a problem. I just couldn't work out how Harriet Horobin could be related to George Brindley at the Star Inn. No matter what I imagined, I couldn't find a plausible scenario to explain it. Eventually, I decided to stop beating my brains out on this question. Possibly, I speculated, Eliza A. Smith was an honorary niece and George her honorary uncle? Such things are not that unusual and in any case people are not always 100% truthful in filling in census forms. So, believing that I had wasted my money, I put this information to one side and carried on looking for other data.

Meantime, I had found William and Ellen on the 1881 census. They were living in Hollington near George and Mary Ann. In their household were a couple more Brindleys - daughter Ann Jane, unmarried and born about 1842, and Emily, unmarried and born about 1858. I noted their names for later, remembering that I had previously seen Emily's death mentioned on a headstone in Hollington churchyard.

At this point, I feel I should mention that many family history researchers encounter indifference or even hostility to the hobby on the part of other family members. During the course of my research I have come across many like-minded individuals. Most of them tell me the same thing - that nobody in their family understands or is interested in what is perceived by them as a ghoulish enterprise; *"How can you enjoy thinking about dead people all the time? Spending hours in morbid cemeteries?"* they say. The truth is that we are thinking mostly about their lives and not dwelling on the fact of their death. Philistines all, I say! Anyway, there is often more life to be found in a cemetery than can be found between the average pair of ears! But I digress.

Pleased that I had made a kind of progress, laterally if not back, by now I was debating with myself whether or not to apply for a copy of Mary Anne's death certificate. By now, I had gained a little experience and had discovered that often death certificates revealed little more than the cause of death. At £11 a time, a copy certificate from the Southport Record office was not best value in my opinion and it could take up to a month to receive it. I wasn't really inclined or happy to gamble on the likely outcome.

The costs can soon mount up and I noted that there was now an entire industry founded on the desire of people to trace their ancestors. These days there are at least three, possibly more, family history oriented monthly magazines. There are hundreds of offers from those willing to research your ancestory for you. Computer programmes abound which claim to make your life easier. You can have professionally drawn up trees. Photo enhancement or portraits can be commissioned. In other words, a thousand ways have been devised to part

Clerk Bank, Leek

The Van Tuyl tomb in St Edward's churchyard - the last resting place of Joseph Brindley, Surgeon

The old Red Lion in Leek Market Place

you from your money. Worthy as some of these services may be, I believe that there is no substitute for doing it your self at a minimal cost. A pencil and notepad allied to an orderly approach is probably all you need. However, it has to be said that some money will occasionally have to be spent. Some costs are unavoidable. Obtaining copies of birth, marriage and death certificates is usually necessary at some stage.

Nevertheless, a niggling doubt still gnawed at me. In an act of recklessness, I stumped up another £11 and spent the next four weeks telling myself off. Four weeks later, a brown envelope dropped through the letterbox and I picked it up feeling a mixture of hope and dread - one quickly turns into a 'post junkie' doing this hobby. I managed to find my specs and eagerly tore the envelope apart. Good! At least there was a certificate in there and not the dreaded rejection slip.

My eyes scanned the data. Mary Ann (née Pountain); Cause of death - Pthysis, or Tuberculosis in modern day terms. But then the detail that made my eleven pounds spent worth every penny: Present at death - Dinah Mart, sister in law. Hurrah! Another family member for George! Slowly, I was reeling them in.

Next day, I attended the Cheshire Family History Society Library in Alderley Edge, but a few miles from where I live. This society must be in the top three such organisations in the country. They seem to have a surfeit of facilities; pleasant, knowledgeable volunteers are always on hand to help and they have more indexes, censuses and parish registers than you could possibly shake a stick at.

I sat down with the GRO microfiche and within minutes found a marriage of Dinah Brindley at Stone, Staffordshire. A few weeks later the certificate duly arrived from Southport. It confirmed she was indeed George's sister. She had married John William Mart, a coachman, of Blythe Bridge, at the Congregationalist Chapel, Stone. Dinah was a cook at Blythe Bridge at this time. It was a case of a Brindley departing briefly from the norm of the Church of England and I couldn't help wondering why. Brides traditionally marry in their home church. So far in the quest, the Brindleys had seemed a traditional Church of England bunch yet here was an example of marrying at a non-conformist church. Perhaps her husband was a Congregationalist?

The marriage certificate showed that her father was William Brindley, a stonemason/quarryman (clearly the one married to Ellen). The 1881 census found her living back in Hollington with her husband and several children near the Star Inn, and near to where William and Ellen lived. When I checked my database, I was quickly able to assemble a snapshot of her history and I have included it in the Brindley Clan biographies later.

Things were going well I thought, but only in a lateral line. Over the last few weeks I had made several visits to Stafford Record Office and systematically checked the parish registers for Alton, Hollington, Checkley, Leigh, Stramshall, Tean, Uttoxeter, and all points around with the exception of Rocester. I had found a lot of Brindleys and noted their details but no sign of my William's marriage to Ellen, nor of his birth or baptism. Some Rocester records were available but nothing after about 1800 to the present day. Furthermore, I had discovered that Hollington burials, Croxden St Giles and Rocester births, marriages and deaths since 1800 were all in the hands of the vicar of Rocester. Early on in my research, I had written to him several times over many months with no response, despite a stamped self addressed envelope being enclosed. On several occasions I had telephoned him but had to leave messages on the answer phone. Unfortunately, no return message was received.

By this time, I was starting to become obsessed with Rocester. More and more, I believed that Rocester would be the key to success, and so it would eventually prove to be. I remembered making the acquaintance of Amy Tatlow, a local farmer's wife, who happened to hold the keys to the Hollington church and I decided that I must call in and see her soon and see if she could help.

4th July 2001

My son Derek telephoned unexpectedly to say that he and his partner Nokomis Pinder had just become parents. *"Speak to your grandson Thomas Owen Brindley"*, he said, and the next thing I heard was Thomas Owen gurgling down the phone! The birth was not due for another five days. Thomas has turned out to be a little star. A few weeks later, he eloped his parents to Gretna Green and got them married. I would soon realise that this Brindley way of doing things was an old established 'in the genes' habit.

It was now August 2001. I had spent the morning at The Sentinel Newspaper Headquarters at Etruria, an area well known to Josiah Wedgwood and the Brindleys, James and John. A sympathetic reporter was interviewing me with a view to doing an article about my quest. She took me to the staff canteen and I noticed a large mural showing a canal barge emerging from under a bridge. The mural carried the legend - Brindleys. How apt, I thought. It was gratifying to see the name being honoured like that. I took a photograph.

There were a few hours left in the day, so I headed towards the Alton area and soon I was back again in the churchyard at Hollington. With new information of Brindley marriages in my head, I found more graves of relatives previously unknown to me. Next to my grandparents' grave was that of Prudence Ellen and her husband James Swinson. Facing was the grave of Clara Ann and her husband Joseph Albert Bull. I realised slowly that more and more of those at eternal rest were in fact related to me.

Having recorded their graves and inscriptions for my growing database of Brindleys, I called on Amy Tatlow. She received me like an old friend - I must say that the people I've met in North Staffordshire seem to be very friendly. She sat me down in the farmhouse kitchen and over a cup of tea we had a good old chat about the area, the difficulties experienced in the upkeep of country churches, and the problem of foot and mouth disease. Almost as an afterthought, I mentioned that I had not yet been able to obtain access to Rocester Parish registers. Amy immediately offered to ring the vicar for me.

She made contact straight away, told the vicar that her 'friend' wanted to see his registers and then she put me on the phone. *"When would you like to come?"* he asked. *"How about now?"* I responded, hopefully. To my great surprise, he immediately agreed and fifteen minutes later I was in the vicarage with the registers spread out around me.

In little over an hour I had perused them all. I found several Brindleys. One entry above all shouted to me off the page. It related to the burial in Hollington churchyard of a William *Horobin* Brindley, of the correct age to match the William Brindley who was married to Ellen and who had been elusive so far. I remembered that Eliza A. Smith's mother was called Harriet Horobin before marriage and the re-occurrence of the Horobin name sent a shiver down my spine. What did it mean? I thought about it all the way back to Manchester but still couldn't work it out.

In bed that night, I kept thinking about this 'Horobin' connection and finally fell asleep still wondering about it. I would have to think long and hard on this one. The next day, after breakfast, I was pondering over a cup of tea when the idea came to me: what if the parents of a child had that child first and married later? I had already noticed that occasionally the first child of the marriage of a particular ancestor was born 'early'. They were either prematurely born or the wife was already pregnant at the time of the marriage. It now occurred to me that, on occasion, a man might well have a reason to wait until long after his child's birth before marrying the child's mother. It could just be down to laziness of course but it was more likely to be a precaution to make sure that the child was his and not some fugitive father's.

Because children often died young in those days, baptisms usually took place soon after birth. If this happened before the parents married, the chances were that the child would be baptised in the mother's name and the father's identity would remain undisclosed. Enthused with this idea, I determined to get onto the internet and see what I could find. I had recently invested in a new computer; "now", I thought, "it's time to put it to the test". I logged on to the IGI site (International Genealogical Index) which is run by the Mormons and is an excellent family history research facility. I entered the name William Burton, selected 'all events' and the year 1837 (plus or minus 5 years). Within seconds a list was on screen. I noted an Alton event and highlighted it. The baptism of a William Burton, base born son of Helen Burton was detailed at Alton in 1837. Was this 'Helen' William Horobin's Ellen? You can bet it would be!

Next I entered the name William Horobin, chose search all records and selected a time frame of five years either side of 1837. In a few seconds a list of events was on my screen. My eyes focused on a Checkley event on 24th September in 1838. I clicked onto the entry to see the details. It was the marriage of William Horobin to Helen Burton. Clearly, this could be William Horobin (later to be Brindley) marrying Ellen.

So, if they were married in 1838, and their son George, whom I had previously regarded as a Brindley, was born the year after, could he be a Horobin too? Within seconds I had him - signed, sealed and delivered. George was baptised as George Horobin at Alton on the 6th October 1839. His parents *were* William Horobin and Ellen.

So, William Horobin and William Brindley were one and the same individual. What on earth was going on? Just to add to the mystery, I had recently found another Brindley son living near to William and Ellen, namely a Joseph Walter Brindley. He really was baptised 'Brindley' and registered Brindley too! (Though somehow he was officially registered, mistakenly, as Walter Joseph) So what I had were three brothers: William Burton, George Horobin, and Joseph Walter Brindley. You simply couldn't make this up. Then I remembered Eliza Ann Smith's mother Harriet being a Horobin and that her father was a William Horobin. George Brindley, my great grandfather, had started out as a 'Horobin' also. That would explain and validate the census information. Harriet Smith, formerly Horobin, must have been George's sister. There was no other explanation.

Whilst I was on a winning streak, I looked for Ann Jane, another child who appeared on the 1881 census as a Brindley. Sure enough, she was baptised at Checkley on 3rd July 1842 as Ann Jane Horobin. Another child I found was Emma Horobin, baptised at Checkley on 26th May 1842. Of course, I expected that I would find Harriet Horobin's baptism just as easily, but there was no trace of it. Going back to the 1881 census, I re-read the data. Harriet had said she was born in New Brighton, Cheshire. Now why, I thought, would she alone of the siblings be born at such a remove? The only explanation that came to me was that she might have been an *illegitimate* daughter of William Horobin. (A case of history repeating itself.) All attempts to find her birth or baptism have foundered to date. If she had been born illegitimately, perhaps to a Hollington woman other than William's wife, I could well imagine that the woman might have gone far way, perhaps to relatives, to give birth. Maybe this unknown woman had Harriet baptised in *her* maiden name. This would explain why I couldn't find the data! Without that maiden name I would never find out.

Of course this meant a trip to Stafford to check with the entries in the registers. You simply can't accept the IGI entries at face value. So, the next day I was off to Staffordshire Records' Office without an appointment. I couldn't wait. It is always a bit risky going there without an appointment because the microfiche machines soon get booked up and without access to one you just can't read the information. Luck was with me this time. Once I had booked in I found the Checkley Parish records. In a few minutes I had found the relevant entry. William Horobin married Helen Burton in 1838 and the best bit, **new** information – father of William Horobin was JOSEPH BRINDLEY, surgeon!

So, that was it! The fog was starting to lift from my mind. These mysterious people had started out in life with the surname of their mother and only later had they retrieved their Brindley name. William Horobin was an illegitimate son of Joseph Brindley. No wonder he had been so difficult to pin down. All the time I was looking for Brindley when he was actually under the name Horobin. Joseph Brindley was not shown as one of the witnesses to the marriage event so I had no proof that he was present at the marriage of this son. I would like to think that he was there but there was no documentary proof to support that hope.

I now had several lines of enquiry open to pursue. I tore myself out of reverie and pressed on. My next task was to look for William's birth. Looking back through the Checkley births data I found him soon enough. William Horobin was the base born son of Jane Horobin, a servant, she being of Hollington. He was baptised on 11th December 1817 at Checkley. Not surprisingly no mention was made of his father. This was normal.

The next information I wanted was Jane Horobin's birth. Yet another surprise was in store. She was born in 1802 to William Horobin and Margaret (née Webb) and that meant she must have been only fourteen when she became pregnant (the age of consent was raised to 16 in 1889). I wondered how old Joseph would have been. My imagination was in overdrive. The ancestors were being plucked like grapes from a vine.

I also realised something else: My great grandfather George Brindley had married Mary Ann Pountain at the Wesleyan Chapel Uttoxeter - *a non-conformist c*hapel. Strictly speaking he was called George Horobin. In the light of his revealed Brindley descent, he must have wanted to get his name registered as Brindley. Had he married at the regular Church of England Church the vicar may have raised an objection. By marrying in a church where he was unknown, all he simply had to do was say his surname was Brindley. So, he walked in a single man called Horobin and came out a married man called Brindley.

On the other hand, his father William Horobin managed the transformation about 1850 when he had his latest child, Joseph Walter Brindley, baptised. This date was not long after the building and consecration of the Church of St John the Divine at Hollington. My guess is that he took advantage of the new circumstance and said at the baptism that he was William Brindley. The Horobin name only surfaced once after that and that was when his son Joseph Walter, who was present at the death, gave his father's full name for the burial register. And that was how it came to be entered in the Hollington death register as William Horobin Brindley. But for that, the subterfuge may never have come to light. However, Joseph Walter didn't mention the Horobin bit when he *registered* the death. This time the name of his father was given as William Brindley. By these simple acts, Joseph Walter confirmed the dual identity of his father and left us the necessary clues to find the truth.

One thing I haven't been able to discover so far is - when and where did William Burton Brindley marry? Did he engineer his change of name in a similar manner? I wouldn't be at all surprised.

Naturally, I was curious to know more about Jane Horobin. Again, the IGI proved useful. I found her baptism on 16th May 1802 at Checkley. Her parents were William and Margaret Horobin (née Webb) of Hollington. If Jane was born not long before her baptism, she could have been not much more than fourteen years of age when she became pregnant with her illegitimate son William and would have been fifteen years old when she had him! (Later, the parish register confirmed her birth was on the 9th May 1802) So, she was actually 15 years and 7 months old, almost to the day, when her son was born. If her pregnancy had run the full term, she must have conceived about the 11th March 1817 when aged 14 years and 10 months. Teenage mothers are apparently not a modern phenomenon!

Jane never married her Joseph Brindley. Both were obviously too young when their first child was born and they probably saw little of each other after their relationship was discovered. Joseph was already apprenticed to an apothecary at Cheadle by then and later moved to another apothecary/surgeon named Chas Chadwick at Leek. Jane remained local to Hollington and, on 5th August 1820, had another illegitimate son, Matthew Smith Horobin, baptised at Checkley. The father wasn't named. However, on 16th October 1823, aged 21, she married a John Bott at Checkley. No trace of children from this marriage has been found. We shall probably never know if John Bott was the father of Matthew Smith Horobin.

The next and last glimpse I had of Jane's life was from the 1881 census. Age given as eighty-one, she was now a widow and pauper living in the Union Workhouse at Cheadle. Her occupation was given as charwoman. I have yet to find her death entry. She is known to have had a sister, Hannah, born about 1798 and brothers George, born 13 August 1814; John, born 28th January 1816; Thomas, born 20th October 1822; James Smith, born 26th April 1824. Her father was a Tape Weaver (probably at John and Nathaniel Philips' Tean factory) and the family lived at Over Tean.

Full to the brim with satisfaction, I walked back to the car smiling idiotically despite the grey sky and the late afternoon rain. Passers-by must have wondered at my demeanour. Never mind the weather, the sun was shining inside me. The fifty odd mile drive back home was a 'breeze', I was so elated.

The preserved Brindley Water Mill at Leek

The Brindley Aqueduct over the River Irwell

Chapter 3
Breakthrough

One problem that besets many researchers into family history is the overlap of area boundaries. It can be very confusing. For example, the Ecclesiastical administrative geography for Hollington means that Hollington is considered to be in or subservient to Checkley Parish but the reality is that today Rocester covers Hollington (but not Checkley) and keeps the records. In turn, Rocester seems to be under the thumb of Uttoxeter. However, for birth, marriage and death registration purposes, Hollington is in Cheadle. Oakamoor lies in the Cheadle district for local government purposes, but is administered locally by Alton clergy. However, it is in the diocese of Lichfield. When you get close to the Staffordshire/Derbyshire boundary the nightmare is compounded. I shall say little more than.... *aaaaarrrgh!* (Just be aware, that's all!)

It was now some eighteen months since I had started the quest in earnest. From the beginning I had kept a note of every Brindley (including variations of the name) I came across. They were all entered on a database I had created which had grown to some twenty thousand entries. This would now prove very useful. Also, recently, I had enquired about any books about Brindleys. In this way I obtained a copy of Kathleen M. Evans' book on James Brindley the canal engineer. Kathleen had done a magnificent job researching not only James but many of his relatives and their descendents. I too had come across many of these Brindleys during my research and had duly entered them on the database.

Following my recent success in solving the Horobin question, I was now looking to find the Joseph who was a surgeon. I wrote to the Royal College of Surgeons and the Society of Apothecaries requesting their assistance in tracing this Joseph. While I waited their response I could do some checking on my database. I sat at my computer and put the name Joseph in. In a split second it showed me all the Brindleys who had carried that name. It did not take me long to spot a Joseph born in Alton in 1801, the son of John Brindley and Frances (née Mellor) his wife. This was exciting because I already knew that this John was a direct descendent of Joseph Brindley of Alton, Millwright and brother of the famous James.

I changed my query to seek all entries of John and Frances and this showed me immediately that they had parented seventeen children. Their first child and son was a Joseph, as mentioned. I wondered if this Joseph could be the father of William Horobin? It would mean that Joseph would have been about fourteen years old when he impregnated Jane Horobin who was a servant at the time of her confinement. Could she have been in the service of the John and Frances Brindley Household? It seemed entirely possible to me. It is only about four miles from Hollington to Alton. In 1817 Frances Brindley would have needed a considerable amount of domestic help. By now she had given birth to about ten children. A couple had died but that still left eight alive, several of them probably still at home needing care or supervision.

I didn't have long to wait for replies from the medical bodies. The Royal College of Surgeons was the first to respond. Indeed they did have a record of a Joseph Brindley of Leek, Staffordshire. His name was on the list of Licentiates of Apothecaries published in 1840. He received the licence of the Society on July 29th 1840. The letter went on to comment on the use of the word 'surgeon'. It said that the word was used rather loosely in the early nineteenth century, often referring to any medical practitioner, and the apothecary's licence was in itself a medical qualification. This welcome information at least confirmed the existence of Joseph and shed useful light on his vocation. What I lacked was some indication of Joseph's age. He would necessarily appear to have attained the age of twenty-one years on qualification but something more explicit was needed.

On the 1st November 2001 I received the response of the Society of Apothecaries. This had more information than the previous body. They said that the Joseph Brindley they knew of qualified on the 29th July 1840 (thus confirming that their Joseph was the same one referred to by the Royal College of Surgeons). He had originally applied for the licence and been examined on 10th May 1821 (so by then was of full age, making his birth about 1801 possible). He had been apprenticed to Henry Langley of Cheadle, Staffordshire, apothecary, for a premium of £70 and his indenture was dated 21st June 1815.

The letter also commented that the age for apprenticeships to begin was usually fourteen years old. There was also detailed information about the nature of an Apothecary's training but now I had seen what I had hoped for. Though not explicitly cast-in-stone proof, this seemed to pin this particular Joseph down to being born around 1801. Circumstantially, at least, he looked likely to be the son of John and Frances. I just needed that extra bit of information. It seems likely that Joseph found himself another apothecary, soon after his examination failure, and probably relocated to Leek around 1821.

Once again I returned to my database. This time I was looking for a Joseph in Leek. I soon found him. Joseph Brindley, a surgeon, had married Harriet Van Tuyl at St Edwards Parish Church in 1840. Prior to his marriage, Joseph was living at Clerk Bank, Leek, which is near to St Edward's Church. According to information on p. 167 of *Olde Leeke Vol. II*, by M. H. Miller, in 1818, Clerk Bank was also the residence of Charles Chadwick, apothecary of Leek, with whom Joseph was connected about this time.

Another reference on p. 221 related a story about the steel stocks opposite the Red Lion in market square. *"On one occasion a man named Matthew Moss was fixed in them, and he did enjoy himself. <$iDrs. Brindley, Walters, and Robins> were in the Red Lion, and during his detention they sent him several pints of ale."* Though this article is undated, it was probably around 1836–1838.

I later discovered that the Clerk Bank properties were owned by another Joseph Brindley (apparently a descendent of a Henry Brindley of Gawsworth, Macclesfield, who is suspected of being the brother of James the canal engineer). This Joseph would have been related to Joseph the surgeon. They were distant cousins. This information was found in a will of the said Joseph Brindley of Gawsworth, dated 24th July 1843; he died 30th January 1848, leaving properties in Leek, Danebridge, Sutton, Macclesfield, Buglawton, and an investment in the Congleton and Buxton turnpike.

It seems more than a coincidence to me that Joseph, the surgeon, was living where he was. The two Josephs would almost certainly have known their family ties and the surgeon might well have taken property there because of the family link.

Others of my family members, part of the James Brindley Clan, were also present in Leek at this time and their presence occurred like this:

Joseph, the 'great mechanik' of Alton Brassworks had a daughter called Mary, baptised at Alton on 22nd August 1758. On 18th January 1779, she married John Cope at Alton. Their daughter Mary Cope (who lived for a time at Wyldgoose House, Bradnop, ancestoral home since 1450 of the original Brundelegh de Brindley descendents), married Joseph Malkin, and their daughter Ann married a James Brindley, a miller of Leek, at St Edward's Church on 29th August 1829. This James's brother Henry was a witness. James and Ann lived at the James Brindley Mill, 112, Mill Street. So, the Brindley name was, in a way, recaptured by Ann, the descendent of Joseph Brindley of Alton. I wonder whom they chose as their doctor?

November 2001

While I was waiting for the marriage certificate of Joseph to come back, I went to Leek Library and asked if they had any useful books on Leek covering the period 1830 to 1850. They presented me with a book entitled Miller's *Olde Leeke VOL I*. I settled down for a good read. The book was a minefield of distracting and interesting tales and information. With difficulty, I forced myself away from reading these and looked in the index. There was a reference to 'Brindley' around page 272.

This contained a paragraph about a section of St Edward's Church in Leek known as doctors' corner. It stated that within the railings of the Van Tuyl–Bullock tomb was an inscription about Joseph Brindley, a surgeon, who died 11th April 1841, aged 39. It said:

"He was associated in business, before he obtained his diploma, with Mr (Charles) Chadwick, surgeon of Leek and was of much the same gay and festive temperament. On the day of his death he was hastening round the turn from Abbey Green to Mill Street, when a stirrup leather broke, and he was thrown violently to the ground and suffered a fatal fracture of the skull. He was very fond of boxing and old inhabitants tell of his exploits in this direction."

Joseph was dead at the age of 39. Sadly, the railings are long gone from the tomb, and the inscription can no longer be read. Thank goodness for Miller's *Olde Leeke!*

Ironically, the last thing Joseph was likely to have seen in the seconds before his death was the famous water mill, created by his great great uncle, James Brindley - Abbey Green at the junction with Mill Street, Leek, is only a matter of yards away.

So, this piece of information confirmed that Joseph must have been born about 1801. All I needed now were the certificates as an extra check, and the proof that he was belonging to John and Frances would be mine. I left the library and walked the short distance to St Edward's churchyard. There was a keen wind but mercifully it had stopped raining. I spent an hour wandering among the headstones, searching for Joseph's grave and that of James and Susannah Brindley, James' parents. Joseph's was there, as mentioned already, but I couldn't distinguish James' and Susannah's grave. Time and neglect seemed to have allowed the inscriptions to weather beyond legibility; happily at a later date I did find them.

In due course I received both certificates. The marriage certificate confirmed that Joseph's father *was* John - a farmer. (In 1841 the John Brindley who married Frances Mellor was indeed a farmer) The death certificate issued by the Burslem Coroner confirmed that Joseph was aged 39 at the time of his death and was killed by "Falling from a Horse".

The proof was now gathered in. As a final attempt to get the last drop of information I could about Joseph, I tried to find his will. Unfortunately, he hadn't made one. I ordered copies of his widow's application for the administration of his estate. The value of it was attested to be less than four hundred pounds. As a last check, I searched my database for any other Joseph who could possibly have been a suspect for being the son of John and Frances Brindley. Happily, there were none. The evidence I had gathered was about as good as it gets. Now I could move on to thinking about John Brindley and his wife Frances.

John Brindley 1780-1852 abt. and wife Frances née Mellor

Once again the Alton Parish Register had the necessary information. John was baptised on the 3rd September 1780 at Alton. His parents were Matthew and Lydia (née Walker) and his father Matthew was leasing and running the Brass works at Alton, a position of some local status. It didn't take me long to establish that John married Frances Mellor on 23rd December 1800 at Alton. She was baptised on the 21st November 1779 at Alton, the daughter of Hugh Meller (sic) and his wife Sarah. The Meller/Mellors were an old established Alton family.

Besides parenting sixteen or more children, John and Frances would experience many difficulties in their life. John must have had a reasonable education because by the time he was in his twenties he was clerk to the wire works in Alton, not far from the smelting mill run by his father, Matthew. He must have had a good income. In 1815, he had high hopes for his first son Joseph who was indentured to an Apothecary and this cost £70, a not inconsiderable sum for those days. It must have been a cause of some consternation for John to discover soon after that Joseph was destined to become a young father. The crisis was somehow resolved. With ten other children to feed and educate, life must have been very full. Their second daughter Sarah, who never married, must have been a great help to her parents. She seems to have remained in the household and was certainly looking after John in his old age.

At first John seemed to make a decent living at the wire works but later, when that business was in decline, he turned to becoming a dyer, improver and colour manufacturer for the pottery trade. However, by 1831 that business was also in difficulties. He was declared bankrupt in 1834, the hearing being on 17th June at the Royal Oak Inn, in Cheadle.

His wife Frances died at Dilhorne on 1st January 1840 which might imply that John may also have been living in Dilhorne by now. He was barely getting over the death of Frances when another death in the family occurred on 11th April 1841. His eldest son Joseph, living in Leek, having finally qualified as a surgeon/apothecary and recently having married well, was killed in a tragic accident, falling from his horse. The 1841 census showed that John was living and farming on five acres of land at Cotton in what must have been very reduced circumstances, probably with his unmarried daughter Sarah looking after him.

We next find him mentioned in the 1851 census by which time he had moved to Checkley. Now aged over seventy, he is described as 'retired' and living with unmarried daughter Sarah. Though his precise address is unclear, he would be close to Hollington and his illegitimate grandson William Horobin. I have speculated on the reasons for the Brindley name being recaptured by William Horobin and his children and believe that there may well have been some kind of family conference on the subject. With so many children to John and Frances, you would have expected that the Brindley name would be in no danger of dying out. However, three had died young; Clement died aged 21 unmarried, no trace of Paul or Isaac marrying has been found nor of Edmund. Apart from Joseph, James married Anne Whitehall at Uttoxeter, on 11th November 1833, and produced heirs named Brindley. So far no marriages have been found for Thomas, born 19th April 1808, or Edward, born 15th May

1810. John, born 28th September 1817, may have married someone called Ann. The others were girls and their surname would be surrendered on marriage. Could it have been old John Brindley's prime concern to make sure that Joseph's illegitimate descendents carried on the Brindley name? I think it likely.

John and Frances had the following children:

Joseph, baptised 16th August 1801;
Sarah, baptised 6th July 1803 who died as an infant;
Mary Anne, baptised 11th January 1804 and must have died young.
Paul, baptised 13th September 1805;
James, baptised 11th May 1806;
Sarah, baptised 3rd July 1806;
Mary Ann, baptised 11th January 1808;
Thomas, baptised 19th April 1808;
Clement, baptised 15th December 1809 and died 1830;
Edward, baptised 15th May 1810 and must have died young;
Isaac, baptised 6th September 1812 at Alton and died at Leek, 1879, apparently unmarried;
Catherine, baptised 1st June 1815;
John, baptised 28th September 1817;
Edmund and/ or Edward (both?) baptised 27th June 1819;
Emma, baptised 24th September 1820;
Frances, baptised 23rd May 1824.

Old John probably died around 1855 at Checkley.

This largely concludes the story of the search for my Brindley roots. Naturally, I have not detailed the many and frequent visits to record offices and libraries in Staffordshire, Derbyshire and Cheshire. The biographies of the rest of the 'James Brindley Clan' - my name for the entire related larger family, in honour of its most famous son - are to be found in the section following.

The old Quakers' Cottages on Overton Bank are seen at the right, opposite Clerk bank c.1900. The Quaker Meeting House - still in use - is behind these cottages. See also the story of Margaret Lucas pp. 70/71.

Above, James Brindley in his later years,
and below, portrayed in a sculpture by John
McKenna as the 'great puddler',
for the Droitwich Canal Trust.

Prudence Ellen Brindley.

George Edwin and Mary Elizabeth
(nee Phillips).

Frederick Arthur Brindley.

Richard Brindley aged 11 with father George Edwin.

The Burton family with George Brindley, 4th from right back row, and Mary Agnes (nee Burton)
BELOW: A Brindley clan gathering in Stoke-on-Trent in 1967.

Evening Sentinel

MONDAY, APRIL 24th, 1967

Mr. Robert M. Brinley (he spells his name without a "d") entertained all the Brindley clan in Stoke-on-Trent yesterday—or at least as many of them as he could muster by telephone calls or through the "Sentinel"—and told them some details of the family history about which he has written a book. Mr. Brinley, a New Jersey banker, and owner of a newspaper in Maryland, claims descent from one of the original settlers who went to America with William Penn nearly 300 years ago, and has traced the family history back to the 13th Century.

IT WAS A GREAT DAY FOR THE BRINDLEYS

Chapter 4
James Brindley Clan

Before 1751, following the Julian Calendar, the church year began on Lady Day, 25th March, and ended the following 24th March. The Gregorian Calendar then came into use, giving 1st January as the first day of the year and 31st December the last. In order to catch up with the alterations in the calendar, in 1751, the 25th March became the 1st day of the year and 31st December the last, giving 1751 only 9 months. In 1752, the year commenced on 1st January and ended on 31st December *but* 14th September followed 2nd September, leaving out eleven days. (Causing riots because some ignorant people thought that it meant their lives would be cut short by that period.) From 1753 onwards, the year remained as now.

MATTHEW BRINDLEY 1749-1820

Matthew was born in Alton about 1749 to Joseph, the Millwright, and Sarah Bennit/Bennett. Matthew married Lydia Walker on 7th February 1770 at Alton. Matthew became Clerk to the Wire Works at Alton and enjoyed an affluent life. A large family followed:

James, baptised 18th March 1770;
Rupert, baptised 18th June 1771 married Catherine Finney 10.11.1817;
Margaret, baptised 1772 who must have died young;
Joseph, baptised 5th January 1775;
Mary, baptised 24th November 1777;
Hannah, Baptised 15th July 1780;
John, baptised 3rd September 1780;
Sarah, baptised 6th April 1783;
Susannah, baptised 23rd October 1785;
a second Margaret baptised 17th August 1794.

The birth of James, early in 1770 is testimony to the fact that Lydia was already with child at the time of the marriage. This was not uncommon in those days. Contraception was virtually unknown. Matthew's siblings were:

James, born 1745, who emigrated to America; who married Elizabeth Ogle in 1779.
Elizabeth, baptised 25th August 1751 at Checkley, who married Thomas Salt at Alton 21st July 1771;
Susanna, baptised 27th May 1753/4 at Checkley, who married Joseph Tideswell on 2nd June 1777 at Alton;
Sarah, baptised 26th January 1755 at Checkley, who married Thomas Alkins on 7th October 1786 at Alton;
Mary, baptised 22nd August 1756 at Checkley, who married John Cope on 18th January 1779 at Alton.

Matthew's father Joseph remarried to Lydia Lightwood on 13th February 1762 because his wife Sarah had died. As a result of this Matthew also had a half sister Lydia, baptised on 25th September 1763 and a half brother Henry, born January 1763. This Henry may be the one who later married Ann Collies. Sadly Lydia died that year and Joseph married a third time to Mary Mobberley, an elderly lady. There were no children of this marriage.

Matthew must have known his disappointments and joys but there is little recorded information to detail. The fact of his and Lydia's local esteem is recognised by a large memorial tablet on the wall of Alton Parish Church which reads:

In memory of Matthew Brindley Late of Alton Mills. He departed this life April 11th in the year of our Lord 1826 aged 71. Lydia wife of the above died January 20th 1838 age 88.

His estate was valued at under £450 on his death in 1820 (probably undervalued for tax purposes). The local paper reported his death on 22nd April and stated his age as seventy-one. (Note: There is a tendency for gravestones to be inaccurate concerning ages, often because the headstone was made and paid for long after the person was interred).

JOSEPH BRINDLEY 1720–1790 Millwright

Joseph was born about 1720, as best we know, the son of James Brindley and Susannah (née Bradbury). Records of Brindley events are becoming sparse at this period, possibly due to church records being lost or damaged or the influences of Quakers; unless there is an unexpected find we shall never know. He is thought to have been the second born after James, his famous brother.

By what circumstance we don't know but he eventually turned up in Alton, having acquired the smelting mill business. However, before that he married Sarah Bennitt/Bennett in Alton on 17th December 1746.

There has been little found to indicate where Joseph and Sarah lived at this time or what occupation he followed. However, I found a baptism at Waterfall, which is not that far from Alton. The entry in the Parish Register is for the baptism of James, son of Joseph and Sarah, and dated 8th May 1748. This now proves to be the first son of Joseph the Millwright of Alton.

Son Matthew followed and was baptised at Alton on 30th October 1748. Soon after that, Joseph and Sarah must have moved to Checkley, because four daughters were baptised there; Elizabeth, baptised 25th August 1751 who married Thomas Salt in 21st July 1771; Susanna, bapt. 27th May, 1753/4, married Joseph Tideswell, 2nd June 1777; Sarah, bapt. 26th January 1755, who married Thomas Alkins on 7th October 1786; and Mary, baptised 22nd August 1756 who married John Cope on 18th January 1779.

How he earned a living at Checkley is unknown. Sarah must have died because Joseph married Lydia Lightwood at Alton on 13th February 1762. Two children of this union quickly followed; Henry baptised January 1763 and Lydia baptised 25th September 1763. Lydia also died and was buried on 11th November 1763, leaving Joseph grief stricken and with two more young children to bring up motherless, in addition to the children of his previous marriage.

Joseph married a third time to Mary Mobberley, a 50 years old spinster, at Leek on 3rd July 1764. This was probably a convenience for both of them rather than a love match. There were no children from the arrangement. Joseph died in December 1790 and was buried at Alton on 26th December. His estate was valued at not more than £3000.

JOHN BRINDLEY: Master Potter of Burslem 1721-1807

Parents: James and Susannah (née Bradbury). John was probably born at Tunstead near Wormhill, Derbyshire. The family later moved in 1726 to Lowe Hill Farm between Bradnop and Leek, near Wyldegoose House/Farm, a home of the original Brindleys from Cheshire. As soon as he was deemed ready, around ten years of age, he was sent to Burslem to learn the potter's trade. In this he became very successful and prospered, mixing with the entrepreneurial classes then making their presence felt on the burgeoning industrial scene.

He knew and did business with Josiah Wedgwood, from time to time providing him with basic pottery ware for decoration and finishing. He had a factory and large three storey Queen Anne style house built at Longport, Burslem, within a mile of Wedgwood's House and factory at Etruria. Only one gatepost of Brindley's house now survives on what is now a modern housing estate.

On 8th October 1748, he married Ann Rogers. A son, Francis, was born in 1749 and baptised on the 13th August, followed by John, baptised 17th May 1752; James,baptised 1st January 1754, who married Catherine Morris on 22nd April 1784 at Church Lawton; and Joseph, baptised 22nd March 1756.

John's wife Ann died in September 1758 and he remarried two years later to Hannah Stevenson, a widow (née Taylor) in September 1760 at Stoke Church. They had two children: Susannah, who only lived two years and Taylor Brindley, born 1763, who died unmarried in 1786 aged 23. His second wife Hannah died in July 1779.

Around 1773 he erected two works at Longport, Burslem, which he leased to tenants. These appear to have remained in the family to the 1840s, when they were sold by Joseph Brindley (his grandson).

John was a churchwarden of St John's, Burslem, and signed his name to a notice the churchwardens issued on 8th July 1788, which pledged to enforce laws restricting the selling of goods on Sunday. They also wanted to enforce the times that public houses were allowed to open and prevent *"illicit tippling"*.

In the list of subscribers to a fund to promote an Act of Parliament authorising the construction of the Trent and Mersey Canal, Thomas Whieldon and Josiah Wedgwood were Treasurers and the document contains the actual signatures of those who promised subscriptions. The deed is dated 27th June, 1765. Most of the leading manufacturers of that day subscribed including Hugh Booth, Humphrey Palmer, Josiah Wedgwood, Anthony Keeling, Thomas Adams, Thos. Warburton, Isaac Warburton, John Brindley, Joshua Heath and others.

From Notes on Some North Staffordshire Families by Percy. Adams.

In 1773, he built a house in Dale Hall, Newcastle, which became the parsonage for the nearby St Paul's. In 1805, he acquired an ironworks at Brockmoor, near Kinver and spent the last few years of his life living at Union Hall, Kinver. He died in 1807, a wealthy man, and was buried in Kinver churchyard.

THOMAS JOHN BRINDLEY 1806-1848

The son of James and Catherine (née Morris), he was born in 1806. The only member of the James Brindley Clan to aspire to a coat of arms (granted in 1828), he was the grandson of John Brindley the potter of Burslem. He died, apparently childless, at the age of 42, in 1848. It is uncertain whether the male line of this Brindley has continued to the present day.

His coat of arms contains three scallops, probably an heraldic reference to the first Brindley arms. This would seem to indicate that the College of Heralds accepted that Thomas John's family were descended from the original Brundelegh de Brindley family.

JOSEPH BRINDLEY married to Ellen Bowman

Joseph is a somewhat elusive and mysterious figure. He married (we believe) Ellen Bowman in 1683. He may have been married previously. His brother in law, Henry Bowman, was a signatory to a Quaker removal certificate relating to a Luke Brindley from Leek in 1684. Luke had emigrated to Philadelphia earlier. It is not beyond the bounds of possibility that Luke may have been his son by an earlier marriage, a brother, or a cousin. Another signator was

Old Brindley homes near Leek. Wildgoose House & right, Lowe Hill.

Hestor/Esther Fallowfield, who was born a Brindley and married in 1666 at Leek. She may have been a sister or cousin of Luke. It seems highly likely that these Brindleys *would* be related. There are only three or four Josephs known who might be candidates to be this particular Joseph. The big problem is that there may be a Joseph who is not actually recorded anywhere. As we know, absence of proof is not proof of absence!

JAMES BRINDLEY of Wormhill and Lowe Hill, Leek

Born around 1684, the only son of Joseph and Ellen (née Bowman), little is known of James' early life. He married Susanna Bradbury at Chesterfield by licence on 25th January 1751, when she was probably aged a little over 21 years. An earlier attempt to marry there had failed because no parental consent had been obtained for her marriage. The Bowmans had Quaker leanings and this may account for the lack of baptisms of their children being found.

The couple's first son was the famous James, engineer and canal builder. They also had John, who became a famous Potter of Burslem and a rich man, and Joseph (of Alton) who also did well. The fourth brother, Henry, seems to have become a farmer and managed to live quietly in Cheshire. He may be the Henry who married Elizabeth (aka Betty) Shaw of Bosley.

The daughters Mary, Esther and Ann all married and lead quiet lives, although I admit to not researching them in depth, thus far.

JAMES BRINDLEY 1716-1772   Canal Engineer. The Old Schemer!

Much has been written elsewhere about this famous engineer of Leek. His birth in Derbyshire doesn't take away from the fact that his family were of Staffordshire and he was more closely connected to Leek than anywhere else. That he was an inventive man, some say genius, tends to obscure or polarise opinions about him.

James Brindley was born in 1716 at Tunstead, Derbyshire, he was the first-born of James Brindley and Susanna Bradbury's seven children.

When he was aged 10 the family moved to Leek and James was employed on odd jobs and farm work. In 1733, aged 17, he was apprenticed for seven years as a carpenter and millwright, to Abraham Bennett of Sutton near Macclesfield. Early on James was chastised by Bennett when he made a mistake in repairing the spokes of a wheel, but from a hesitant start he learnt quickly and, when making repairs at a silk mill in Macclesfield, aged 19, the superintendent observed that he was an excellent workman.

A couple of years later he was skilled and experienced enough to complete the repair work of a paper mill on the River Dane, on behalf of Abraham Bennett, who by this stage was placing great reliance on James's skill.

Such was James's enthusiasm that one Saturday night he is said to have walked twenty-five miles to Manchester, to view and note details of new machinery at Smedley Mill on the River Irk, before walking back for work on Monday morning.

When Abraham Bennett died James carried on the business for the Bennett family, until the business was wound up in 1742. He now returned to Leek and built (? rebuilt) a substantial mill on Mill Street, near Abbey Green. This mill still stands today as a museum, celebrating James and his achievements.

In 1750, he rented a workshop near Burslem through the Wedgwood family and began his long-term association with the 20 year old Josiah Wedgwood.

In 1755, he was engaged to attend to the machinery in a silk mill under construction in Congleton. Another man had responsibility for the whole operation, but it soon became obvious to everyone that the man was not capable. Brindley declared himself better able to do the job and the mill owner agreed, letting him take charge. Brindley made design improvements to the machinery which led to reduced costs in production and which were eventually taken up by the cotton industry.

His work at the Clifton Colliery, which suffered from flooding, started in 1750, and was to enhance his reputation further and lead to his involvement with the Duke of Bridgewater.

In 1757 he constructed a flint mill at Tunstall for Thomas Baddeley, and he went on to build many others. One, which still survives, is the Cheddleton Flint Mill.

In 1758, he inspected and overhauled pumps for Earl Gower and did work on a flint-grinding windmill for J & T Wedgwood at Burslem. His diary mentions work on a mobile water engine, and he patented a steam-engine boiler. And in this year he began surveying for the Trent & Mersey canal, which would eventually lead to his great project of the Grand Trunk System.

In 1759, he visited Coalbrookdale iron foundry and met Abraham Darby II. He was engaged with steam engines at Cheadle, Staffs, Bedworth and Little Wyreley, for Phineas Hussey and was called in by the Duke of Bridgewater to survey the Bridgewater canal, Worsley to Manchester Section.

1760 saw him acting as a Parliamentary witness, in his capacity as engineer of the

Bridgewater Canal. He worked on a mill at Tatton for Samuel Edgerton, worked at Congleton and purchased a share in the Turnhurst Estate and Goldenhill Colliery. He also became a partner with his brother John, the Potter, in the Longport Pottery.

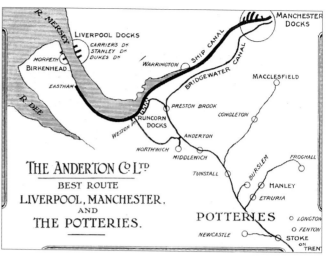

The illegitimate son of Mary Bennett was born this year in Burslem; some said that James was the father. This is discussed later in the book.

Brindleys earliest canal work.

1761 saw the Barton Aqueduct completed and opened for traffic. Considered to be a wonder of the age, if not the world, the structure showed some signs of strain at first, as small cracks appeared when the water was first introduced. James was overcome with anxiety and stress to the point that he had to return to his lodgings in Stretford, and take to his bed. In the event, the viaduct held up and gave many years of reliable service.

In 1762 his work rate continued. He was engaged on surveys for the Chester Canal, the branch canal from Sale Moor to Stockport (it was never made), and he again visited Parliament as a witness, in his capacity of Chief Engineer to the Bridgewater Canal. He surveyed for navigation from Chester to Shrewsbury, and from Rotherham to Doncaster. He also entered into an association with John Henshall.

1763: He spent ten days surveying the Lower Avon navigation, advising George Perrott on improvements.

1764: Engaged supervising construction of the Bridgewater Canal.

1765: He married and took up residence at Turnhurst. He was appointed Engineer to Calder and Hebble Navigation. He planned and constructed the portion from Salterhebble to Sowerby Bridge. 30th December: The first public meeting was held for the Trent and Mersey Canal Company. Josiah Wedgwood said:

'BRINDLEY was called upon to state his plans, BROUGHT THEM FORWARD WITH SUCH EXTRAORDINARY LUCIDITY OF DETAIL AS TO MAKE THEM CLEAR TO THE DULLEST INTELLECT PRESENT.'

Brindley urged that it should be called the GRAND TRUNK CANAL, as he judged that it would be the main artery from which other canals would branch.

1766: Work started on the Grand Trunk Canal.

1767: Engaged in surveying the Bradford canal, Rochdale canal and Stockton to Darlington canal. In September, a contemporary of wrote (concerning Harecastle tunnel):

'Gentlemen come to view our EIGHTH WONDER OF THE WORLD, the subterraneous navigation, which is a cutting by the GREAT MR BRINDLEY, who handles rocks as easily as you would plum pies, and MAKES THE FOUR ELEMENTS SUBSERVIENT TO HIS WILL. HE IS AS PLAIN A LOOKING MAN AS ONE OF THE BOORS OF THE PEAKE, OR ONE

OF HIS OWN CARTERS; BUT WHEN HE SPEAKS, ALL EARS LISTEN, AND EVERY MIND IS FILLED WITH WONDER, AT THE THINGS HE PRONOUNCES TO BE PRACTICABLE.'

1768: Surveyed for the Leeds and Liverpool Canal.

1769: Surveyed for the Leeds and Selby Canal and the Oxford Canal.

1770: Prepared scheme for Thames Navigation improvements.

1771: The Chesterfield Canal started construction.

1772: Surveyed for the Lancaster Canal.

He died on the 27th September. After a long day surveying the Caldon canal to Froghall, James had stopped for the night at an Ipstones Inn and was given 'damp bedding'. He became ill and died after a few days. He had developed diabetes a few years before and this would probably have been a factor. Wedgwood wrote: *"Poor Mr Brindley has nearly finished his course in this world. He says he must leave us, and indeed I do not expect to find him alive in the morning".*

Wedgwood. who visited Brindley at Turnhurst Hall every day during his last week, said that his death *"...will deprive us of a valuable friend, and the world of one of those great geniuses who seldom live to see justice done to their singular abilities, but must trust to future ages for that tribute of praise and fair fame they so greatly merit."*

That he was an inventive man, some say a genius, tends to polarise opinions about James. Sharing the same Y chromosome, I feel in a position to empathise with him. James knew well the feeling we today call stress from overwork. He was single-minded, determined, yet modest, too. His portrait shows a kindly face with honest eyes. In some ways he has been cruelly put down. It is stated that he could not read or write. As Kathleen M. Evans rightly pointed out in her book, he could do both perfectly adequately. Some of his notebooks have survived and can be seen to prove the point - he wrote in a practised and confident hand. That he spelt phonetically was characteristic of his era - even educated clergy were apt to spell erratically, rendering different versions of the same name at subsequent baptisms.

Some critics have also taken exception to his rough manner of dress. Quite how they expected a 'hands-on' outdoor engineer to dress is hard to imagine. The man led by example, as much as anything else, and was always likely to find himself wading in muddy canal beds to demonstrate puddling. He was out in all weathers, and being on a horse, sometimes for hours, is well known to impart a certain odour and dishevel one's powdered wig quite awfully!

And people raised in Mayfair drawing rooms, who never had to get their hands dirty, were not noted for their insight into real life. They took exception to James's honest Staffordshire accent and dialect. To James' credit, he does not seem to have been tempted 'to put it on'. He would have been well aware of how the refined London accent sounded. He kept both his feet firmly on the ground and did not give in to such vanity.

Some people believe that James was the father of an illegitimate son called John Bennett, from whom the writer Arnold Bennett was believed to have been descended. I enquired from the Arnold Bennett Society if there were any direct male descendents of Arnold. Unfortunately, the answer was no. However, there may well be direct male descendents of John Bennett through Arnold's brother, Frank. I hope to be able to have our DNA compared, if I can trace a willing male descendent, to prove or disprove the assertion.

James married Ann Henshall and had two children: Ann, who died at sea returning from

Australia, unmarried; and Susanna, who married James Bettington and emigrated to Australia. They had descendents, including James Brindley Bettington who married Rebecca Lawson on 7th June 1830 at Castlereagh, New South Wales, and became a very wealthy man.

James Brindley Bettington Snr. arrived in Sydney on the Brig *"Ionia"* on 19th December 1827. He at once began the business of a shipping agent as well as representative of the London firm of John Bettington, Sons & Company, general merchants, in which he was associated with his father John Bettington and brother John Henshall Bettington. Being closely identified with the mercantile interests of the community, he was elected in 1828 to the directorate of the Bank of New South Wales and remained on the board for many years.

He was appointed a magistrate of the Territory in 1831 and, during the period 1851-53, represented the Pastoral Districts of Wellington and Bligh, in the Partly Elective and Partly Non-Elective Legislative Council of New South Wales. Between 1834 and 1839 he acquired several purchase grants for pastoral purposes, giving to those situated in the county of Brisbane the name 'Brindley Park', provided for in the deed of grant for a comparatively small area near Merriwa. The property was considerably enlarged in subsequent years.

About 1840, he purchased Oatlands House, near Parramatta. James was a shrewd businessman; at the time of James Brindley Bettington Jnr's, death in 1915, his will left £6,000,000. When James Jnr's wife, Caroline Sophia, died, her will left over £7,000,000.

Their other children were: John Henshall Bettington, 1839-1850; William Lawson Bettington, 1842-1883; Susannah Caroline, born 1848; and Rebecca, born 1834. Today, there are numerous descendents of James, through the female line, in Australia.

Today there is a canal side development in Birmingham named after James Brindley, there is a statue remembering him at the waterways marina in Stoke on Trent, and Coventry also have recently erected a statue in his honour.

Dr Erasmus Darwin MD wrote an eulogistic poem to James:

So with strong arm immortal Brindley leads
His long canals and parts the velvet meads
Winding in lucid lines, the waiting mass
Minds the firm rock, or loads the deep morass;

While rising locks a thousand hills alarm,
Flings o'er a thousand streams its silver arm;
Feeds the long vales, the redding woodland laves,
And plenty, arts and commerce freight the waves.

Nymphs, who erstwhile on Brindley's early bier,
On snow-white bosoms shed the incessant tear,
Adorn his tomb. Oh: raise the marble bust,
Proclaim his honors and protect his dust

With urns inverted round the sacred shrine,
Their ozier-wreaths let weeping Naiads twine:
While on the top mechanic Genius stands,
Counts the fleet waves and balances the sands.

BRINDLEY'S FLINT-MILL AT THE PRESENT DAY.
Brindley's derelict wind flint mill from Metyard's
Life of Wedgwood

WILLIAM BURTON BRINDLEY 1837-1889

William was born at Alton and baptised on the 8th October 1837, the base born son of Helen Burton. His father was not mentioned on the baptism entry. However, his mother married his father William Horobin (later Brindley) the following year, thus legitimising him.

Little is known about William Burton Brindley's early years. Combined evidence of gravestone inscription and census information indicates that he moved to Rocester around 1864 and is assumed to have married a woman called Charlotte. (Marriage not yet found) Charlotte's death was registered in the Uttoxeter registration district. She died at Rocester on 3rd January 1880, aged 45 years, of acute phythis (tuberculosis). The death certificate says that she was the wife of William Brindley who was present at the death.

William and Charlotte lived at 16 Churnet Row and raised a family. In 1881, William, now a widower, was working as a stonemason and had the following children:
Alfred Edward (also called himself Alfred Henry) baptised at Rocester 30th April 1865, married twice:
1. Sarah Jane Gaunt on 23rd December 1888 at Uttoxeter and 2. Jessica Burton, in 1906 at Uttoxeter;
Joseph, born about 1871 at Rocester and who married Ellen Gaunt on 15th August 1896 at Rocester. Joseph died and was buried on 26th April 1911 at Rocester;
Samuel, born about 1877 at Rocester and appears to have remained a bachelor; Anne, born at Rocester about 1867, who married Samuel Burton on 10th June 1889.

William died 8th April 1896 and was buried in Rocester churchyard alongside Charlotte.

GEORGE BRINDLEY 1839-1904

George was born at Alton, Staffordshire in 1839 to Helen 'Ellen' Horobin (née Burton, later to assume the Brindley name) and baptised on 6th October 1839 at Alton in the name George Horobin (p.33). Parents William Horobin (later Brindley) and mother Ellen.

George married Mary Ann Pountain on 27th November 1875 at the Wesleyan Chapel Uttoxeter, using the name George Brindley rather than Horobin. The choice of a non-conformist church was probably because he intended to use Brindley as his surname rather than Horobin. Had he gone to Alton church, the vicar would be likely to know that he was baptised as 'Horobin' and might have insisted that he be married in that name. The birth of their first son, George Edwin Brindley, on 25th February 1876, indicates that Mary Ann was already pregnant when they married.

George worked in a local quarry as a stone-getter and mason, probably working in the same quarry as his father who may have got him the job. By 1880, he and Mary Ann were able to buy the Star Inn, on Main Road, Hollington. I suspect that his father in law, John Pountain, may have been able to give financial assistance.

Three more children followed: Clara Ann, baptised 3rd November 1878; Prudence Ellen, baptised 28th March 1880; and William, baptised 1881, who died within a few weeks.

Mary Ann's premature death from tuberculosis in October 1882 must have been a great blow to the family. She was buried 26th October, in Hollington Churchyard, leaving George to bring up the children by himself. No doubt relatives pitched in. George's sister Dinah Mart was nearby, as was Joseph Walter Brindley, his brother. George never re-married and lived on to 1904, by when he had the satisfaction of seeing all his children married and settled.

His death certificate says he died from haematemesis, syncope (vomiting of blood). He was buried in Hollington churchyard on 29th September 1904, alongside Mary Ann.

HARRIET HOROBIN 1844-?

Father William Horobin (later Brindley)

Harriet, of Hollington, was born about 1844 at New Brighton, Cheshire. Her marriage at Hollington on the 23rd August 1864 to John Smith, 19yrs, labourer of Broadgate Hall Farm, revealed that her father was William Horobin, a stonegetter. This is without doubt the William Horobin *Brindley* of Hollington. Later baptisms at Hollington clearly show the family links to validate this belief, as does the 1881 census for Hollington and Checkley. The curious detail about Harriet is the location of her birthplace. When all her brothers and sisters were born within four miles of Hollington, why was she born at such a remove?

Research to find her birth or baptism has been fruitless to date. It occurs to me that there could be one possible explanation for this. Suppose she was the result of an affair? If her father William had a relationship with a woman of Hollington other than his wife, that woman might feel the need to go away to have the child where people didn't know her. Then, that woman could have had the baby baptised in *her* surname and that would explain why I couldn't find Harriet's baptism. Later, when time had passed, and the dust had so to speak settled, she might return to Hollington. Life would go on and, if not forgotten, the people concerned could adjust to the facts. Harriet and John Smith had a large family:

Eliza Ann, born 1864;
Elizabeth Ellen, baptised 9th June 1867 when he was a stonegetter of Hollington;
William? Born 1868 abt;
Harriet, born 1872 abt;
Kate, baptised 27th December 1874;
John Edward, baptised 25th March 1877;
Mary Ellen, baptised 21st September 1879;
George, baptised 9th October 1881;
Ethel May, baptised 13th April 1884;
Emily, baptised 10th April 1887;
Clara Jane, baptised 18th August 1889;
George, baptised 11th December 1889 and died 26th January 1890;
Harry, baptised 26th August 1891 and died 27th September 1891;
Harriet Ann, baptised 29th April 1895 and died 12th May 1895;
Lily, baptised 26th June 1898
Alice Cecilia, baptised 22nd June 1902.

Some later entries show her husband as John Thomas Smith, and some as John Gould Smith. The reason for this is not known. The place of Harriet's death was probably at Hollington.

JOSEPH WALTER BRINDLEY 1850 -?

Joseph Walter was born in Hollington on the 9th March 1850 and was the first of William Horobin Brindley's and Ellen's (Helen née Burton) children to be baptised at Checkley and registered in the Cheadle registration district with the Brindley surname. He was actually registered as Walter Joseph, a mistake, as, ever after, he was to use the names in the order Joseph Walter. Who made the mistake we can't know, but mistake it was.

My first glimpse of him was in the 1881 census. He was then living at High Ridges, Checkley and farming 13 acres. He appeared to have five children, but, I quickly worked out that if he was the father of the eldest, he would have only been fifteen when she was born. It took the usual patient process of careful checking and sending for certificates to work out the true position. The marriage certificate revealed that he had married a widow - Catherine Beardmore at Oakamoor Holy Trinity Church on 9th March 1874. She was actually born Catherine Barker at Cheadle about 1843.

Further checking eventually showed that his wife brought with her two children from her previous marriage: Catherine Beardmore and Ernest W. Beardmore. The census entry was therefore slightly inaccurate. These were step-children and not strictly his son and daughter. The census showed them as Catherine B. Brindley and Ernest W. B. Brindley. One wonders if Ernest retained the 'Brindley' surname in later life.

Joseph Walter and his wife Catherine (Hollington Parish Register entries also have her as Katherine and Kate) had the following children together:

Joseph Barker, born 13th December 1874 at Green Dale, Cheadle, who married Beatrice Ethel Maude Barker on 22nd May 1899 at St Giles RC church, Cheadle. They lived at Well Street at the time of marriage and he was an insurance agent. One wonders if they were cousins because of the recurrence of the Barker name. They had a son, Victor Lawrence William, born 1902 at Cheadle. At this point, Joseph Walter was a quarry foreman by occupation.
Sarah Ellen, baptised 15.12.1876 at Checkley.
Gertrude Blanche, born 1879 and baptised 4th May 1879 at Checkley.
William James, baptised 25th March 1883 at Checkley.
Frederick George, baptised 5th April 1885 at Checkley.

Joseph Walter was present at the death of his father in 1889 and confirmed that his name as William Horobin Brindley; the key information needed to solve the Brindley/Horobin puzzle.

DINAH BRINDLEY 1852-?
Parents William Horobin Brindley and Ellen (Helen) née Burton.

Dinah Brindley was born about 1852 in Hollington to William Horobin Brindley and wife Ellen (née Burton). She would have had a typical country girl's upbringing, helping her mother with household tasks and looking after younger siblings. She must have had a reasonable education by the standard of the day because she signed her name to her marriage certificate in a confident style. By 1871, aged around nineteen, she was employed as a kitchen maid at Huntley Hall, in Cheadle. Later, she progressed to being a cook in a household in the Blythe Bridge area of Stone.

Some time prior to 1873 she met John William Mart, a coachman, also of Blythe Bridge. They fell in love and married at Stone Congregational Church, Gatherville Terrace, Stone, on the 29th December 1873. She was aged just twenty-one. Witnesses were George Brindley, her brother, and Anne Brindley, almost certainly her sister. The couple soon moved back to Hollington, living near her parents William and Ellen. Children soon arrived:

Ann Ellen Mart was baptised on the 20th March 1875 at Checkley;
Dinah Ethel on 24th June 1877;
Eliza Ann on 15th April 1879 at Checkley;
John William on 21st June 1880 at Hollington;
Charlotte May on 27th August 1882 at Hollington when they were living at Castle Hays, Burton on Trent, and John was a waggoner;
Florence Elizabeth on 8th November 1885;
Ernest William on 31st October 1887, who died within a fortnight on 13th November 1887;
Alice Ethel Maude baptised 15th June 1889 who died a few days later, on 23rd June.

Dinah's death has not been noted to date.

GEORGE EDWIN BRINDLEY 1876-1968

Described as medium to stocky build, 5ft 6ins tall, blue eyes, brown hair, red nose George Edwin was the eldest born son of George (Horobin) Brindley and Mary Ann (née Pountain). We don't know if he was aware of his father's name change to Brindley. The first born of four children, he was named George after his father and Edwin after his mother's brother. He was born in Rocester, Staffs, on 25th February 1876, at the maternal home in Back Lane and baptised at Hollington on 7th May that year. In 1880, his father and mother acquired the Star Inn at Hollington where George Edwin and his siblings, Clara Ann, Prudence Ellen and a younger brother, William, who died shortly after birth, were brought up.

It is believed that he lived for a time in the Burton household at Rocester and that may have been where he met his wife to be. As well as helping his father at the inn, he also worked in a local quarry where his father also worked during the day. Quarries were numerous in the area and an obvious alternative to agricultural employment which was poorly paid.

After his marriage to Mary Elizabeth Phillips at St Mary's Church Uttoxeter, on 18th September 1902, the couple lived at Ground Hollow, Hollington, which is about fifteen minutes walk from the Star Inn. Mary Elizabeth was born 27th March 1876 at Uttoxeter to Richard Phillips and Elizabeth (née Dougherty).

He claimed to have ridden stagecoach as a boy. Later in life he improved his income and his status locally by leasing Red Quarry, also known as Field's Park Quarry, Croxden, from John Fielding. He ran this enterprise from 1929 to his retirement in 1949. At its peak it employed 35 men and produced good quality red Staffordshire sandstone for which there was a big demand after the First War. George Edwin's quarry supplied the stone for St Edward's Catholic Church, Macclesfield, built around 1930 in memory of Edward Lomas, a local mill-owner's son. The new Coventry Cathedral also used Hollington stone in its construction.

George Edwin working at Field's Park Quarry, Croxden.

According to Colin Shaw, a quarryman of Ground Hollow, (January 2002 visit to Hollington), George Edwin also quarried at Beggars Well Quarry. The Field's Park Quarry still exists but is not worked. Rumour has it that it may be worked again soon.

The Great Gate cottage might have been tied in some way to the quarry. Later, he was able to buy it and he lived there until after his wife Mary Elizabeth, known as Mollie, died in 1955. Soon after her death, he went to live with his daughter Ivy Mary Belfield, her husband George Arthur Belfield, and grandson Edwin Arthur, at the Waterworks Cottage, half a mile away on the road to Cheadle.

I remember that he would call his wife 'mother' and she would call him 'Dadda' which I thought eccentric. He was a strange character with a perverse, if not cruel, sense of humour. One of his tricks was to place the hot spoon on your hand after he had stirred his tea. - I speak from experience. Another tale I heard was about one of the quarry workers, into whose tea he secretly added laxative. The poor man suffered the obvious results soon after, and George Edwin thought it an hilarious prank.

In later life he had a bloated red strawberry-like nose. This was said to be due to stings received when he disturbed a hornet's nest, a prank that misfired. He had noticed the nest in the hedgerow and beckoned one of his workers who was a bit simple-minded, to *"come and look"*. The man duly came and George Edwin poked the nest with a stick, expecting that they would frighten the man. Instead, it was he who received the wrath of the hornets.

Despite being regarded as a difficult and obstinate old grouch by almost all the family, his wife Mary Elizabeth was devoted to him. She would remove his boots when he came home and put on his slippers for him. She was an exceptionally kind woman, loved by everybody. She was always for peace and neither my father nor mother ever remembered her losing her temper.

George Edwin, like most Brindleys, enjoyed a drink. He always had a bottle of whisky in his bureau, yet he never was seen drunk. Possibly this contributed towards his red nose. Once, he suffered from rheumatism and bought the crop of one year's apple orchard to make cider, apparently an old country recipe. Anyway, the plan appeared to work because his rheumatics disappeared, never to return. He had hernia problems early in life and wore a truss.

He followed and played cricket, as did his sons. He would have been appalled at the modern cricket phenomenon of unruly crowd behaviour and colourful outfits. He was definitely a traditionalist and a Victorian. He was also a follower of Stoke City football club. In his last years, during the early 1960s, Michael Gent of Great Gate recalls taking him to see them play. George Edwin could be quite grumpy. *"If someone blocked his view during the match, he'd strike them with his walking stick"!* That sounds just like him.

He is believed to have sold the family bible to visiting Americans in the early fifties. They were apparently staying in Cheadle and made contact with him. Ivy remembered him showing the visitors into the parlour. Shortly after the visit, Fred noticed the bible's absence and, despite he and brother George grilling him, he wouldn't admit to parting with it. We assume the bible is living comfortably with an American Brindley, and have never been able to discover who they were. We don't especially want it back but would dearly like to know the data it contained, as family names were dutifully recorded in it. So Fred, in New Jersey, if you're still there… how about it?

Life in the cottage at Great Gate was primitive in certain respects. Even as late as 1950, the lighting was by gas or oil. There was no hot running water and the toilet facility was a hundred yards up the hill from the back of the house. It comprised a stone built shed in which there was a wooden 'plank' with two holes cut in it. If you were lucky, the pit below would have been emptied recently. As a boy I would sit and count one-two-three.... until I heard the impact! If it was nearly full, that was something else! On a wild night in wintertime, you really had to be motivated to go 'up the field'. Forward planning was everything.

Taking a candle to bed was, from a child's point of view, a great adventure. The flickering flame threw gigantic dancing shadows across the walls. It gripped the imagination. Outside, the screech of an owl or distant sound of water over pebbles added to the mood. In the morning, the air was like wine and one could see rabbits frolicking on the opposite hillside.

If you wanted a bath, you had to fetch the galvanised tin contraption from where it hung on an outside wall, set it out in front of the fire, and wait for ever while kettles of hot water were poured in it.

There were good aspects to being there, though. My grandma made preserves and jams, bottled her own pickles and salted hams. Fresh vegetables came from the garden, while seasonal wild fruits, just begging to be picked, grew close by. Mushrooms that sprang up overnight in the field opposite would often appear on the breakfast plate, and these had real taste, unlike those available in the shops today.

George Edwin's lifetime spanned a period of unprecedented advance, almost from the age of the horse to the space age. In 1876, when he was born, most roads in England were narrow, primitive and unlit. Aircraft were unknown. Women had no vote. Fridges, radios, televisions were in the future. By the time he died, motorways were commonplace, electricity was everywhere, and man was just about to land on the Moon.

George Edwin died peacefully from old age on 17th February 1968, just a few days short of his 92nd birthday. He was buried in Hollington churchyard and lies with Mary Elizabeth née Phillips, first grave on the right from the lych gate.

CLARA ANN BRINDLEY 1878-1945

Parents: George Horobin Brindley and Mary Ann (née Pountain).

Clara Ann was born in 1878. She was baptised on 3rd November 1878 at Hollington. On 18th October 1895, she had an illegitimate son, John Edward, known as little Jack, baptised at Hollington. She was seventeen years of age. The father's name was not mentioned. John Edward died when an infant and lies in Hollington churchyard.

She married Joseph Albert Bull at Hollington on 17th December 1902. Her first son of the marriage, also called John Edward, (known as Bertie) Bull, was born 1903 and died in 1905. He was also buried in the churchyard.

Clara developed diabetes late in life and was treated at North Staffordshire Infirmary. She was blind in her last years due to her diabetes. Clara Ann Bull died on 8th April 1945 and was buried in Hollington churchyard facing her parents' grave.

8.35 pm Monday 11th February 2002

Just received a telephone call from my good friend and genealogy researcher Ivy Mary Brunt of Tean, Staffs. She knew of my family interests and had good news. A friend had called to see her - Val Bull. In conversation, Val mentioned that her grandmother was Clara Ann

Brindley! Ivy gave me her phone number and by 9 pm I was having a conversation with my newly discovered relative. I then found, at a stroke, all Clara Ann Brindley's descendents, of whom I was previously totally unaware.

Clara Ann and her husband had a son, George William Brindley Bull. He married Frances Camwell about 1928 and they had two daughters, Valerie and Rose Bull.

Valerie had recently married a Mr Manion. Rose had married Bramwell Aubrey Hurst and they had two sons, Andrew and Philip. I spoke to Philip and he told me about his two sons, Robert, born 1985, and Jonathan, born 1988.

Joseph Bull and Clara Ann also had a daughter, Clara Ellen (known as Nellie) who married Arthur Kinder. Their children were Mary, Ronald Arthur, David, Gerald and Sandra.

I would soon meet my 'new' cousins and exchange news and photographs. One never knows the moment in family history research! I hope I have the same success with tracing Prudence Ellen's descendents.

PRUDENCE ELLEN 1880-1947

Parents: George Brindley and Mary Ann (née Pountain).

Prudence Ellen, known as Nellie, was baptised on 28th March 1880. She married James Swinson at Checkley Parish Church on 14th April 1903 at the age of 23. He was a quarryman. Witnesses were Mrs Elizabeth Whieldon and William Swinson. They continued to live in the Hollington area. Nellie developed breast cancer late in life and her breast turned black. She didn't mention it to anyone until she was past any medical assistance. The couple's grave is in Hollington churchyard.

Their possible descendents are unknown at this time.

WILLIAM BRINDLEY 1881-1881

Parents George Brindley and Mary Ann (née Pountain). Baptised 10th June 1881 at Hollington, and died within a few days of birth.

GEORGE BRINDLEY 1904-1968

George was the first-born son of George Edwin Brindley and Mary Elizabeth (née Phillips.) His birth was 12th July 1904 at Ground Hollow and he was baptised at Hollington church on 11th September 1904. He was very much like his father in appearance.

When he was about 14 his father arranged for him to work for a farmer, whose name we don't know, in the Alton area. George was unhappy there. He missed home terribly and, after a few days, absconded during the night and walked about five miles through the unlit countryside to home. He arrived, according to his own account, around three in the morning. It took him ages to arouse the household. His dad, George Edwin, was unimpressed and promptly marched him back to the farmer.

Soon after, at his father's insistence, George was made to work in the red quarry, Great Gate, Croxden, run by his father. During this period he got sandstone dust in his lungs and it caused him ongoing health problems for the rest of his life.

Later, he became 'engaged' to Mary Agnes Burton of Alton (born 21st December 1907, baptised 19th January 1908 at Alton RC chapel, parents Francis Richard Burton (known as Dick) and Maria Agnes (née Hammersley), always known as Polly (nb many early baptism names are 'latinised', a practice continued in Roman Catholic churches today).

Mary Agnes (née Burton) died 8th May 1988, aged 80 of congestive heart failure. Her siblings were Katherine (Kitty), Hilda, Winifred (Winnie) born 21st November 1904, George, Nellie, Francis (Frank) and Joe. Her Hammersley descent has just been established and is traceable back to Richard Hammersley, born 1695 at Uttoxeter, who married an Ann.

When Mary Agnes became pregnant, George had to break the news to his dad. Just to make things worse, he had to admit to George Edwin that Mary was not only pregnant but was a Roman Catholic. For some reason, George Edwin was prejudiced against that religion. As George told the story:*"The next day I had to visit the vicar who had me on my knees all day. In fact I had no skin left on them because I was up, down, up, down for hours, praying for forgiveness."* (Source: Margaret Mary Brindley)

He married Mary Agnes Burton at Alton Catholic Church and had four children:

George Richard, born 5th June 1932, married Emily Barkes in 1956, died from brain cancer 13th June 1978, aged 46, and had one son Anthony Neil;

Mary, born 21st November 1929, who married 1. Jack Peaty and had five children, Angela, Richard, Bernard, Christopher and Julia.; 2. Barry Deeming, with whom she had: Joanna, in 1971;

Margaret, birth registered at Uttoxeter on 31st January 1934, born 18th December 1933, died 20th June 1988. She married Donald William Walker, a sales rep. on 12th September 1953 at St John's Chapel, Alton RC Church. They had no children;

Francis Edwin, born 27th September 1943 at 3 Saltersford Lane, Tithe Barn, Alton, who married 1. Kathleen Elizabeth Smith, who died from cancer. 2. Jennifer Matthews. Edwin has a daughter, Elizabeth Anne from his first marriage.

George was a keen and much respected cricketer, playing for Hollington and Alton cricket clubs. He also played football for Hollington. His father George Edwin was believed to have lent him some money to enable him to obtain the tenancy of the Royal Oak Inn in Alton near Horse Road. Later in life he had bronchial problems related to silicosis.

Unknown to George Edwin at the time, George converted to Roman Catholicism around 1955. According to grandma, the family had tried not to mention it to George Edwin, knowing how touchy he could be about such things. George once told my parents about his desire to convert but said he didn't think he would do so while his parents were still alive because he thought they might be upset.

In 1967, George attended a Brindley reunion in Stoke, organised by a visiting American Brinley, who was researching his roots. The Staffordshire Sentinel had publicised it and subsequently over 200 Brindleys turned up, more than the venue could hold. Sadly, George died on the 24th April 1968 aged 63, and was buried on 30th April in the Catholic cemetery, on the outcrop above Alton, overlooking the Churnet Valley.

RICHARD BRINDLEY 1908-1990

Richard, known always as 'Dick', was named after Richard Phillips, his mother's brother. Born 13th March 1908 at Ground Hollow, Hollington, the second son of George Edwin and Mary Elizabeth (née Phillips) of Uttoxeter. Baptised 19th April 1908 at Croxden Church, overlooking the ancient Abbey ruins.

He had a quiet personality, well mannered, a dry and mischievous sense of humour.

He married Margaret Mary Lynch (born 24th January 1914, the descendant of Peter Lynch and Jane Elliot of Ireland who settled in Macclesfield about 1830 and had a furniture broker's shop in Back Wallgate) on 20th August 1937, at St Giles, Croxden, Staffordshire.

Always interested in sport, he was particularly keen on cricket. Aged 11 he won a scholarship to Uttoxeter Grammar School, an achievement of which he was immensely proud.

He left school age 15 years. Rather than work locally on a farm or in a quarry, he opted to go to Manchester where his parents had arranged for him to work in J & N Philips' Textile Warehouse in Manchester. The Philips family were well known to the Brindley family and had a tape factory in Tean. He had digs with the Waterman family in the Moss Side area.

Dick found that he had a talent for snooker and became a member of the Birch Lane, Club in Longsight, Manchester. He once famously played in an exhibition match at the club with Fred Davis, World snooker champion. Dick looked like making a decent break when a voice from the spectators announced that it was Fred they had really come to watch!

He played cricket for his work's team and also in a local team on visits home. On one such occasion he was fielding close to the wicket when he received a severe blow in the face from the ball. It hit him just above the right eye and he fell pole-axed. He was rendered unconscious for several minutes and carried a scar the rest of his life.

On the outbreak of war, he was called up to serve in the Gordon Highlanders Regiment, based in Aberdeen. Overall, he had a good war but an incident at Rosehearty when a German bomb killed several people, including a family of young children, caused him to lose faith in God. He was Lance Corporal in charge of the digging party that uncovered the bodies. He was later mentioned in dispatches for courage and prompt action in suppressing a fire at an ammunition dump.

His wife Margaret Mary was employed as a parachute packer in Macclesfield during the war. She once told of Dick attempting to get her to put his slippers on for him, just like his mother did for his father. Margaret replied, *"You might be from the Potteries but you're not going to make a mug out of me!"*

Dick was demobbed in 1946 and resumed his pre-war job at J & N. Philips. He eventually moved to a firm called McAdams, a retail drapery shop in Longsight and worked the South Manchester area on a pedal cycle loaded up with suitcases full of goods.

Two daughters came along in the mid-fifties - money was so tight he stopped smoking then. For his 53rd birthday, in 1961, his son paid for driving lessons. Luckily, he passed the test first time, so he got a firm's vehicle and no longer relied on pedal power.

In 1970, he suffered a strangulated hernia, requiring emergency surgery. Luckily, son Gordon just arrived at his house at the right time and a quick dash to Withington Hospital, Manchester, saved Dick's life. Several feet of Dick's intestine were removed.

The night his mother died, he was working late and cycling through Reddish, Stockport. He glanced at the clock in Houldsworth Square to see what the time was and he saw his mother's face where the clock face should have been. When he got home his wife opened the door to him; he said, *"You don't need to say anything. My mother died at 8 o'clock. She's been in front of me all night."* Later in life, when he had his operation, he said his mother came to him - he had stretched out his arms toward her and she had gestured him away, as if to indicate that the time was not yet.

In late retirement, he had a stroke and his mental state deteriorated noticeably after that. He had to be admitted to Cheadle Royal Hospital for care, and died there on 19th July 1990. He was cremated at Manchester's Southern Cemetery. He was eighty-six.

FREDERICK ARTHUR BRINDLEY 1913-1979

Fred, as he was always known, was the youngest son of George Edwin and Mary Elizabeth Brindley (née Phillips). He was born in 1913 and baptised on 13th June at Hollington Parish Church. Of the siblings, he was probably the one least intimidated by George Edwin; Fred always had an extra bit of individualism. Like his brothers, he enjoyed cricket but he had other interests too. Like many men, he had an early interest in motor vehicles and in later life collected vintage model cars.

During the war he was in the RAF, driving heavy transporters. After the war, he started his own haulage business, F.A. Brindley Haulage. Starting with just one secondhand lorry, he gradually built up the business to six trucks and employed four or five men.

He once told me that he had been driving across the Yorkshire Moors in his lorry on a night that was misty and horrible when a strange figure suddenly came into his headlights. Fred decided to offer the man a lift. There was something odd about this man, he thought. The stranger did not speak and Fred started to feel uneasy. Suddenly, the man asked him to stop the lorry. As Fred pulled up, he stared at Fred with piercing eyes and told Fred that he would never come to harm driving lorries - and then simply disappeared. Fred said he didn't know how he was able to continue driving - he was convinced the man was the devil!

Fred was very popular with the fair sex and never seemed to be without a girlfriend. I remember that in 1952, at the time of my grandparent's golden wedding, he had a long-term girlfriend called Mabel but they eventually went their separate ways. It appeared at one time that he might turn into a confirmed bachelor, but he met and married Hilda Mary Smith in the 1960s and they had a daughter called Pamela. Soon, after Fred married, he sold the haulage firm and worked in the garage business of his father in law at Kingsley Moor.

He was a good uncle to me. I remember him occasionally taking me out with him for the day in his lorry, a real treat for me. He turned up at my house with an old 1934 vintage Bugsy-Malone type car when I was eighteen. He said I could use it for a while and then sell it for him. When I sold it he shared the profit (£10 each, as I recall).

When my grandma, Mary Elizabeth, was ill at the end of her life, he would take her out for little trips, even though she was paralysed and couldn't speak. He also tended to her while Ivy was out at work. A real nice guy, was Fred. He once told me that his philosophy was - *"Don't run if you can walk, or walk if you can sit, or sit if you can lie down!"*

Fred died of cancer on 22nd February 1979. After a funeral service at St Werburgh's Church, Kingsley, he was interred at Cheadle Municipal Cemetery.

In Fred's household were two Alsatian dogs. After he died, the dogs would go missing. When found, they would be sitting by Fred's grave. How they were able to find him at such a distance from his home is a mystery.

IVY MARY BRINDLEY (later Belfield) 1910-1996

Ivy was born 16th April 1910, and baptised on the 29th May, the only daughter of George Edwin Brindley and Mary Elizabeth (née Phillips).

Being brought up a country girl, you might have expected that she would have noticed where milk came from. Strangely, she only discovered this fact in her early teens when sent to get a jug full from Walters' farm, a mere hundred yards up the lane from the Great Gate house. She got the milk but noticed a cow being milked; horrified, she complained bitterly to her parents about not being informed earlier and she never drank milk again.

As a young woman, she sometimes worked in domestic service locally. For a while, she was in service at Grays, Essex. At one time, she worked in a nearby factory.

Eventually, she met, and on 19th July 1941, married local lad, George Arthur Belfield (1911-1992), who was in the RAF as ground crew during the war and worked for the Water Board after. Their only son, Edwin Arthur, was born in 1945. Ivy worked in the Hollington school preparing meals for the children. She also did voluntary work for the local WVS.

Ivy had long looked after her parents. Following her mother' death in 1955 she had the continuing burden of George Edwin for twelve years until his death in 1968. In her later years, Ivy lost the vision of one eye and had a leg ulcer that wouldn't heal. She started to become confused about 1993. She died on 13th September 1995.

RICHARD GORDON BRINDLEY 1944-

Parents; Richard Brindley and Margaret Mary (née Lynch). Born 27th March 1944 at 6 Maywood Avenue, East Didsbury, Manchester.

Educated at Beaver Road Primary School, Didsbury, then Chorlton Grammar School, Chorlton cum Hardy, Manchester.

First worked as builder's clerk before joining the Civil Service as a Clerical Officer. Both jobs lacked excitement so joined Manchester City Police in 1963. Promoted Sergeant 1978, and retired in 1991.

In late teens played piano and guitar, part of a trio called the Grasshoppers, in working men's clubs around Manchester and the King's Arms Pub in Oldham. Spent a few years in hospital radio at Wythenshawe Hospital, Manchester, then Stepping Hill Hospital, Stockport.

1983 degree course, Open University, graduating in 1986 BA.

After writing of police experience and travelling, he worked for the Automobile Association for two years. Since then involved in genealogical research.

Married Jean Shepherd of Rochdale in August 1968 - they met on a bus while on holiday in Venice. Children, Tina, born 20th March 1970 and Derek, born 12th February 1972, both at Withington Hospital, Manchester.

Lives in Gatley near Cheadle, Cheshire.

HAZEL BRINDLEY 1953-

Parents: Richard Brindley and Margaret Mary (née Lynch)
Born 5th October 1953 at 6 Maywood Ave, East Didsbury, Manchester, baptised at St James Parish Church, East Didsbury. Godparents Fred and Dorothy Stott of East Didsbury.

Educated at Broad Oak Primary School, East Didsbury, and Wilbraham High School, Chorlton-cum-Hardy.

1st husband, Michael Worsley, married 1973 at St James' Church, East Didsbury; amicable divorce in 1980. 2nd Husband, Andy Hague, a computer consultant. They live in Cadishead. Married in 1999 at Alpharetta near Atlanta, Georgia, USA.

Hazel never intended to have children, her main love being for animals. She is always willing to take up the cause of an ill-treated animal. She also has a degree of second-sight and can tell many interesting stories of her experiences. Here are a couple:

"From time to time, when I was a child, the locked door on the old wardrobe in our

bedroom would swing open by itself. Objects on the dressing table would then be swept onto the floor, as if by an invisible hand. The wardrobe always had a weird smell and had its own horrible atmosphere. It had been bought, second hand, when my parents first set up house.

After my divorce, I was living in a ground floor flat that was part of an old Victorian house. One morning, I was awakened by my bedroom door opening. The doorknob was loose and rattled when turned. I turned to face the doorway, thinking that one of my dogs had found out how to open it. In walked an old woman, appearing to walk about a foot above the floor. She was in her late sixties, plump, with grey hair tied back severely in a bun. She wore a white blouse and a full-length skirt. Over her arm she carried an old-fashioned wicker shopping basket. She turned to me, and shook her head with a sad expression on her face. Then, she moved across the room and disappeared into the opposite wall.

Some time later, I was at my Mum and Dad's and we were looking through old photographs when I came across a picture of this lady wearing the same clothes I had seen and her hair in a bun. When I asked my mum who she was, she said it was her grandmother, Martha Lynch.

I can't think why she had come to me but, strangely enough, after her visit I had a run of bad luck. Maybe she was trying to let me know things were going to get bad?"

YVONNE ELIZABETH BRINDLEY (later LONG)

Parents: Richard Brindley and Margaret Mary (née Lynch). Born 10th July 1956, 6 Maywood Ave, East Didsbury, Manchester. Educated at Broad Oak Primary School and Parrs Wood High (Comprehensive) School, East Didsbury, Manchester.

Briefly at The Lancashire Cotton Institute, Didsbury, Manchester (also known as The Shirley Institute), she then worked for the GPO before venturing into the travel business.

She married in Texas to Michael Long, an English computer expert and businessman, and both have lived Stateside since. Denver, Colorado, was their first home and more recently they have located to Alpharetta, near Atlanta, Georgia.

TINA BRINDLEY 1970-

Parents: Richard Gordon and Jean (née Shepherd)

Born 20th March 1970, at Withington Hospital, Manchester. Educated at Kingsway Comprehensive School, Cheadle. She has a particular talent for art and is musical.

In 1999, she decided to work abroad and obtained an administrative position with a holiday company in a small village near Chania, Crete. Whilst on the island, she met Cecar Yanchev, a Bulgarian similarly working abroad. They married at Kazanlac, Bulgaria, in March 2001. Soon after, they moved to England and bought a house in Woodley, Stockport.

DEREK BRINDLEY 1972-

Parents: Richard Gordon and Jean (née Shepherd)

Born 12th February 1972, at Withington Hospital, Manchester. Educated Kingsway Comprehensive, Cheadle.

Leaving school, apprenticed to Henry Simon Engineers, Cheadle Heath. Subsequently lived in Amersham, Bucks, for two years.

In 1995 Derek was in a bad car smash when his vehicle skidded off the road in bad weather and hit a tree. He suffered severe injuries. Luckily, he survived and after a long spell in hospital made a full recovery. His girlfriend and future wife, Nokomis Pinder, was also injured in the crash.

Undaunted, Derek found himself a job with Astra-Zeneca, at Alderley Edge, Cheshire, where he is a now a design engineer, and he and Nokomis have a house near Macclesfield. They married at Gretna Green in Scotland. One son, Thomas Owen, born 4th July 2002.

EDWIN ARTHUR BELFIELD 1947-
Born 28th January 1947 Stoke on Trent, the only child of George Arthur Belfield and Ivy Mary Belfield (née Brindley). He was brought up in the Great Gate-Hollington area of Staffordshire. Attended London University where he obtained his BSc degree. He then obtained a post as a scientific officer with the British Ceramic Research Association.

He married Carolyn Paula Thomas, a nurse, born 30th October 1946 at Cheddleton, daughter of Mr and Mrs J.W. Thomas of Oak Ave, Cheddleton. Carolyn was a nurse at Stallington Hospital, Blythe Bridge.

Married 5th December 1970 at St Edward's Church, Cheddleton. Two children, Paula Jane, b. 23rd June 1974 at Solihull and Gareth Thomas, b. 7th July 1976 at Shotley Bridge.

They have lived in North Wales and more recently in Tenbury Wells, Worcester.

GEORGE RICHARD BRINDLEY
Parents: George Brindley and Agnes Mary (née Burton)

George was born 5th January 1932 at Alton, the eldest son of four children. He was educated at St John's Roman Catholic School, Alton. He played both cricket and football at county level. In the 1950s he played in a local side that actually beat Stoke City Football Club! He was raised in a pub, the Royal Oak, Alton.

He did his National Service and spent a long period at Aberystwyth, Wales. He met and married Emily Barkes in 1956 and had one child, Anthony Neil Brindley.

He became a master bricklayer and was proud to be involved in restoration work on the beautiful Italian tiled Alton Castle roof.

He was a governor of St John's RC school. He intended to set up his own business but contracted brain cancer. He was a practising Catholic. A sincere man who led by his actions rather than his words, George Richard is buried at the St John's Catholic cemetery, Alton.

ANTHONY NEIL BRINDLEY 1959-
Born 12th September 1959 at Alton, Staffordshire, son of George Richard Brindley and Emily (née Barkes). He was confirmed on 11th February 1968 at Alton Catholic Chapel and was given the saint name of George.

Known as Tony, he had a good Catholic education at St John's school, Alton before moving on to higher education. He currently works as a senior buyer for JCB at Uttoxeter.

On 16th March 1991, he married Elaine Lesley Eccleston at Alton Catholic Church.

He still lives in the Alton area and he and Elaine had a lovely little boy born on 5th September 1996 called George Kieran Brindley.

Clara Ann Bull (nee Brindley) with some of the Croxden
and Hollington Show Committee c. 1930

Ivy Mary Brindley's marriage to George Belfield.

Chapter 5
James Brindley's Clan Pedigree

Generation 1
Joseph (= Ellen Bowman)

Generation 2
James 1763D (= Susanna Bradbury)
Esther (= John Ludford)
Hannah (= Thos. Linnis)
Prudence (= George Walker)

Generation 3
James 1716B (= Ann Henshall)
Joseph (= 1. Sarah Bennett; = 2. Lydia Lightwood; = 3. Mary Mobberley)
John (= 1. Ann Rogers; = 2. Hannah Stevenson, widow)
Mary (= Abraham Birchenough)
Esther (= Samuel Simcock)
Ann (= William Allen), son Thomas emigrated to America with James Brindley.
Henry (= ? Elizabeth aka 'Betty' Shaw)

Generation 4
From James 1716B above:
Susannah (= John Bettington), many descendents
Ann (unmarried). Rumour: John Bennett, illegitimate son

From Joseph, above with Sarah Bennett:
James, 1748C (= Elizabeth Ogle)
Matthew 1749B (= Lydia Walker)
Elizabeth 1751C (= Thomas Salt)
Susannah 1753C (= Joseph Tideswell), numerous descendents including Nigel Cope, alive
Sarah 1755C (= Thomas Alkins)
Mary 1756C (= John Cope)

From Joseph with Lydia Lightwood:
Lydia 1763C (= James Hammersley)
Henry 1763B (= Ann Collies) - descendents

From John with Ann Rogers:
Francis 1749C
John 1752B
James 1754B (= Catharine Morris), many descendents
Joseph 1756C

From John with Hannah Stevenson:
Susanna 1761C
Taylor 1763C

(Speculation) From Henry who married Elizabeth aka 'Betty' Shaw:
James, 1756B
Joseph, 1765B (= Elizabeth)
David, 1779B (= 1. Martha Lawton; 2. Elizabeth Siddorn)
Samuel, 1773C (= Martha ? Shaw, 1797 m. Astbury, Cheshire)
Henry 1821D (= ?)
Children from Mary, Esther, and Ann in Generation 3 have not yet been researched.

Generation 5
Grandchildren of James, canal engineer:
Via Susannah who married John Bettington, several children and descendents partially researched.
Grandchildren of Joseph and Sarah Bennett:
From James, born Waterfall, (1st son of Joseph and Sarah Bennett)
From Matthew, 1749B:
  James 18.3.1770B
  Rupert, 1771B (= Catherine Finney 10.11.1817M), children
  Margaret, 1772B abt (= Joseph Salt);
  Joseph of Longport, 1775B (= Catharine Brindley 1805M), children

John, 1780B (= Frances Mellor 1800M), 14+ children
Hannah, 1780C (= John Cope? 19.12.1805M)
Susannah, 23.10. 1785B (= Robert Smedley 13.12.1803M)

From Elizabeth, born 1771B (= Thos Salt):
Joseph
Ester
Mary who married Joseph Malkin and had Ann.

From Susannah who married Joseph Tideswell – descendents to Nigel Cope, alive.

From Sarah, 1755C, married to Thomas Alkins – not researched.

From Mary, 1756/8C, married to John Cope, 1779M - not researched.

Grandchildren of Joseph = Lydia Lightwood:
From Lydia, 1763C, married to James Hammersley, not researched.
From Henry, 1763B Jan, who married Ann Collies:
Ann, 1792C
Joseph 1793C, died young
John 1795C, died young
Joseph 1797C
George 1799C.

Grandchildren from John, the potter via his son James 1754B, married to Catharine Morris:
Thomas John, no children
Catharine 1789B, no children
James 1785B, m. Blanche Jones, ? children
William of Great Chell 1791B, m. Elizabeth, children Catherine 1818, Eliza 1819, Blanche 1821,
John Jakes 1822

Joseph 1788B = Caroline Pargeter, had Catharine; Caroline
Joseph Pargeter- unmarried

Generation 6

Rupert who married Catherine Finney 10th November 1817, had two children:
William, baptised 16th April 1819, who married Ellen Bonsall,
Maria, born 3.10.1820
Alice, born 30.3.1823
Benjamin, born 4.3.1832, who married Mary:
Elizabeth, baptised 19.3.1822. No further information.
(William may have married a 2nd time to Mary Harvey. ? two children, Edward and Emily Mary).

Children of Joseph of Longport = Catharine Brindley:
Ann, baptised 19.12.1811, died 1834
Catherine Lydia 31.5.1807C
James John 1809C
Joseph 16.3.1814C
Mary 17.12,1816C
John 18.8.1818C
Sarah 12.6.1821C
Frances 9.6.1824C
Margaret 9.6.1824C
James Aug 1829C
Caroline 20.6.1827C
Blanche 20.9.1830C

Children of John = Frances Mellor:
James, born 11.5.1806 = Ann Whitehall:
James, born 1833
Thomas born 1834, both at Uttoxeter.

Children of John, born 28.9.1817, probably married Ann Salisbury on 30.12.1844:
William 1847B 25.4 who married Louisa Grundy, they in turn having: Maria, Louisa and William.
Emma, baptised 24.9.1820, had illegitimate son Anson, baptised 1st November 1840, at Cauldon.

Top: Harold Hulme Brindley in 1888, seen 3rd from the left back row,
and, below, in the early 1940s when he was in his late 70s.

Thomas Brindley of Manchester b. 1840

Isobella Brindley, b 1839, Thomas's wife

Elizabeth Brindley (nee Goulding)

William Brindley b. 1881

Macclesfield Brindleys

Below: Frederick A., George Edwin
and Richard about 1940

The appeal of local history

A tattered document — written more than 100 years ago — has turned out to be a piece of Post Office history.

It was unearthed by retired Wombourne engineer Mr William Brindley, aged 83, of Station Road (pictured). And it has turned out to be the public appeal launched on behalf of his great grandfather, Thomas Brindley.

Top left: Kezia Brindley of Cauldon Lowe, on the left,
taken when she was 19.
Top right: Martha Brindley of Buxton.
Bottom left: John William Brindley, Macclesfield, b. 1878.
Bottom right: Arthur Brindley of Manchester, in the First
World War; grandfather of Ann Sent.

Martha Ann Brindley of Hotspur, Victoria, Australia (1873-1934) seen with her friend Rachel Annie Burgess, and marrying Henry Hiscock in 1894.

George Edward and Rosa Elizabeth (nee Barber), with baby Basil Brindley

The Damask Napkin, the gift of Charles Edward Brinley to the Philadelphia Museum of Art. According to tradition this was part of a set of linen which were a gift from Charles I to Thomas Brinley (1591-1661).

Chapter 6
Notable and Interesting Brindleys:
The Original Brindley Family

That we have so well documented a family tree of the early Brindleys is largely thanks to John Beavis Brindley, first Recorder of Hanley in the 19th century.

As a barrister, he was well placed to find obscure legal documents and records of legal proceedings. With such skilled and privileged access, over thirty years he gradually compiled the Brundley/Brindley data upon which those of us who came later have been pleased to rely.

His son, Harold Hulme Brindley, a distinguished Cambridge Don, also added to the information.

Following the Norman Conquest of 1066 and William of Normandy's consolidation of his possession of England by 1086, lands all over the country were given to loyal supporters as a reward and as a safeguard for William against the possible revolt of local Anglo-Saxon populations. Among the Norman families who were granted land were the De Praers and Veneables families. Both these names appear on lists of supporters of Duke William. They may or may not have been present at Hastings or battles soon after - there is no proof either way. The Normans were not an ethnically pure race and many of William's allies were non-Norman, e.g. Bretons - descendents of those who had fled Britain earlier under Saxon pressure - Frenchmen and Flemish. There was also a small French and Norman presence in England prior to the Conquest.

A branch of the De Praers family, given land at Stoke near Nantwich, Cheshire, started calling themselves De Stoke. A family believed descended from the Venables family, given land at Brereton, started calling themselves De Brereton. These families settled down with their new holdings and over the next hundred years or so became gradually anglicised, although they remembered their Norman descent and conspired to inter-marry with others of similar background and origins.

About 1272, a marriage was arranged to unite two families. Gilbert de Stoke, son of Randle/Ranulphus/Rani de Praers (born 1038, also Baron of Criche, Derbyshire) was betrothed to Isolda de Brereton, daughter of Sir Ralph Brereton who might have been a Venables descendant. (see George Ormerod, *History of Cheshire*) In 1086, Brereton, (which seems to have contained Brindley within it since 'Brindley' is not separately recorded in Domesday) was owned by Gilbert Hunter alias Venables who had two unnamed tenants using land there.

As part of Isolda's marriage settlement, land at Brundelegh, next to Brereton, was given to Gilbert. Brund Legh was Old English/Anglo-Saxon, meaning burnt pasture.

Ranulphus de Praers was descended from Hubert de Rie/Rye in Normandy who helped found Colchester Abbey about 1096. George Ormerod cites Rogeri de Praers as father of Ranulphus, however some modern research cites Hubert as father. Hubert appears to have been the son of Eudes; Eudes was son of Geoffrey, Lord of Rie near Bayeux, Normandy.

Little is known or recorded about Gilbert and Isolda other than that their first son came into possession of the land in the course of time and that it was he who decided to call himself

Brundelegh de Brundeley/Brindley. The spelling of the name was erratic for hundreds of years but refined gradually to Brindley or similar by the 18th century. Whether or not Brundelegh had other children is not recorded. The name of his wife is also unknown.

The early Brundeleys seemed to have led quiet, undistinguished lives, farming their land, and having sons who passed on the name. By the 15th century, they had multiplied and spread into Staffordshire, and seemed particularly suited to the area of North Staffordshire known as the Moorlands. From then on their name suddenly becomes much more in evidence in places such as Leek, Alstonefield, Hartington, Stoke-on-Trent, Cheddleton and an apparent population explosion occurs.

Gilbert de Stoke had brothers Rogerus and Hugo and at least one half-brother called William because his father Randulphus married twice; from these beginnings, the Stoke families founded many collateral lines who prospered and spread all over England and eventually to America and Australia. The Brindley descendents will share the same ancestral male chromosome with many of these Stoke families, who ultimately trace themselves back to Ranulph de Praers of Stoke township, near Nantwich, Cheshire.

John Beavis Brindley 1827-1890

John Beavis was born 22nd December 1827 at Newcastle Under Lyme to John Brindley and Mary (née Brough). His baptism was on 1st January 1828 at March Independent or Congregational Chapel. Little is known of his early years but he was well educated and married Mary Brough at Leek on 29th April 1863 at the age of thirty-five. It was a case of Brindley genes reuniting, because Mary was herself a five-generation direct descendent from the marriage of Edith Brindley to Thomas Brough at Grindon on 30th March 1702. Both she and John Beavis were from the same root-stock, namely the Brundelegh de Brindley clan.

John Beavis was ambitious and studied law. At first he lived at 1 College Hill, Highbury, Islington. The 1881 census found him living at 25 Aubert Park, Islington, with his wife and children, and he was recorded as *"of Highbury and Gray's Inn, a barrister"*.

John Beavis was interested in his family origins and later Brindleys who are interested in their genealogy owe him a great debt, because he was uniquely placed to search for and explore ancient legal documents. It was a painstaking task which enabled him to compile the Brundelegh de Brindley family tree and prove his descent from the founder.

In 1880 he was appointed the first Recorder of Hanley, Staffordshire and he fulfilled this role until his death in 1890.

According to the Metropolis Newspaper, 23rd June 1886, he stood as a Liberal candidate for Member of Parliament for Newcastle under Lyme, but he failed to get elected.

Harold Hulme Brindley 1865-18th February 1944.

A direct descendant of Brundeley de Brindley, he was born on 17th June 1865, at 1, College Hill, Highbury, Islington, Middlesex.

His father was John Beavis Brindley, barrister at law and first Recorder of Hanley, Staffs. His mother was Mary née Brough from an accomplished local Staffordshire family.

After being educated at Mill Hill School, he was accepted as a 'Pensioner' student at St John's College, Cambridge on 22nd April 1884. 'Pensioner' was the 2nd of three admission ranks at that time.

Like his father before him, he was interested in his family history and he updated the comprehensive family tree that his father had painstakingly researched.

He attained his B.A. in 1887, his M.A. in 1891 and was made a Fellow in 1931. He had an outstanding academic career at Cambridge, involved in Biology and Zoology and being an examiner from 1913-1934; and at Glasgow University 1915-1918, 1924-9, and 1931-4. He was President of the Cambridge Antiquarian Society 1915-16; F.S.A. Head of the Seal Room, National Maritime Museum, Greenwich, 1935; Vice-President of the Navy Records Society and the Society of Nautical Research. He lived at 25, Madingley Rd, Cambridge.

He married Gertrude Roberta Froggatt Brindley between July and September 1896 at Christchurch, Hampshire and had two children, Dorothy and Beavis William.

She died in 1921 and he then married Maud Doria Haviland, an ornithologist and another Fellow. They had a daughter, Avice Haviland Brindley.

Harold Hulme had a great sense of humour and could bring interest to the dullest of topics. According to the Eagle Magazine's obituary *"he never thrust his views forward in such a way as to dominate a conversation."* During the General Strike of 1926 he was reputed to have driven a passenger train at express speed from Liverpool and, when congratulated upon his fast time, replied *"dammit, I've only just discovered how the brake works!"*

Thomas Brinsley

Matriculated pensioner from Christ's College, Cambridge, c. 1592.

John Brinsley 1565 abt -1601 abt

Matriculated sizar from Christ's, Cambridge University, March 1580-1; Scholar; BA 1584-5; MA 1588. Ordained deacon & priest, Peterborough, 10th April 1588. Headmaster of Ashby de la Zouch School till about 1619. Was suspended for his Puritan opinions. He went to London and lectured there. Then he taught at Great Yarmouth. He married Miss Hall, sister of Bishop Joseph Hall. He was author of Ludus Literarius, and other scholastic works. He had one son, John.

John Brinsley 1600 abt - 1665

Son of John (above). Mother née Hall. Admitted sizar at Emmanuel, Cambridge University, 23rd May 1615. Was born at Ashby de la Zouch School where father was headmaster. Matriculated 1615; Scholar; BA 1619-20; MA 1623. Minister and schoolmaster at Yarmouth, 1625-7. Town preacher, 1644-60 (ejected). Rector of Somerleyton, Suffolk, 1632-44. Rector of Ashby, 1632-44. Author of religious works. Died 22nd January 1664-5, aged 64 years. Had one son, Robert.

Robert Brinsley 1638 abt-1670 abt

Son of John (above). Was admitted sizar at Emmanuel, Cambridge, 15th June 1653. Born Somerleyton, Suffolk. Matriculated 1653; B.A. 1656-7; M.A. 1660. Fellow 1659; ejected, 1662. Adm. Extra-licentiate Royal College of Physicians, 6th June 1664. M.D. of Leyden, 1668. Practised at Yarmouth. (Munk, 1. 315.)

Thomas Brinley 1636-1672

Son of Thomas Brinley and Ann (Wase), he was educated at Eton College, Eton, before going up to Cambridge University. He was admitted to King's College 10th August 1653. He gained his B.A. 1657 and his M.A. 1661. He was a Fellow in 1656-72, and was Ordained Deacon (Ely) 10th March 1665-6. He died April 20th 1672, apparently unmarried. A direct descendent of Brundelegh de Brindley.

His will, dated 12th April 1672

In the name of God Amen, I Thomas Brinley one of the fellows of King's Colledge in the University of Cambridge being sicke and weake in Body but a sounde perfect Mind & Memory doe make and declare my last Will & Testament in manner & form following FIRST I bequeath my Soule into the hands of Allmighty God trusting to bee saved through the meritts of Jesus Christ & for my worldly Estate wch it hath pleased God to bestowe upon me I doe give & bequath the same in manere & forme following viz FIRST I doe give & bequeath unto Mr. John Wase Cittizen & Lynnen Draper of London All that messuage4 or tenem[ent] situate & being in Horton in the county of Bucks nowe in the occupancy of Richard Sharpe together with the Ozier plot & Meadow ground thereunto belonging or [therewith] used & allsoe all those my twoe Closes of Meadowe & pasture called Hogg Lane Close in Horton aforsd & in Hanwell in the county of Midd[lesex] And alsoe my two Closes of Meadowe & pasture sometimes being both in one calles [Hoay?] Close or Closes being in Hanwell aforesd And allsoe all that my close of Meadowe called Cotterills being in Hanwell aforesd which severall closes are nowe in the occupation of John — or his assigns. And I do hereby declare my Intent & meaning to bee the [paper damaged, assume John Wase, very faint] as soon as may be convenient — as may be after my decease sell all my sd Estate & all other my reall & — estate — for the best price he canne gett for the payment & satisfaction of all my Debts Legacies & funeral Expenses And the — & surplus of my Estate after my debts funeral Expenses & the legacies hereafter mentioned bee discharged upon sale therof I doe give & bequeath unto my twoe Brothers Ffrancis Brinley & William Brinley & bee equally divided between them. ALSO I give & bequeath unto Ralph fflyer Doctor of Phisicke the sum of ffive pounds of Lawfull money of England. ALSO I give and bequeath unto Jane Walton widdowe my Beddmaker fforty shillings AND I doe hereby nominate and Appoint the sd John Wase to bee my sole Executor and do give him as a Legacy for his care & paines in performance of this my will the sum of fifty pounds IN WITNESS whereof I have hereunto sett my Hand & Seale the Twelfth day of April in the yeare of our Lord One Thousand Six Hundred Seaventy Twoe Thomas Brinley signed sealed published & declared by the Testator to bee his Last Will & Testament in the presence of Edward Mitchell/Wingell? Robert Yarde John Allison

Samuel Brinley 1624-1695
Samuel was the son of Lawrence of London, merchant of Ironmonger Lane and cousin of Thomas above. Baptised 2nd July 1624 at St Mary, Aldermary, London. He was admitted as a pensioner to St John's College, Cambridge, 20th September 1644. He previously Matriculated from New Inn Hall, Oxford, 26th May 1642 and got his B.A. in 1645-6; his M.A. 1649, became a fellow of St John's 1647. Rector of Alphamstone, Essex, 1654-62; ejected. Afterwards, he lived in London. 1672, licensed (P) at Dedham, Essex. Minister at East Bergholt, Suffolk, 1689-94. (Wallis, Cal.Rev. 75;Holman 52). Died about 1695. (Calamy,1. 495; Visitation of London, 1634.) He was a direct descendent of Brundelegh de Brindley.

Joshua alias Joseph Brindley 1657 abt-1700?
Son of John and Mary (née Whywall) of Kingsley. A direct descendent of Brundelegh de Brindley. He was born at Whiston Eaves, Kingsley, Staffs.

Was admitted as pensioner at Clare, Cambridge University, April 7th 1671. Matriculated Easter 1671 as 'Joseph Brinley'; BA 1674-5. Parish Curate of Cheddleton, Staffs, c.1676-96.

He married Sarah Whywall and had three children, Mary, born at Horton and bapt. 27th January 1681 at Biddulph; Sara, bapt. 29th August 1683 at Cheddleton; and Anna, bapt. 14th July 1685 at Cheddleton. Joshua probably died in 1696.

Joseph Brindley 1687 abt-1795
Joseph Brindley was buried at Huntington, Cannock, Staffs, 22nd February in the 109th year of his age. (Staffordshire Advertiser 1795) Makes him probably the oldest Brindley recorded.

1655 Walter Brindley of Lapley - Licentiousness!
There had been Brindleys in Lapley since at least 1550 and many were called Walter. Almost certainly they were descendents from the Cheshire founding dynasty but many records of this period were lost and it is difficult to prove this as a fact. However, as there have never been any Brindleys found of a different descendency at this time, this assumption seems reasonable.

Walter's and his sons' claim to fame or notoriety came to light in the record of a court case at Stafford Assizes in 1665 concerning events at Lapley, Staffordshire, on the 5th May. This was during the Commonwealth period when Oliver Cromwell was in power. The local vicar, John Jackson, made the complaint. It seems that Walter, a husbandman, and his sons, Edmund, John and Matthew were responsible, among others, for several misdemeanours, including - failing to attend church, frequent drinking, licentiously Morris dancing, and causing great commotion. (Perhaps their true offence was being Papists.) Over several days they had been seen going in and out of several houses where they had drunk freely and engaged in boisterous horseplay and singing. One had also been found lying drunk outside the church. The main complaints were that they partook of licentious dancing and failed to attend the established church. The court seems to have been slightly bemused by these

Thomas Brindley and his wife Selena (née Scrivens), and daughter, descendents of
Walter Brindley of Lapley. C. 1945

allegations and, unimpressed, took a neat legal route out of the situation by binding over the men concerned to be of good behaviour for the next twelve months. Reverend Jackson later had the indignity of being dismissed from his living and being replaced by his predecessor.

Brindleys remained in or near Lapley from the late 16th century to modern times. There seems to have only been one or two families, at most, throughout this period.

Alice Haskins (née Brindley) has contributed much of my Lapley information and she and her family were born, and have lived many years, in South Wales. She is probably directly descended from Thomas Brindley, a farmer, and Jane Adams (also spelt Addams). Thomas and Jane had their son Walter baptised on 10th October 1706.

There is a gap of possible Walters hereafter but we know that the descent is certain from James Henry Brindley who married Mary Paget. Their son Thomas married Alice Scrivens at Bedwellty in 1901. They had Henry James who married Dorothy Chant and their daughter was D.A. Alice Brindley who married George E. Haskins.

They have two sons, Robert and Richard, who have provided eight grandchildren.

Margaret Lucas (Brindley) 1701-24.6.1769

The testimony of the Friends, at the quarterly meeting in Staffordshire, held by adjournment at Leek, the third of the fifth month, 1770. There it is stated how Margaret Lucas, of Leek, was educated in the national worship, and strictly conformed to the rites of it, and that she afterwards frequented their meetings. She departed this life the 24th, and was interred in the Friends' Burying Ground at Leek, on the 26th of the 6th month, 1769, aged near 68 years.

She was born in 1701, in Fleet Street, London, the daughter of James Brindley of Fleet Street, a China merchant who died when she was seven. Her mother died before that. She was one of fourteen children. Aged 12, she was put in the care of her father's married sister who lived in Leek. She was sent to school in Deansgate, Manchester, but in 1714 returned to Leek and lived with her uncle and aunt. About 1717 they left their little, though convenient house, and took a larger one opposite the lych-gate of the church.

When she was about seventeen years of age a bishop visited Leek to hold a confirmation, and she was confirmed. At the age of eighteen, on the advice of her uncle she purchased the shop occupied by S. Taylor who was going to live at Stafford. Apparently, mistress Taylor was a Quaker, and Margaret's uncle had so good an opinion of the Quakers that he left the appraising of the goods entirely to her. This led her to attend the Quakers' meeting, and that brought the parson (Mr. Samuel Leay) down upon her. Shortly afterwards Parson Bennet sent for her to Widow Bruerton's and tried to reason her out of her persuasion.

On account of her uncle using threats toward her she henceforth lived at her shop instead of lodging with her relatives. Again Mr Leay interested himself and offered to answer her scruples, or if he could not to get the Bishop to do so.

After the separation from her relatives she seems to have relied upon the advice of the Tofts (three brothers; Joshua, whom she called uncle, Samuel, and John). Her aunt commenced to persecute her, and a P. Mellor invited her to Whitehough for three months.

Besides her shop she had a kind of school, but it was not an advanced one. Her aunt was undoubtedly cruel to her, for one market day she followed Margaret behind the counter and pinched her arm so severely that it swelled prodigiously. Dr. Grosvenor's daughter happening to go in the shop saw what was up and fetched her father, and he attended the girl.

Margaret arranged to board with Thomas Turnock, who occupied the living part of her shop premises. On one occasion her aunt chased her towards the Friends' Meeting House, and she nearly fell headlong down the precipice (now Mill Street). At the age of twenty-four she became the wife of S. Lucas, and subsequently became the mother of several children. She kept true to her faith, and after many struggles became a preacher.

<$iSarah Penelope Brindley

Alias 'Stanley'> she is cited in 1796 as having served as a soldier before her eventually being discovered to be female. - *The New Newgate Calendar ...memoires of notorious characters convicted of outrages on the laws of England.* 5 vols. London [1826?]

1816: Isaac Brindley - Tried for Murder

On Tuesday 15th April 1816, at Warwickshire Assizes, Isaac Brindley was arraigned for the murder of Ann Smith in the Parish of Over Whiteacre on the 10th last:

Isaac Brindley was a servant in the employ of Mr Weston. Ann Smith was also in Mr Weston's employ but was leaving. She was seen carrying a bag and heading along a local footpath. Brindley was also seen to be following after her. Next day her body was discovered in the shrubbery near the footpath, apparently having been strangled. Evidence of the circumstances was given but Brindley could say little for himself but protest that it wasn't he who did it. One gets the impression that he was somewhat lacking in intelligence. He was quickly convicted and sentenced to death, to be executed on Thursday and his body to be dissected. Presumably that occurred.

The Times

1824: Thomas Brindley - Suicide

The Times Newspaper 8th September 1824:

Mr Thomas Brindley, a confectioner, residing in Hackney, and generally very respected, on Sunday evening, about five o'clock, hanged himself in his own stable. He was discovered after he had been hanging about an hour, when every attempt which surgical skill could suggest was made to recover him, but without success. Mr Brindley was about fifty years of age; he has left behind him a widow and a young family.

For several months previous to his committing the melancholy act he manifested symptoms of a disordered mind. On Saturday he was particularly wild in his language and manner. On Sunday he went upstairs, requesting he might not be disturbed, as he wished to sleep. He came down afterwards without his shoes, and was found as we have stated.

1838: He, She or It?

From a report in The Times Newspaper 14th February 1838:

A poor old person who has been well known for the last twenty years in the neighbourhood of Wolverhampton and Dudley as an itinerant pedlar, and who usually passed by the name of John Brindley, died last week in the workhouse of Dudley. On being laid out, previous to being enclosed in the coffin, it was noticed that poor "John" was a woman!

Although the deceased slept for some time, while in the workhouse, with a man who was a fellow inmate, neither he nor anyone else had the least suspicion regarding John's real sex until after death. For the last four years he lodged with a woman named Catherine Dudley, better known as the Old Pottery Bear Woman (from having kept a bear).

She avers that she was ignorant of the deceased's sex. Various are the rumours afloat as to the reasons which induced her so long and so closely to maintain her disguise, but as they appear to be merely conjectures, we forbear at present to publish them.

Staffordshire Advertiser

John Brindley: Headmaster Resigns

John Brindley has resigned. Twenty guineas subscribed by the clergy and other inhabitants of DUDLEY was presented to Mr Brindley a few days since, in acknowledgement of their gratitude for the noble and successful stand he has long made and continues to be making against the wicked and blasphemous doctrines of Robert Owen and his emissaries.

Worcester Journal. 7th September 1839

Thomas Brindley (Old Tom) - First Postman of Wolverhampton

Thomas, "Old Tom", Brindley was born in 1763 to Daniel and Mary Brindley. He was the 3rd born of nine children. He became a well known figure around the city and had a long life of service. He married Mary Williams at Sedgley, Staffs, on 24th April 1783. They had the following children: Mary Anne, baptised 12th May 1788; Sarah, bapt. 1789; Thomas, bapt. 19.09.1789, who probably died young; Thomas, bapt. 19.09 1791 at St Peter's church; Maria, bapt. 31st May 1798; Sophia, bapt. 31st May 1798; William, bapt. 9th May 1803 at St Peter's church; James, bapt. 3rd June 1805 at St Peter's church; William, bapt. 9th May 1805, St Peter's church; and Louisa, bapt. 28th February 1807 at St Peter's church, Wolverhampton.

Old Thomas Brindley.
Courtesy of Wolverhampton Archives

His obituary in the Wolverhampton Chronicle in May 1855 summed his life up :

LONGEVITY

Our obituary this week records the death of an old and faithful servant of the town in the person of "Old Tom Brindley, the postman". He died Friday last, in the 92nd year of his age. He had for nearly half a century, and that expired years ago, day after day visited the doors of our forebears, and brought intelligence of weal and woe.

Born in 1763, after being 46 years in the service of the Post Office, he was in the year 1845, when 82 years old, discharged, being incapable of further duty, owing to the infirmation of age. As a proof of Brindley's industry and strength of constitution, we may mention that for some years he was a watchman by night as well as a distributor of letters by day.

Old Tom had been Wolverhampton's first and lone letter carrier, starting in 1789.

This only took up part of his morning, for the rest of the time he worked as a groom for Mr. John Lewis, a Queen Street linen merchant and was also a night watchman until an evening delivery of mail became necessary. In 1789, the post office was part of a chemist's shop in Queen Street.

In 1840, when the penny post was introduced, he was unable to cope alone with the ever-increasing number of letters. In 1846, after 56 years of service, he was dismissed. There were no post office pensions then, and an approach on his behalf to the Postmaster General brought an icy response that there were no funds for that sort of thing. Fortunately, there were kindly folk in Wolverhampton who raised subscriptions to pay the old postman a weekly allowance of 12s. for the rest of his life.

He died 17th May 1855, age 91 years and was interred at Merridale cemetery, Jefflock Road.

He had a grandson called William Brindley but the intervening names have not been researched.

Joseph Brindley - Still Here! 1858

Several of my friends being under the impression (from the report yesterday) that the whole of my stock was injured and business suspended, I beg to state that such is not the case, the building and contents damaged forming but a small portion of my premises and stock in trade. Trusting you will insert this in your columns.

I am sir, yours obediently, Joseph Brindley, Slate Merchant. Bermondsey Wall, April 9th.

The Times

1860: William Brindley charged Manslaughter

Report in The Times Newspaper 1st August 1860:

In the criminal court before Mr Justice Byles, William Brindley, engine driver, surrendered to take trial upon a charge of manslaughter, in causing the death of John Jones on the 2nd May 1860 (by gross negligence in not attending to a danger signal and stopping the train). On the 2nd May last, at Whitchurch his passenger train ran into a goods train killing the guard. The jury found him guilty but recommended mercy on account of his good character. He was sentenced to one year's imprisonment.

1885: Private James Brindley – Homicide at Woolwich

Extracts from *The Times Newspaper* of London, 11th February 1885.

Yesterday afternoon, an inquest was held at the Hornet Military Hospital, Shooters Hill, relative to the death of Private James Brindley of the ?? Battalion Shropshire Regiment, quartered at Woolwich who was bayoneted by a sentry at the Government Powder Magazine on the marshes below the Royal Arsenal, Woolwich early on Sunday morning last, under circumstances already reported.

Colonel S.M. Beadon, commanding the Battalion to which the deceased belonged was present and the sentry implicated, Private Botham occupied a seat by the side of his solicitor, Mr Greening. Corporal Ledyer repeated the evidence which he gave on the previous day at the police court and in reply to the Coroner, further said, - During the night the deceased had been for two hours on sentry duty at number 2 post (the gun cotton magazine) but he had no business to go there whilst Botham was in charge. He had not left anything in the sentry box, and it is not usual for sentries to do so.

The sentry box is close to the outer gate, and the tramway comes in across the marshes. It is the duty of the sentry on that part to walk between the gate and the next sentry, and also to go round the gun-cotton magazine. If he saw or heard a stranger approach he should challenge him three times and then come to the charge at once. From the gateway to the spot where he found the deceased in the arms of Botham was about twenty yards.

The rifle and bayonet carried by Botham were both produced and the witness showed the jury the action of "coming to the charge".

There followed a cross-examination and the coroner asked if the deceased was fond of practical jokes. The answer was "no".

The surgeon, Mr Dodd, described the deceased's injury: - the bayonet entered the chest one and a half inches above the left nipple…piercing the heart and left lung and leaving a six and a half inch deep wound.

After a half hour deliberation, the jury exonerated Edward Botham, finding that the deceased James Brindley was justifiably stabbed. They commended the sentry for the performance of his duty.

1896: James Brindley charged with Murder

On the 1st September at Cannock, James Brindley and his wife Louisa were charged with the murder of Arthur Workman. The child was handed to them at Penkridge in February last, £9.10 s being paid for its adoption, and had not been heard of since. Mary Workman, mother, identified clothes but the body has not been found. The accused were remanded in custody.

James Brindley, Mayor of Buxton 1874- ?1954

James was a man of energy and conviction. He was a son of Josiah Brindley, born Marylebone, London (according to the 1881 census, but evidence suggests this was a transcription error for Marple, Cheshire) and Mary Ann (maiden name unknown) of Ashton under Lyne, Lancashire. He was industrious and did well. He learned his trade and worked his way up to become a self-employed Master Builder and built up a thriving local business. He was interested in local affairs and eventually he became an Alderman of Buxton and a Justice of the Peace. From 1932 to 1933, he was Mayor of Buxton.

James was born on 9th February 1874 and baptised at Marple Primitive Methodist Chapel on 26th September 1874, the son of Josiah Brindley and Mary Ann, both living at Buxton. Josiah was the son of Samuel Brindley and Mary Ann Kirk of Marple.

James married Ellen Lear of Tunstall on 25th March 1899, and died about 1954. His siblings were:

James Brindley, Mayor of Buxton 1932/3.

Elizabeth A. born 1870; Sarah, born 1872; Mary Anne, born 1875; Frank, born 1880. James and Ellen had the following children: Frank, born 1904, who married C.E.F. Hayes and was a well respected builder of Buxton. He died in 1989; Edith, born 1906; Florence, born 1907 and currently retired in Cornwall; Marion, born 1910. Frank had three children: Beryl, born 1932, (who kindly provided the information) later married to Mr. Thompson, and had children - Nigel; Karen; Adrian; Gail; Christopher David, born 1936, died 1994, who had a daughter Maria; David's twin sister - Anne Lorraine; and Christine born 1940, who has three children - Caesar, Bruce and Ptolemy.

Bolton's First Gay Marriage Friday 16 August 1996

The Reverend Peter Brindley officiated at Bolton's first gay wedding yesterday. This took place at the Town Hall between Sharon Smith and Leanne Jones who took part in a "rite of blessing". The ceremony was watched by members of the gay community. Sharon's two teenage daughters and Leanne's mother were among the guests.

From the Internet

Report 11th June 1999. Love Triangle. Joint Suicide

An inquest heard how Stuart Brindley, aged 75, of Wellington Court, Hanley, argued with his 52 year old son Paul after the younger man asked homeless Ann Dykes to move into their flat. But within days, Miss Dykes, age 44, formed a sexual relationship with Stuart Brindley which angered his son. The inquest heard how Stuart Brindley hit his son over the head with a rubber mallet when he complained about Miss Dykes sleeping with his father. On May 1 last year, Stuart Brindley and Miss Dykes signed a joint suicide note saying they could no longer stand the arguments.

Staffordshire Sentinel

Hot Stuff! 15th July 1999

Timothy Parker, age 27, was convicted by a jury of using a cigarette- lighter to set Dean Brindley ablaze. The jury was told that Parker now accepted that Mr Brindley had not been in his flat. Burns victim Dean Brindley told today how his life had been ruined after being torched by his best friend. Dean, 30, suffered injuries to his upper body and head when bodybuilder Timothy Parker doused him in petrol and set him on fire.

Staffordshire Sentinel

Lynne Brindley: Chief Executive of the British Library

Lynne Brindley took up her appointment as Chief Executive of the British Library on 1st July 2000. Her career spans a range of management roles at leading academic institutions including the London School of Economics and Aston University. She has also worked as a senior management consultant with KPMG, with the British Library (1979-85) in both Bibliographic Services and as head of the Chief Executive's Office, and has played a leading role in initiatives designed to modernise library provision in higher education.

Commenting on her appointment, the Chairman of the British Library, John Ashworth, said: "*I am pleased to be welcoming Lynne to the British Library. Lynne fought off stiff competition from a superb field of candidates from both inside and outside the library community. I am delighted that for the first time in its history the Library has a Chief Executive who is also a professional librarian.*"

Following the successful move into the St Pancras building, the British Library stands as an unique symbol of the cultural and economic importance of libraries. Lynne will be able to take the development of the British Library forward as it addresses the challenges of both meeting the Government's policies of access, education, excellence and enterprise, and the ever rapid changes in information technology.

Lynne Brindley said: *"I feel enormously privileged to be taking on the job at such a critical time. I will seek to build a range of imaginative partnerships and collaborations to ensure the library fulfils its potential to support UK plc, educational and research activity at many levels, and widens access to the Library's rich heritage resources."*

Lynne was previously Pro-Vice-Chancellor and University Librarian at the University of Leeds where she had been since 1997.

Bill Brindley - 2001: Last Pilgrimage for our Heroes of Dunkirk

Due to age and infirmity the 3000+ strong Dunkirk Veterans association has now disbanded. The war cemeteries of Northern France are full of Bill Brindley's friends and comrades that never made it home. The 79-year-old Sergeant was with the North Staffordshire Regiment. Bill, of Forrister Road, Longton, remembers things he saw on the beaches:

"There are lots of graveyards for soldiers but when I go to Dunkirk I know lots of them

because they were in my regiment. Out of 1,000 men only 300 came home and I knew most of the lads that never came back. Standing there among all those familiar names is very poignant - it is the one thing that gets me."

"Our colonel said 'here you are lads, make your own way home - there are the ships.' My mate and I volunteered to carry the wounded on stretchers to the hospital ship. That was torpedoed and we had to abandon ship. I was rescued by someone on a tug who pulled me out of the water and gave me a mug of cocoa."

After Dunkirk, Mr Brindley joined a reconnaissance corp and fought in the Middle East, Africa, Sicily and Italy, before becoming one of the first British troops to march into Austria.

After the War, he returned home and worked in the pottery industry. He married Joyce, had two children, four grandchildren and one great grandchild.

Thomas and Lawrence Brinley - A Tale of Two Brothers and the English Civil War

This story illustrates how a family can pull together and survive 'interesting times'. Both were sons of Richard Brinley of Willenhall and Exeter, who married Ann Reeve.

Thomas was born in 1590, at Exeter and married Ann Wase. Lawrence was born in London, in 1592 and married 1. Mary Minnifee; 2. Elizabeth Beard.

The first brother, *Thomas, Esq*, was well known by virtue of his being appointed Auditor General to King Charles I of England and, after an interruption of twelve years during Oliver Cromwell's Commonwealth Interregnum, was reinstated to the same position by and to King Charles II when his Crown was restored.

Thomas (later he seems to have been dubbed 'Sir' Thomas by some but no evidence of knighthood has been found) was probably the first Brindley/Brinley since the founding of the name to have noticeably advanced himself socially. He seems to have achieved this by strategic marriage and an ability to make friends in high places. How and why he moved to Datchet in Buckinghamshire is not recorded but he found the place suited him very well. His father Richard was a successful merchant at Bristol and Thomas doubtless made his initial contacts through the medium of trade.

After his marriage into the Wase family, he was soon to be found working for Mr Budd Wase, his brother in law, in the Auditors' Office. He must have showed flair because he was appointed to be the next Auditor General following the retirement of the current holder. He had to wait about four years for the position but it was well worth it. His salary was £20 a year but it was expected that he would use his position to advance his wealth, and he did. Quite how he achieved this has never been explained. Was he ruthless and without scruples in seizing lands and property? Was he a fair man? We cannot know for sure. The fact is, he did amass lands and property all over the Country. Eventually he had land at Newcastle under Lyme, Wakefield, Yorkshire, and many other places.

His fortunes dipped when Oliver Cromwell took over and he was allegedly forced into exile, though there is no substantiating evidence of him being seen outside England. He may have just kept a low profile, relying on his brother Lawrence to help him survive political misfortune. His lands and properties were confiscated. Thomas tried to avoid losses as much as possible by having some money transferred abroad in the names of friends or business acquaintances. Some went to Spain (nothing changes, does it?).

After Charles II regained the Crown, he started to have his possessions restored to him, but unfortunately died within a year and not all the former estates were recovered.

Nevertheless, his will, 13th September 1661, with codicil of 16th October 1661, proved 11th December, 1661, gives us a glimpse of some of his wealth:

"My third of tenements in the town of Newcastle upon Tyne, and two thirds of the manor of Burton in Yorkshire, to eldest son Francis Brinley and his heirs. My half of the township or manor of Wakefield, heretofore parcel of the *Lordship* of Raby, and my lands and tenements in Wakefield, county and Bishoprick of Durham, purchased in the name William Wase of Durham and of Robert Worrall, lately deceased, and of Michael Lambcroft, lately deceased and of John Maddocke, of Cuddington, co. Chester, in trust for the use of me, the said Thomas Brinley, and the said Thomas Worrall and our heirs and assigns forever, to my wife, Anne Brinley, during her natural life; at her death to eldest son, Francis Brinley.

My lands in Horton and Stanwell, in the several counties of Middlesex and Bucks, & c., by me purchased of Henry Bulstrode of Horton, to wife Anne for life; then to my second son Thomas Brinley, a lease of 99 years. Certain other lands, &c., lately bought of James Styles, the elder, of Langley, to wife Anne; at her death to my third son, William Brinley. A legacy to daughter Mary Silvester, widow, and her daughter, my granddaughter, Mary Silvester the younger, who are both left destitute of subsistence by the decease of my said daughter's late husband, Peter Silvester, &c.

To the children of my daughter, Grissell, the now wife of Nathaniel Silvester, gentleman, dwelling in New England, in the Parts of America, in an island called Shelter Island, one hundred pounds within one year after my decease.

The witnesses to the will were Robert Style and Rose Baker. In the codicil he bequeathed legacies to his brother Lawrence Brinley and Richard Brinley, Lawrence's son, both of London, merchants, to the intent that they shall with all convenient speed sell that half of said lands, &c. (in Wakefield) for the best rate and value that they can get for the same.

The witnesses to this codicil were William Wase, Budd Wase, William Carter and William Brinley. The will was proved by the widow, Anne Brinley.

Clearly, Thomas was an extremely wealthy man. The above reference to the Lordship of Raby may explain why he was referred to by some as 'Sir'! Could his ownership have conferred on him an automatic right to a title? Had he lived longer, Thomas might have been entitled, by virtue of his lands, to an Earldom.

Meanwhile, his brother Lawrence, who was a successful merchant of London, a haberdasher of Ironmonger Lane, had been gaining influence with the Roundhead politicians. His religious preference was toward Prestbyterianism. He was in fact an activist and petitioned Parliament for a stricter form of Presbyterianism. He rose through the ranks to become a Warden in 1656, and was the Company Master in 1657, a highly prestigious position. As such, he was an honourary Governor of the Adams Free School, in Newport, Shropshire.

As matters came to a head in the clash between Parliament and King Charles, his loyalty was clearly on the Parliamentary side. Indeed, he served on Oliver Cromwell's Commonwealth Committee. There is some evidence to suggest that he made good use of his position to give some discreet aid to his brother, Thomas, in making financial deals and watching his back, but times were risky and there was a thin line he dare not cross. While Thomas appeared to have fled the Country and was losing property and possessions, Lawrence was making use of his position to consolidate gains. However, at the Restoration of the Crown, the tide turned again and it was Lawrence who was wrong-footed.

Lawrence's will of 1669, gives some indication as to his wealth:

To Mary Limbrey twenty pounds; to Philip Limbrey of Virginia, twenty pounds; to my sister, Susan Gregory, of Exon (Exeter), widow, ten pounds; to my cousin Elizabeth Brinley, of London, widow, and her two daughters, twenty pounds apiece to buy them a ring; to *Master Calamy*, my dearly beloved pastor and faithful minister of Jesus Christ, five pounds; *to poor Prestbyterian ministers out of their places for conscience sake, thirty pounds, to be disposed of according to the discretion of my executors with Mr Calamy*; to my daughter Jenne Jackson, the wife of —, the sum of twenty pounds, and, in case Weaver's Hall money cometh in, eighty pounds; to my daughter in law Elizabeth Earnly, widow, the sum of twenty pounds; to my son Nathaniel Brinley fifty pounds, when he cometh out of his time. I do constitute and appoint my two sons Samuel and Richard Brinley to be my executors, and give ten pounds apiece to them. The residue, &c, to my five children, viz., Nathaniel, Susannah, Hester, Philip and Isaac Brinley, according to equal proportions. My real estate of land in Ireland and England, after my decease, to be sold according to the uttermost value, for the payment of my wife's and the children's portions.

The witnesses to this will were William Webb, Richard Brinley and John Jackson. Clearly, Lawrence was worth a few bob, if not as much as his brother Thomas.

It has been said that the brothers did not always see eye to eye, to what extent is unknown, but there is evidence to suggest that they did put family interests first:

KEW Document Reference C5/386116: In the case of Bland versus Brinley, Middlesex, 1650, a Bill of Complaint was made by John Bland, as follows:

In all humble manner complaining sheweth to your good lordships your daily orator John

Bland of the City of London merchant that whereas Anne Brinley wife of Thomas Brinley of Eaton by Windsor in the county of Berkshire did about November in the year of our Lord God 1644 come unto your orator with her then apprehensions of the dangers of the time and therefore being desireous to instruct some moneys in the hands of some friends beyond the seas and the rather for that she further acquainted AND PRETENDED to your orator that her brother (in law) Lawrence Brinley was become a very unkind brother (in law) and would destroy her and her husband if he could discover any of their state that he could seize on and thereupon did earnestly entreat and importune your orator TO RECEIVE £400 of the same as a great courtesy from your orator whereupon your orator in kindness and good will was endured to accept of the same, and according to his best will and advice did by exchange in the year aforesaid SEND THE SAID MONEY FOR THE KINGDOM OF SPAIN and that returns were made of the same in pieces of eight and account thereof given to the said Thomas Brinley husband to the said Anne who accepted and approved of the same as may appear by letter to your orator bearing the date about the 9th of December 1645 subscribed by the said Anne with an acknowledgement of good engagement he your orator for his favour and care in the business and contending further desires of adding £60 more to the said moneys and that your orator would again employ the same as by the said letter and content thereof may appear whereupon your orator out of further love and kindness to your said Thomas and Anne in the year 1646 did again dispose of the said moneys beyond the seas and that returns thereof were again made and that your orator did likewise give an account of the sam to the said Thomas Brinley who liked and approved of the same, and your orator further showeth that the said Thomas Brinley and his wife did further desire your orator,etc.

Anne and Thomas have got all these letters in their possession; with William Wase, brother in law of Thomas, PRETEND THAT THE MONEYS WERE WASE'S AND WANT A RECEIPT ACCORDINGLY.

Molest and harass the orator.

Answer of Thomas Brinley, Anne his wife and William Wase, defs.

1642 - 1644 defendants were apprehensive of the danger of the times.

Thomas and Anne, having then 9 children unprovided for, they were solicitous to dispose some money that they had got together for their children. So that the children might have something on which to survive whatever might happen to Anne and Thomas, Anne went to the plaintiff and acquainted him with the situation. Leave it with friends across the seas.

But Anne DOTH DENT (deny) THAT SHE DID DESIRE ILL IN RESPECT OF LAWRENCE BRINLEY as in the said bill is alleging.

I think it is clear that the brothers were not letting politics get between them but had to put a face on things for political reasons. They looked out for each other in spite of being on opposite sides of the political spectrum. Obviously, It would have been against both their interests to admit that they put family ties before political allegiance, though that is what they seemed to do. The very fact that Thomas left Lawrence a bequest in his will, would seem to indicate that he felt no sense of grievance or injury at all.

Recently it was discovered that the Philadelphia Museum of Art held some table linen that once belonged to THOMAS BRINLEY. The museums description is as follows:

"During the seventeenth century the weaving of fine, figured linen damask reached its artistic and technical height. In addition to the traditional floral and checked designs, such linens were often decorated with armorials or coats of arms... This Flemish linen napkin is one of a set of three each one with a different scene from the Old Testament story of Judith and Holofernes...... Large damask tablecloths and napkins, regarded as luxury items and status symbols, were often given as official gifts. One napkin in this set is embroidered with the initials TAB [presumably THOMAS and Anne Brinley]; according to family tradition, the linens were a gift from Charles I of England to THOMAS BRINLEY, his Auditor General of The Revenue."

The linen is dated circa 1630 and measures 36.5" x 27.5". It was a gift to the museum by Charles Edward Brinley and Miss Katherine Faneuil Adams in 1937. How it came into their possession we do not know, however Katherine Johnstone Wharton may have one time owned it. In 1920 in *The Old Newport Loyalist*, read before the Newport Historical Society, she tells us:

"My Great Grandfather who dyed in 1661, was the Auditor General to both King Charles y'e first and second, used to ride the Northern circuit [not to be thought vain). He was personally known well by their Majesty's, particularly the old King [I have considerable table linen now in the house, how or by what means I don't pretend to know, only as soe mentioned in my Grandfathers pocket book amongst other things] and for his loyalty as a great sufferer. For obeying his Princes Command to come to him at Oxford, he had all they could find of his estate seized and an order from the Then Parliament to apprehend his person, soe was forced to abscond for near 4 years, until his Majesty King Charles y'e 2nd of Blessed Memory came to England in 1660, when he was possest of his office again. He was with his Majesty in his exile, but being ancient upwards of 70 years, dyed less than a year, soe had little or benefit, or recompense which he expected [and ought to have had] from his Majesty for the following loss, and still due from ye Crown to his family if common justice could be distinguished properly. Had he lived undoubtedly would have happened."

The gift of the table linen may appear to be rather plain, however the old King was known for being devoid of humour; he was often described as *"glacial, withdrawn, and prudish.... he was an inaccessible King except to his small band of confidants."*

To demonstrate just how much potential wealth was lost by Thomas at the fall of the monarchy, a copy of a special charter granted to him and his associates is shown here. It involved a vast tract of land, some ten thousand acres; at a nominal yearly stipulation. The land was located in Yorkshire, and its southern borders included villages, churches, and all accompanying privileges. If nothing else, it surely demonstrates the esteem at which Charles the first, held Thomas.

Thomas was buried at Datchet in 1661. His tombstone in the Isle of Datchet church says:

Here Lyeth the Body of Thomas Brinley Esq., being one of the Auditors of the Revenue of Kinge Charles the First and of King Charles y Second.

Lawrence died on 26.6.1662 and was buried in London.

Children of Thomas Brinley and Ann Wase:

1. Ann, born around 1626, married William Coddington.
2. Richard, buried St James's Clerkenwell, 11.7.1625.
3. Rose, born around 1628, married Giles Baker, Lord of the manor of Riple (?) Kent, in 1649.
4. Grissell, baptised 23.9.1631, died young.
5. Mary, baptised 26.11.1632. Married Peter Sylvester around 1656.
6. Patience, baptised around 1632. Married Richard Hackle Esq., 1653.
7. Francis, baptised 11.11. 1633, at St James' Clerkenwell.
8. Thomas, baptised 26.12.1634 at St James's Clerkenwell. Will dated 12.4.1672.
9. Grissell, (2nd) baptised 16.1.1635 or 6.1.1636 at St James's Clerkenwell.
10. John, buried 26.4.1636. (St Mary's Aldermary.)
11. Elizabeth, baptised 6.1.1638.
12. William.

[Notes: 1. Tombstone says 5 sons and 7 daughters.
2. At time of the 'Money to Spain' incident 1642-1644, they were said to have 9 living children.
3. Richard and John are likely children to Thomas and Anne but not proven.
4. John was buried at St Mary's Aldermanbury and the reference says 'of his brother'. I am assuming this is an unaccounted boy of Thomas and Anne.]

Children of Lawrence married to Mary Minifee, 1623 in Stepney:

1. Samewell, baptised 11.7.1624.
2. Marye, baptised 6.8.1626.
3. Larance, baptised 20.4.1628.
4. Daniell, baptised 27.4.1632, buried 28.4.1632.
5. *Anne*, baptised 21.5. 1633. Married Rev. John Jackson, 21.7.1653.
6. George, baptised Duiwich College, 14.7.1636, buried 1.5.1637.
7. Joseph, baptised St Martin Pomeroy, 23.3.1637.

Children of Lawrence married to Elizabeth Beard:

8. *Suzanna*, baptised 11.1.1645 at St Lawrence Jewry and St Mary Magdalene, Milk Street, London.
9. Rebecca, baptised 19.2.1646 at St Lawrence Jewry and St Mary Magdalene, Milk Street, London.
10. Easter! *Hester* baptised 13.6.1647 at St Lawrence Jewry and St Mary Magdalene, Milk Street, London
11. *Philip*, baptised 2.7.1648 at St Lawrence Jewry and St Mary Magdalene, Milk Street, London.
12. *Isaac* baptised 23.5.1651 at St Lawrence Jewry and St Mary Magdalene, Milk Street, London.
13. Mary (2nd) born 14.8.1654, baptised 23.8.1654 at St Mary the Virgin, Aldermannbury, buried 8.9.1656
14. *Nathaniel*; no date of birth but mentioned in the will.
15. *Richard*; no date of birth but mentioned in the will.

Those in italics are mentioned in Lawrence's will. A Richard is also mentioned in Thomas's will. Lawrence also mentions his daughter 'Jenne' Jackson and the will is witnessed by a John Jackson. See Anne (No 5) - is she calling herself Jenne rather than Ann?

There was a marriage on 24th September 1656 at Aldermanbury of a Richard Brinley to Mrs Katherine Chase of St Peter's, Cornhill. They had Mary, baptised 4.7.1658, and Sarah, baptised 11.10.1659. (I have not established the connection, if there is one, of this couple to Lawrence Brinley)

HERE LYETH Y BODY OF THOMAS BRINLEY
ESQ: BEINGE ONE OF THE AVDITORS OF
THE REVENNVE OF KINGE CHARLES THE
FIRST AND OF KINGE CHARLES Y SECOND
BORNE IN THE CITTY OF EXETER HEE
MARRYED ANNE Y DAVGHTER OF WILLIAM
WASE OF PETWORTH IN SVSSEX GENT
WHO HAD ISSVE BY HER FIVE SONNES AND
SEAVEN DAVGHTERS HE DYED Y 18TH DAY OF
OCTOR IN THE YEARE OF OVR LORD 1661

HERE ALSO LYETH BVRIED Y BODY OF THE
ABOVESAIDE WILLIAM WASE WHO DYED
THE 29TH OF SEPTR 1642 AGED 62 YEARE
AND 5 MONETHES

Datchet Church.

Above and below, the
Thomas Brinley gravestone
in Datchet Church.

X

Charter granted to Thomas Brinley by Charles I.
Original document at the Public Records Office at Kew

The King to all whom etc. Greetings. Know that we, as well in fulfillment and performance of a certain contract or agreement by indenture sealed with our great seal of England, dated 27th day of December in the 4th year of our reign, made between us with the advice of the Lords and others of the privy council of the one part, and Cornelius Vermuyden Esquire, of the other part, as for consideration of an annual rent to us by these presents reserved the divers and other good causes and considerations—us at the present specially moving of our special grace and of our sure knowledge and certain will give and grant by these presents for us our heirs and successors, at the nomination and request of the said Cornelius Vermuyden, to our chosen William Curtenie, Knight, Robert Cambell, alderman of London, and to our chosen and faithful servants Charles Harbord, Esquire and our supervisor general, **THOMAS BRINLEY**, one of the Auditors of our Revenue, John Lamote, merchant, and Timothy Vanvleteren, clerk, their heirs and assigns all those parts portions and parcels of land lying and existing within or near the Chace of Hatfield in co. York or within the plain called Levell of the same Chace in cos. York aforesaid, Lincoln, and Nottingham, and within the manors or parishes of Snath, Cowick, Crowle, Missen, Miscerton, and Eringley or any or either of them in our said counties of York, Lincoln, and Nottingham, or any or either of them, lately inclosed or to be inclosed and reclaimed or to be reclaimed with certain water ducts, ditches and divisions, and improved or to be improved by the said Cornelius Vermuyden, his partners or assigns from the waste lands there, except all those parts of the said waste lands belonging to the several vills and people having common within the chace & palm aforesaidor allowed by reson of the said contract or agreement for the enclosure and improvement of the said Chace and plain i.e. all those lands called Haxey Carr or South Carr lying in Epworth, Haxey and Stockwick, lately inclosed, abutting upon the water called Bickersdike and a certain close of Miscerton [??] on the south upon the wastes or commons called Stockwith Common , Owston and Haxey Commons on the east and north and upon the old water course of Jew on the west, and all those other lands called Holmes Carr, Starr Carr, Thornbush Carr and Belton Plaines in Epworth Co. Lincoln, also lateley inclosed, on both sides of the new way or ditch leading from the pond called Iddlestopp to Crowle Causeway and abutting from the pond called Iddlestopp to Crowle Causeway, and abutting upon the said old water course of Jew to the west, and upon the waste land called Rosse Common and other common land and enclosures of Epworth on the east and south and upon the manor of Crowle and the old water course of Dunne in the north, including within it's boundaries a certain lake called Messey Mere and a place called Santofte and Ben Jutach, all which premises in Epworth, Belton, Hazey, and Stockwick co. Lincoln contain in all 7,407 acres of land or thereabout, and all that land called Starr Carr in Crowle and Belton co.Lincoln abutting upon the ditch leading from Iddlestopp to Crowle Cause Way on the south and upon the said old water course of Dunn on the west and upon the common other land of Crowle on the north and east containing in all about 718 acres of land, and all those lands in Missen cos. York and Nottingham lately inclosed on both sides of the said new ditch leading from Iddlestopp and abutting upon the said old water cours of Jew and a certain place called Parsons Cross on the east, and upon the manor of Wroote on the north, and upon the common land of Missen on the west, and south containing about 1,518 acres of land and a certain parcel of land in Missen adjoining the above, not yet inclosed but to be inclosed, and containing 282 acres at the least, all which premise in Missen are parcel of the Duchy of Cornwall. Also certain other land lying in Miscerton and Eringley co.Nottingham, lately inclosed, abutting upon the said water called Bickers-dike and part of the manor of Everton on the north and west, and upon the common land of Miscerton and Eringley on the south and east, and containing about 2,133 acres, and all that land lying in Snath, Cowick and Rowcliff co.York, abutting upon the great bank called Dikesmarch, on the west, upon part of the manor of Hatfield on the south, and upon the common land of Snath on the east and north, containing about 401 acres of land — We also give to the said **THOMAS BRINLEY** etc. all messuages houses, buildings, stables, dovecots, orchards, gardens, lands, meadows, pastures, wastes, furze heath, moors, marshes, waters, water courses, mines, quarries, goods and chattels of felons, fugitives, outlaws and attainted and condemned people, waifs and strays, bond tenants and villeins and their families, and royal privileges belonging to the above premises. Also all woods, underwoods, wooded lands, and trees growing upon the said lands, and revertions and remainders of any part of the same waste lands which have been granted in fee tail or otherwise for a certain term of years, and all rents and profits reserved on such grants, and all other rents and profits from the premises. Further we grant the said THOMAS BRINLEY etc. may impark or unclose any of the above lands and shall have free warren with all priviledges belonging to the said lands, and that no one shall enter the warren to hunt of disturb the deer or stags or do anything which could be damage to the said warren without the license of the said THOMAS etc. under penalties provided in the statutes for preserving free warrens and under pain of forfeiting 10 pounds. Further we grant to the said THOMAS BRINLEY etc. all the above premises as fully, freely and entirely as they came into our hands, and they shall have hold and enjoy the same quit of all people claiming through us our heirs and successors, and of all officers, ministers and keepers of deer claiming any state title or interest in the same through us or any other person. Further know that we by this charter have deafforested and de-warrened the premises from hunting deer and expeditating dogs and from all which to forest chase or warren belongs so that no justice, forester or other officer or minister of us our heirs or successors shall enter the same for anything belonging to the forest chase or warren.

Except always to us and our successors the advowsons of all rectories, churches, vicarages, chapels and other benefices, and except all royal mines, mines of lead and stone in and upon the premises and except all Knight fees, wards and marriages. Having holding and enjoying the above lands and privileges to the said THOMAS BRINLEY etc. to the sole work and use of the said THOMAS BRINLEY etc, holding of us our heirs and successors as of our manor of East Greenwich co. Kent by fealty and in free and common socage, not in chief nor by military service, rendering yearly for the said lands in Epworth, Belton, Hazely, Bringley, Miscerton, Snath, Cowick, Rowcliff and Crowle in Cos. Linclon, York and Nottingham £462 and 17 shillings, and for the premises in Missen £281, at the Exchequer at Westminster on the bailiffs or receivers of the same premises for the time being, at the feasts of the nativity of St. John The Baptist and the Birth of the Lord by equal portions, for all other rents or exactions and demands whatsoever.

And if it shall happen that the said rents so reserved or any part of them remain unpaid for 30 days after either of the said feasts, the said THOMAS etc. shall forfeit £20 each month that the rent is in arrears.

And if the said THOMAS etc. do not cause these letters patent to be enrolled before our Auditors for our several counties aforesaid within six months after the date of these presents, they shall forfeit 20 pounds and the same sum every six months until the letters patent are enrolled, and that it shall be lawful for us our heirs and successors by our Receiver General for the same counties or his sufficient deputy to enter into the above premises or any part thereof and distrain there until we our heirs and successors are paid the said rents and-arrears and forfeitures. And further we grant to the said THOMAS BRINLEY etc. that we our heirs and successors will exonerate and acquit as well as the said THOMAS etc. as the said waste lands, marshes, tenements and hereditamets, and all the premises granted above, from all corrodies, fees, rents, services and annuities, pensions, portions of pence, sums and all things whatsoever from the premises or any part thereof issuing or payable to us or our successors, except from the rent reserved above, the arrears of rent if they shall be due the demise and grant of the premises or any part thereof before this make , and the agreement and condition in the same existing, and the agreement and charge which any farmer or farmers of the premises ought to perform and discharge by reason of any indenture or demise. And moreover from the agreement above in these presents made and by the said THOMAS BRINLEY etc. to be done and performed. Wherefore we with and command as well the Treasurer, Chancellor and barons of our Exchequer for the time being as all the singular the Auditors, Receivers, and other officers whatsoever for the time being of us, our heirs and successors, that they each of them upon sight of these letters patent or the enrollment of the same without any other writ or warrant shall make from time to time cause to be made for the said THOMAS BRINLEY etc. full allowance and exoneration from all such corrodies, rents etc., except the rents etc. reserved above. And these letters patent or the enrollment of the same shall be yearly and from time to time, as well for the said Treasurer, Chancellor and Barons of the Exchequer, as the Auditor, Receivers and other officers, sufficient warrant and discharge in this behalf And further we will and command, and give grant of absolute power and authority to Treasurer, Chancellor and Barons of the Exchequer, that they and each of them from time to time, at the request **THOMAS BRINLEY** etc. may make or execute or cause to make and executed, according to the said Exchequer, that they, and each of them, from time to time, at the request of the said **THOMAS BRINLEY** etc., may make or execute or cause to be make and executed, according to the custom of the said court of Exchequer, all reasonable acts and things whatsoever which may be required of them for the better confirmation of the premises according to the true intention of these our letters patent and for the quiet and peaceful possession of the same.

And that the said **THOMAS BRINLEY** etc. shall have and take full and entire advantage and benefit of these letters patent according to our true intention in the same expressed and declared. And these our letters patent or the enrollment of the same shall be to the said Treasurer, Chancellor and Barons of the Exchequer for the time being and each of them sufficient warrant and discharge in this behalf

And further we grant the said **THOMAS** etc. that at the next Parliament or Session of Parliament of us our heirs or successors held within this realm of England we, upon humble request to us made, will give and grant our royal and free assent to any act of Parliament, Petition or Bill brought into the same Parliament for better confirmation, assurance and security of all and singular the said lands granted above, according to the true intention of these letters patent and the contract mentioned above.

And further we grant that if and as often as any doubts or questions shall happen to arise concerning the validity of these our letters patent to any clause, matter or thing whatsoever concerning the estate title and interest of the said **THOMAS BRINLEY** etc., of in or to the premises or any part thereof that then and so often, upon humble petition of the said **THOMAS** to us our successors presented, and upon notice and certificate of the attorney general for the time being of the defect required to be amended, we will grant other letters patent to the same **THOMAS** etc. with such amendments, explanations, amplifications as by the same attorney General shall be seen to be fit.

And whereas the said **THOMAS** etc. of their singular devotion and piety propose and intend to build one or more chapel or chapels within the limits of the said lands and other premises, in the more convenient places, and to sustain in the same, sufficient ministers to celebrate divine service there to the glory of Almighty God, and have prayed for our royal license and assent we, very much favouring the pious and praiseworthy plan of the said **THOMAS** etc. grant them full faculty, license, power and authority at any time hereafter and in any convenient place or places within the limits of the said lands or anywhere which shall seem to them more convenient, with the consent of the ordinary of that place, to build one or more chapels and to maintain in the same one or more ministers to celebrate divine service either in English or Belgian, according to the form of religion established in England, and this without any other warrant or commission to be obtained from us or our successors.

Notwithstanding the wrong naming or not naming or wrong reciting or not reciting of the said premises or any part of them. And notwithstanding the not finding or wrong finding of the office or offices inquisition or inquisition of the premises or any part thereof by which our title ought to be found before the conferring of our letters patent. And notwithstanding any defect in not reciting or wrongly reciting any grant concerning the premises, and notwithstanding the not naming or wrongly naming of any vill, hamlet, lake, parish or county, in which the premises or part of them lie. And not withstanding any defect in wrongly naming any tenant, farmer or occupier of the premises or any part of them. And notwithstanding any variation, discrepancy, or difference in anything, matter, name or form between these letters patent and any particular or survey of the premises, or any record of the same. And notwithstanding any defect in not mentioning or not rightly mentioning the true yearly value of the premises or the true yearly rent reserved, specified in any particular survey or account, before this made or afterwards to be made, of the premises. And notwithstanding that the premises or any profits thereof ever were of better or greater annual value than is specified in these letters patent or any particular of the premises. And notwithstanding the Statutes I Parliament made 18 Henry VI and 1 Henry IV. And notwithstanding any defect in not naming or not rightly naming the nature, quantity and quality of the premises or any person who before this was seised of the same or any state tail to us or any of our progenitors or any indenture or annexation of our late father, or any of the Kings and Queens of England.

The 'Datchet-style' house of Colonel Francis Thomas Brinley.

Trinity Church, Newport, Rhode Island.

PART II
NEW ENGLAND

Chapter 7
Francis Brinley: 1632-1719

Francis Thomas Brinley 1632-1719 was the son of Thomas Brinley, Auditor General to Charles I and II, and Ann Brinley (née Wase). It was said that he was for a time attendant on the fortunes and revenues of Charles II during his exile; records exist for this period but none refer to Francis or Thomas. It could be that the family or friends destroyed the records referring to the Brinleys; possibly, the records were lost; or perhaps the stories are unfounded.

After the restoration, he grew tired of pestering Lord Clarendon for relief and reminding the King of the promised and ample compensation for his (father's) services and sufferings. In consequence of the losses sustained by his father for faithful adherence to the royal family, *"he accepted a grant of lands or office in the island of Barbadoes"*. (Though, there is no record of him actually holding land there!) The climate was not suited to his habits and constitution, and so it is said *"he came early to Rhode Island with money in his pocket."*

We know that the 1st Earl of Clarendon served as the King's Chancellor of the Exchequer during the war and went into exile in 1646, settling eventually with the future King Charles II in France. After the Restoration, he became Lord Chancellor.

If Francis did attend the King, as claimed, it could only have been for the three years between 1649 (as he turned 17) and 1652 - the year he left for America. Any lobbying that Francis carried out with Clarendon must have been at least eight years later, after the restoration of the Monarchy in 1660. In 1652, Clarendon would have been in no position to grant lands, or office, being in exile himself.

There have been several reports of Francis travelling to Barbados in the company of his newly wed sister Ann Coddington and his soon-to-be-married sister Grissell. However, there are differing accounts of the route they took from there to America. Here are quotes from different sources:

"They first touched Barbados whence they sailed on the "Golden Parrott" for Shelter Island, arriving about the middle of 1652." A contrary reference states, *"After nearing the coast of New England on the Swallow, they were shipwrecked, losing most of their goods."*

We also have another report that Francis, Grissell, and Nathaniel, were aboard the shipwrecked *Swallow,* as it headed towards Shelter Island. This was presumably en route from Rhode Island, because Ann and William were not on board. Certainly, if the high profile Mr. William Coddington had been shipwrecked, it would have been written about for decades.

No passenger manifest can be found for either of these ships, so there is no evidence either way. We know the party went to Barbados to visit Constant Sylvester, and we are certain that Grissell and Nathaniel Sylvester were married in America and not England or Barbados. That being said, they must have married in Rhode Island and travelled on to Shelter

Island from there. There was no one qualified to marry them in Shelter Island at the time and it is inconceivable that Grissell would have left the protection of her guardian, William Coddington, before being married. Therefore, that would make their route England-Barbados-Rhode Island-Shelter Island. Maybe, one day, we will know the full tale of their shipboard adventures!

One way or another, Francis arrived in Rhode Island in 1652, and we know from his own hand that he stayed with Grisell and Nathaniel in 1653. A letter he wrote in 1654 states that he had "*been on Shelter Island for a year.*"

In 1655, he sailed for England and returned to America on the ship *Speedwell*, arriving in Boston on July 27, 1656.

A short time after his stay on Shelter Island, Francis decided to make his home in Newport. He first settled in a two-room, two-storey residence on the corner of Farewell Street and Marlborough Street, on land adjoining the estate of his sister, Ann and her husband.

In 1657, Francis married Hannah Carr, of the family of Governor Caleb Carr. They had two children, Thomas and William. We have discussed Thomas and William elsewhere, however it should be remembered that Thomas was the favourite son and, William had incurred his father's displeasure when he married contrary to his father's wishes. Francis eventually made his grandson, the son of Thomas, his heir and beneficiary.

In 1674, Francis and Hannah sold the property on Farewell Street to William Mayes Senior, who quickly turned the former residence into the White Horse Tavern - one of America's oldest inns. We are not aware of where they lived next, but he held land all around town and Newport is small, so it is likely that their new residence would have been only a short distance away.

Over the years, there are many land transactions recorded in Francis's name but, for the purposes of this book, they tell us little more than that he had large land holdings.

In 1684, we have a report of Francis shipping gold and silver to London aboard the "*Francis*", its master being Peter Bennett. Apparently, the *Francis* sailed from England in 1682 to Jamaica and cruised through the West Indies. In St. Thomas, the crew came across a pirate ship called *The Trompeuse* which was on fire and adrift, and it eventually was forced into New England for a refit. The Trompeuse was impounded for piracy and Peter Bennett was later questioned as to his own cargo of gold and silver. This is probably because both ships came into Newport around the same time and the authorities suspected they were in collusion (which they were not). As part of his rebuttal of being a criminal, Bennett revealed to the arresting magistrate, Major Dyer of Boston, that the gold and silver in his custody belonged, in part, to Francis Brinley.

Francis was much respected in his day. Business led him frequently to England. He was, as it were, the organ of intelligence and remittance between the colony and the mother country. Upon his return from England, on one occasion, he came unexpectedly into the quarterly town meeting, then in session - '*whereupon (says the record) all the Freemen rose.*' (Redwood Library Address, by the late Hon. William Hunter, of Newport)

He pressed the authorities in London to do something about the increasing lawlessness prevailing in Rhode Island at the latter part of the century. Newport was gaining a reputation as a pirate's haven.

In 1686, he was appointed Justice of the Peace in Newport and in 1687 (in the reign of

James II) he was appointed a Judge of the Court of Common Pleas for Rhode Island. He occasionally resided in Boston, with a large estate at the corner of Hanover and Elm Streets.

By 1687, French Huguenots arrived on Rhode Island and the Anglican Church was formed. There was deep unrest. In 1690, Francis wrote to his son Thomas in London:

"At New York, Jacob Liesler rules at his will and pleasure, puts in prison whom he pleases and keeps them. We are here in great confusion: John Coggeshall styles himself Deputy Governor and John Greene, of Warwick, calls himself Assistant [both being of the Governors council] and intend next week to call a General Assembly and rule by sword. It is high time His Majesty would settle a government over New England. We can never govern ourselves with justice nor impartiality unless there be good government established here, as in the other plantations. I must remove." He continues *"Three days since we heard that a town above Albany was cut off by French and Indians; where seventy people were killed, and the rest carried captive."*

Many leading opponents vigorously objected to Francis corresponding with London and it was well known that he, together with Peleg Sanford, relayed nearly every act of lawlessness that they were aware of; continuously soliciting a respectable form of government. Obviously, this did not suit some. However, decent citizens of the region held Francis in great esteem and respect.

Around 1696, we learn that Rhode Island maintained its reputation as a notorious resort. One infamous figure of that era was Captain William Kidd, who started in official defensive operations against pirates before turning to piracy himself. Others who turned pirate about this time included William Mayes Junior and Thomas Tew.

Francis wrote a history of the transactions of Rhode Island, Massachusetts and the King's Province, that is, Marrangansett, which may be found in the Massachusetts Historical Collections, 1st Series, 5th volume, page 216. It is dated October 26th, 1700.

He had established himself at Newport, Rhode Island, fourteen years after its settlement, which was in 1638. From that time until his decease in 1719, aged 87, he was always active.

In 1709, Francis's son William, following his elder brother's example of being involved in founding King's Chapel, Boston, signed a petition calling for a clergyman to come to Newport. This was the beginning of William's involvement with Trinity Church. In 1699, his neighbour Robert Carr donated the land that became the site of the first building.

Trinity Church stood adjacent to land owned by the Brinley family and, by 1720, a year after Francis's death, a Francis Brinley of Boston sold it. We assume that this was his grandson, Colonel Francis living at Roxbury.

In 1715, Francis dictated an elaborate account of the purchase of Conanicut Island, the reason being that he was the *"only proprietor living that is now concerned"*. The original document, signed by him, is held at The Newport Historical Society.

He died at Boston in 1719, aged 87, and was buried in the King's Chapel Burial Ground, on the spot where the family tomb now stands. He probably chose to be buried here because his favoured son, Thomas, had been a founder of the Church.

His large estate passed to his grandson, Colonel Francis Brinley, and his grand-daughter Mrs Elizabeth Hurtchinson, because he outlived his children.

He also left a large collection of books including many on Law, Divinity, Philosophy, History, that included copies of Homer's *Iliad*, Plutarch's *Lives*, Sir Walter Raleigh's *World*,

English Chronicles, The Greek Testament and the Works of Virgil.

His will bequeathed most of his estate to grandson Francis and included *"lands in Horton and Stanwell, Co Middlesex and Bucks, England, mentioned in my father's will. And messuages at Quononaguntt Island alias James Towne."* He attached a codicil to prevent Francis inheriting until he became *"solid and sober"*. Francis's mother kept the codicil secret for nineteen years before handing it over to her son. By that time, he had come to his senses!

This seems to tell us that, despite Francis's heavy drinking - and he was by his own admission a *"sad and rakeing dog"*, his grandfather still loved him very dearly and wanted him to have what was rightfully his, once he became more disciplined. Francis, writing in later years, appears to have held no grudge whatsoever about the codicil; and seems to support his grandfather's decision.

Although the younger son William had died in 1704, nowhere in Francis's will does he refer to William's family by marriage; yet we believe there was at least one child. It leaves the impression that William and his father were never reconciled.

For a final farewell, grandson Francis elaborately arranged the funeral and, in his own handwriting, describes mementoes such as scarves, gloves and rings to be purchased for the guests. Amongst those who were invited were the Governor, Colonel and Lady Phipps, Byfield Lyde, Mrs Hutchinson, Madam Sylvester and Mr Homeaudieu. The attending ministers were Dr. Mather, Mr. Miles, Mr. Coleman and Mr. Harris.

No doubt, it was a splendid and fitting send off for this extraordinary character, who witnessed so much and begat the Brinleys of New England.

He was descended from the original Brundelegh de Brindley family.

From the diary of Susan Rothschild

The following poignant extract is from the diary of Susan Rothschild, who was born in Devon, England, on April 30th 1598. She married William Carr of London on May 16th 1619. The wilderness she is talking about is *Rhode Island*. Her descendant was Hannah Carr who married Francis Thomas Brinley, founding father of the Boston and Rhode Island Brinleys. Captain Roger Williams abandoned the sea in 1636, and joined the pioneers at their settlement. It was he, who would first welcome one William Coddington to Rhode Island after he left Boston.

"It was a summer day, in 1621, as I stood upon our ship's deck beside my husband with my infant son closely folded to my breast, while our noble captain Roger Williams, stood by our side. I took a last view forever of my native isle, and forever bid it adieu, and all the scenes of my childhood home. My heart ached while bitter tears blinded my eyes. Never shall I forget the scenes that day, as we took a last farewell of our friends with many promises that they would join us in America.

Then the order was given by our captain to cast off our moorings, and our ship stood out in the Thames. After all sails were spread, we took our course down the river. Each spot along its banks was dear to my soul, and while I was sad, the passengers, there being thirty-five, were singing and making merry that we were going to America. I could not join them for my heart was very sad.

We had a very pleasant sail down the Thames. Still I gazed upon my native isle with tearful eyes, and watched it when far out to sea, until the last mountain vanished from my view. Our voyage was very pleasant for twenty days out to sea, and then we encountered a storm, which lasted all the afternoon and the following night. The weather was pleasant the rest of the way and on the 6th day of November 1621, the anchor was cast at dark some way out to sea for fear of unseen rocks.

Next morning the boats were lowered and we landed, but what was my surprise! Lucinda, George Carr's wife, had died the spring before. My husband and George his brother and myself went to view her resting place. There with tearful eyes I viewed the last resting place of poor Lucinda Devenport, whom I had known in England. She had died in a foreign land of privation and cold, and was buried side by side with many others who had shared the same fate. My heart sank within me to think that I should never see Lucinda again. I had anticipated many happy hours with her, but my youthful hopes were forever blasted.

We lived with my brother George through the winter, living mostly on what game we caught. It was a cold, tedious winter with deep snow. Game was plenty such as deer and moose.

On June 1, 1622, husband started southwest for a warmer climate, with pocket compass and an Indian guide. Brother George went a two days journey with us, and then returned home. I carried my son George in my arms and on my back through a dense forest settled only with wild beasts and Indians, but we met few of the former and none of the latter. After being forty-eight days on our journey, July 18, husband concluded a stop to build a log cabin to settle for life. In four days, husband, the Indian and myself, finished our log cabin, covering it with poles and peeled bark. My journey through the forest and the hard labour I had done in helping build our cabin, had its effects on me. I felt nearly worn out.

I had left my rich parents in England and my only brother Robert in England, and faced the storms and perils of the ocean with my noble companion, and travelled with him forty-eight days through the forest. To my companion I had given my early love and pledged my hand for life. He was ever kind to me. We both belonged to the Society of Friends.

Before leaving England, father gave me £100 in gold coin, my brother gave me two doubloons in gold. This gold coin I sewed into the wadding of my petticoat. Mother gave me her gold diamond ring, which cost £16. She took her gold watch from her pocket and gave it to me. It cost £25. She also gave me her gold locket and the gold chain that she wore with her watch, and bade me keep them to remember her by. The locket cost £10, and I lost it in my journey through the wilderness in coming here, but it was found by an Indian hunter in 1625, and returned to me. I had many happy days hunting deer with my husband, as there was plenty of them in the forest, but I often thought of home and dear ones there. We had fine times hunting with the Indians, they were friendly to us. Our bedding and clothing were nearly all skins and furs like the Indians, but in all these years I was mindful to educate our son George, although we were in a nameless wilderness."

Colonel Francis Thomas Brinley,1690-1765, painted in 1729 by Smibert, a famous Scottish portrait painter of his day who went to America and painted many portraits there.

William Coddington, 1601-1677, married Ann Brinley, daughter of Thomas Brinley, the Auditor to Charles 1, and sister of Francis Brinley. William became Governor of Rhode Island. This image is a subject of controversy (see text).

Deborah Brinley (née Lyde), wife of Francis above, with baby Francis who later married Aleph Malbone.

The pictures of Francis Brinley and his wife Deborah are reproduced by kind permission of the Metropolitan Museum of Art, New York. The picture of William Coddington is by kind permission of the Redwood Library and Atheneum, Newport, Rhode Island.

Chapter 8
'American' Descendents of Auditor General, Thomas Brinley
Ann (Brinley) Coddington

Thomas, the Auditor, has been written about at length earlier in this book. This however is the story of three of his children, Francis, Ann, and Grissell, all of whom were destined to lead prosperous and privileged lives, becoming prominent in the development of their fledgling communities, namely - Boston, Rhode Island, and Shelter Island.

Unfortunately, of the girls, little is known of a personal nature; so we shall attempt to tell their story through the knowledge we have of their partners in wedlock. Luckily, Francis is another story; much has been recorded on his account, as well as the lives of his children and that of future generations. Francis founded the Brinley family in both Boston and Newport.

Every attempt has been made to check facts where they are available; however, much of this information has been passed down in time by recollections of family members and other witnesses to key events. No doubt, there have been exaggerations and distortions along the way. Regardless, these stories have been recorded here alongside the facts, and it is largely for the reader to decide on the "truth." We are fortunate though, that several early Brinleys took an active part in trying to trace and record the family history for posterity.

Apart from the three clearly defined American family lines that are featured in the following chapters it should also be acknowledged that the author is aware of early Brinley families living in Southold, Long Island; Perth Amboy, New Jersey; and in Pomfrit, Connecticut. I hope that more details will follow in a second volume.

Ann Coddington 1632-1719

In order to understand more about Ann Brinley's marriage to William Coddington, and her life thereafter, it is necessary to go back a little and delve into her husband's character and his adventures in America before Ann arrived as his bride.

William Coddington was born in Boston, Lincolnshire in 1601; and from the earliest, he had religious leanings. We know that his regular place of worship was St. Botolph's Church in Boston. We also know from his own recollections that, as a young man, he became a thorn in the side of King Charles; for Coddington was one of the few Lincolnshire businessmen who, on principle, refused to tender money to the spendthrift King, and thereafter claimed *"he suffered because of it"*. What he endured, we do not know, but it is not surprising that Coddington was tired of England and dreaming of a new life far away from the King and his courtiers.

With a clear purpose in mind, he managed to arrange a position as a Commissioner with the Massachusetts Bay Company, which had secured a Royal Charter under seal of the King. The Charter was broad in scope and not only conferred the right to land, but also powers of government as well. On the 7th April 1630 William Coddington left for America, setting sail aboard *The Arabella* leaving from Yarmouth. He took with him was his first wife, Mary Mosely.

On 13th June 1630 the colonists from *The Arabella* arrived in America. They had to become organized before winter set in and lost no time in making a permanent settlement in

Boston, which was then called Trimontaine. Unfortunately, the sickness and disease endured during the sea voyage, coupled with lack of provisions, proved fatal for many of William Coddington's fellow adventurers, and some 200 perished. The harsh winter that followed only served to make matters worse and it is believed that Mary Coddington died that first year.

On the 17th September 1630, Trimontaine formally became known as Boston, named after the English hometown of William Coddington and many of his companions.

In 1632 William Coddington returned to England to settle his affairs, and while he was there he married his second wife, whose name we do not know. It was during this visit to his home country that he first established his reputation as a man of *"remarkable generosity"*; having liberal ideals and a strong commitment *"to improve the condition of lowly man."*

Back in America, Boston was growing rapidly; in fact, records state that over a ten-year period, 21,000 people arrived from England in 298 ships. With this mixed influx of *"new blood"* came a growing number of Puritan Ministers whose fanatical religious doctrines began and ended with the words *"Thou shalt not!"*

Meanwhile, due to his natural business acumen, William Coddington was becoming affluent, and in keeping with his status he built the first brick house in Boston. At this time, his close circle of friends included John Cotton; who was previously the Rector at St. Botolphs and Ann, wife of William Hutchinson. Much has been written about his relationship with Mrs Hutchinson; for a short time their fates were interlinked due to their deeply held religious values.

In 1637, Mrs. Hutchinson was imprisoned for her *"radical"* religious teachings and was eventually brought to trial. Thereafter she was excommunicated from Boston. The court case was a highly controversial event in its day and attended by many; what transpired is a matter of record, and it was reported that William Coddington appeared on the last day of the trial and in public *"forcibly entered his protest"* at the nature of the proceedings. He was very definitely in the minority.

Following the judgment to expel Mrs Hutchinson he sensed he must make a choice. He resolved to support her and leave the puritanical hypocrisy of Boston behind - as well as his home, his friends, his job, and all his business interests.

In March 1638, William Coddington led a small group of *"outcasts"* and braving the winter weather, they set sail to find a fresh start in an unknown place. Having no firm destination in mind, the group eventually set down in Providence, which was already home to a man named Roger Williams, and twelve other neighbours. It was lucky that Williams and his associates were pleased to have more company and eager to assist, he hastily helped his new friends find suitable territory; a place called Aquidneck Island, which they purchased from the Narragansett tribe for *"forty fathoms of Wampum"*.

In March 1638, the new community of eighteen families formed a government, unanimously electing William Coddington as Governor. As the year passed, others joined the settlement, but by this time matters were not going well between William and Mrs Hutchinson; he also now regarded her as a troublemaker. In 1639, several factions in this new society were at odds with one another and eventually Ann seized her chance to grasp power by forcing her mild-mannered husband William to overthrow Coddington.

Optimistic as ever, William Coddington looked on this event as an opportunity to rid himself of the Hutchinsons, and to form a commonwealth in a much better location at the southern end of the island. So, on the 16th of May 1639, a new settlement was established, a place that is now known as Newport, Rhode Island.

A formal administration was quickly created and the town of Newport was laid out in four-acre plots; plots large enough to accommodate decent sized farms for its principal inhabitants. The town was settled on both sides of a bountiful stream that ran down Tanner Street, to Marlboro Street and into a cove. William Coddington's house was built on the north bank of the stream on Marlboro Street, directly opposite Duke Street. Marlborough Street is still a prominent thoroughfare in Newport today.

Over the next few years, more people arrived in Rhode Island and the flourishing towns and communities experienced much in the way of political turmoil. That being said, William was elected to office year after year, and managed his government as a forward thinking modern democracy. Meanwhile rival states such as Connecticut were beginning to seek administrative control of the region, and the liberty of Newport and Rhode Island was now under constant threat.

In 1647, things changed dramatically when John Coggleshall was surprisingly elected President of the Province, which by that time included Portsmouth, Newport, Warwick, and Providence. In the reorganization of power, Coggleshall wanted William to be his assistant for Newport. He declined, not wanting to be a part of the new regime and fearing for the political independence of Newport. Considering what he had already experienced, no doubt he was also nervous of losing his much-treasured spiritual freedom.

By this time, he was a widower again; so, he made up his mind to leave and register his objections by lobbying the Commissioners of State in England. Shortly afterwards, leaving his farm and his business interests in the hands of a representative, he set sail with his daughter, Mary. He arrived in England in the autumn of 1648 and found the country embroiled in Civil War. For unrelated political reasons, more than a year would elapse before he was able to state his case to those with authority. Finally, on the 20th March 1650, he was able to present his petition to the Committee of Foreign Affairs under Sir Henry Vane. A fellow Rhode Islander and political opponent, Edward Winslow was also present to challenge his position.

William Coddington's political motivation for seeking permanent office under the protection of the English Crown is still much debated by Rhode Islanders today. Nonetheless, the decision took over a year to make and favoured him. He was appointed Governor of Rhode Island for life. Like most things, it was not to last, but the diplomacy he displayed, during this traumatic period in English history, became legendary. Those who knew William at the time widely acknowledged him as a born leader.

[Note: In 1903 the Bishop of London presented the original copy of William Coddington's Commission to Colonial Archives Office in Washington, D.C.]

William Coddington remained in England for nearly three years and, in the intervening time between business meetings, he mixed socially with many prominent families of similar ilk including that of Thomas Brinley, and his wife, Ann.

It is evident that under difficult circumstances Thomas established a meaningful relationship with William while he was in England, for not only did he give permission for him to marry his daughter Ann he also entrusted him with guardianship of her sixteen year-old sister, Grissell. We can only assume that Thomas and his family were either in semi-hiding, or at the very least were keeping a low profile, because it also fell to William to *"negotiate"* Grissell's marriage to Nathaniel Sylvester. It is presumed that Thomas did not entrust his son Francis with the task of guardian because he himself was at risk; either that or he had already left England for Barbados at the time.

We know as a matter of record, that the security of their family was of great concern to both Thomas and Ann, so it must have been a great relief for them to know that the last two of their unmarried daughters would soon be several thousand miles away, and in the relative security of solid relationships.

Ann Brinley was born about 1626 and baptized at St. James's Church in Clerkenwell, London. The cherished daughter of Thomas and Ann Brinley, she was born into a house of privilege and social standing, mixing in London society and royal circles at the Court of King Charles and Queen Henrietta Maria.

At the age of 24, Ann became the wife of a powerful and much respected man sixteen years her senior; with two previous marriages behind him. In marriage, Ann also acquired a young step-daughter to care for.

From the Faculty of the Archbishop of Canterbury, the Marriage License states:

"Coddington, William Esq. Of the Isle of Rhodes, beyond the seas, widower, about 40, and Anne Brindley, about 24, daughter of Thomas Brindley of Eaton, co. Bucks, esq. Alleged by John Mayer, of St. Bennet, Paul's Wharf, London, Gent - at Datchet, co, Bucks. 12 Jan.1649/50 F.

Flushed with political success, William returned to America with his new wife and his daughter. Ann quickly settled into the house on Marlboro Street and was well received into society. He, too, was welcomed back enthusiastically and at first there was no indication of the unhappiness his recent appointment created; or of what was to happen next. A powerful reformer, William quickly resumed reins of Newport governorship, feeling protected by the British Government for the first time.

No doubt Ann's highly developed social skills proved an asset; although what she first thought of this provincial *"back-water"* called Newport compared to the frantic activity of life in London, we shall never know. What we do know is that she never journeyed back, and lived in Newport many years after William died; so she must have grown to love the island town and view it as home.

Ann's growing family was obviously the most time consuming aspect of her early-married life. On the 18th January 1651 she gave birth to her first son, William, and the couple went on to have seven more children over the next twelve years. Two of their children died within a short time; Noah was born on November 12th 1658 and died a month later, and Ann was born on June 6th 1660, and died on June 26th.

Inevitably, political intrigue remained rife and trouble arose once more. In 1652, John Clarke and Roger Williams succeeded in having William Coddington's Commission revoked, and he was effectively deposed. There was much mayhem at the time and his life was threatened. That same year, Francis, Ann's brother, arrived in Newport and undoubtedly his arrival must have been of great comfort to them at this very stressful time.

Despite being desperately disappointed at losing office and unconvinced at the wisdom of this development, William supported future governments when needed. Semi-retired he was still keen to lend his expertise to public life.

More children came along and Ann gave birth to Nathaniel, named after her brother-in-law Nathaniel Sylvester, on the 23rd of May 1653. Mary followed; born on the 16th May 1654. Mary went on to marry Governor Peleg Sanford in 1674. Thomas was born on November 5th 1655 and John in December 1656. John died aged 23 years on June 1st 1680. Lastly, Anne was born; their second child of the same name; on July 20th 1663. Anne lived to marry Andrew Willet on May 30th 1682.

Together with Ann, William now devoted himself to his family and to agricultural pursuits on their farm at Coddington Point. The land was very fertile and they used professional farming techniques brought from England. They raised sheep and horses, and sold many *"best of breed"* to the West Indies where they were in much demand.

Eventually William accepted the new regime and appeared before the assembly of Commissions in March 1656 as representative Commissioner for Newport; declaring, *"I, William Coddington, do freely submit to the authority of His Highness in this Colony as it is now united."*

About this time he was accused of selling guns to the Indians: *"....in 1656, guns showed up in the hands of various Indians were much like those Mr Coddington brought over."* This challenged his strong Quaker beliefs which forbade ownership of weaponry.

William was encouraged to take up office again. In 1666, he acted as Commissioner, and then Deputy Governor. In 1675, he was appointed Governor of the Colony, and later, he died holding that office.

By this time, the Coddingtons had become the wealthiest family in Rhode Island and it is reputed, in all of New England. The couple remained devout and had become increasingly attracted to different ways of worship and expression. Soon they converted to Quakerism; which George Fox, a fellow Englishman, had founded.

The Coddington residence on Marlboro Street became a regular Quaker meeting place and William and Anne continued to expand their social existence by entertaining Quakers as they visited the Rhode Island from places such as Jamaica, and Barbados. There were many colonists in the West Indies at the time and they frequently made trips to America for trade and provisions.

In 1672 George Fox visited the Coddingtons at their spacious home on Marlboro Street which was called *"New Lodge."* At this point, nearly half of Newport's population was of the Quaker faith and many people congregated at the house to hear Fox preach in the Great Room. It is known that at the same time as Fox was there, Governor Bellingham of Massachusetts was also staying at New Lodge. It was recorded that *"he and his company were royally entertained for ten days."*

After this event, the Coddington home became revered as place of worship and the couple continued to host meetings and annual gatherings. Ann continued with this practice after her husband's death. We know from the Friends' records that *"In 1678, a man's meeting was held at the widow Coddingtons."*

Around 1673, one of America's oldest inns was built. The White Horse Tavern was situated close to the Coddington home on the corner of Farewell and Marlboro Streets. The White Horse, with its prominent painted sign after the English fashion, quickly became a popular *"watering hole"* for many Friends after meetings. Although we can be confident that Ann would never have crossed the doorstep; it is likely that William did!

The White Horse Tavern

By 1689 the Friends began breaking away from the Coddington house *"never to return"*. It was written *"It is agreed that the Yearly Men and Women's Meeting which useth to be at William Coddington's shall be ye first part at ye Meeting House and later part for ye fayers of ye Church to be at Walter Newberry's"*.

Although one was in existence earlier, by 1699, the Quakers had built a larger Meeting House where it stands today, and as the movement expanded, there were additions built in 1729, 1807, 1857, and 1867. The Meeting House is situated on the corner of Farewell and Marlborough Street, close to the location of Coddington's home.

William Coddington passed away aged 76, on September 27th 1677, and is buried in the Friends' cemetery, which is located on the aptly named Farewell Street. Coddington donated the burying ground to the Quakers and, interestingly, the stone that now marks his grave was provided by the townspeople; it is not known what happened to the original, maybe it just crumbled or was lost.

Ann died thirty-one years later on the 9th May 1708 in Newport. She was aged 80. In the burial ground a stone is marked William Coddington's wife. This is probably the grave of Ann, but could also refer to their son William's wife.

There is no doubt that William Coddington was a controversial figure, not only in life, but also after his death. One debate that still provokes much controversy is that of his *"alleged"* portrait that hangs in the gallery of the Redwood & Athenaeum Library, Newport.

This portrait attracts much speculation because of several reasons; firstly, there was no artist in America that could have painted it. However, it could have been painted during his visit to London in 1651, but as the wearing of a periwig did not become fashionable until much later, it is unlikely. More critical to the question is that it would have been unforgivable for a Quaker to be featured wearing a sword. Some attribute the portrait to the Scottish artist John Smibert [1688-1751]. Interestingly it was Smibert, that painted Francis Brinley and his wife and child - see page 92. The question remains whether this was indeed William Coddington, or whether it was the second William; or even his grandson, also named William who was born in 1680 and died in 1755.

Chapter 9
Grissell (Brinley) and Nathaniel Sylvester

Grissell, daughter of Thomas and Ann Brinley, was baptized St. James's, Clerkenwell, on either January 16th 1635 or January 6th 1636. Confusingly, official church records show two baptism entries for Grissell which may be why her birth date is often shown as "1635/1636" in publicly accessed sources such as the IGI. The church year, back then, ran from April to the following March, which could explain the confusion.

Grissell was the couple's second child of the same name. We know that there was an earlier child named Grissell, who was baptized on the 23rd September 1631, also at St. James's church. This child must have died in infancy, although we have no record of the burial. Certainly, Ann and Thomas are accredited with having twelve children altogether and this first Grissell would account for the "missing" daughter. Thomas's gravestone at St. Mary's in Datchet quotes, *"Hee marryed Anne Y Daughter of William Wase of Petworth in Svssex Gent. Who had issue by her of five sonnes and seaven daughters."* Of the females, we can confidently trace Mary, Ann, Rose, Elizabeth, Patience, and Grissell. This leaves one girl unaccounted for - the first Grissell.

Grissell arrived into the world at a very turbulent time, a period of deep and desperate intrigue that would eventually divide many prominent families such as theirs. As seen in chapter 8, Grissell's father Thomas supported the King, while her uncle Lawrence's allegiance was to the puritan, <$iOliver Cromwell. We know that the two brothers were close, though for a long time it was necessary to appear publicly estranged from one another, so it is difficult to know if, as a child, Grissell socialized with her many cousins. Certainly she would not have been short of company as she had her own brothers and sisters to occupy her.

Family life was always complicated by politics and their situation and security was constantly at risk. When Grissell was about six, civil war broke out in England and her father was at the epicentre of events. When she was eight years old, in November 1644, her parents approached John Bland of London, attempting to send funds to Spain in the name of William Wase. The money was for their children, by way of financial protection should they both meet an untimely end. Because of this transaction, there was a dispute between Bland and the Brinleys, which is now a matter of public record.

In 1646, her father's protector, the King, was arrested and, after fleeing for a time, was beheaded on January 30th 1649. It is ironic that, while her father's fortunes fell, those of her uncle Lawrence were in the ascendant.

It says something if Grissell's parents had permitted their daughter Ann to wait until she was twenty-four to marry, or maybe there was no choice. This was after all a perilous period. Nevertheless, by the year 1652, Cromwell was poised to rule England. King Charles II would remain in exile for another eight years and the Brinley family was in danger. Thomas and Ann swiftly needed to arrange a sanctuary, through marriage, for their daughters.

Arriving in England at just the right time and earning the trust of his prospective parents-in-law, William Coddington proved the perfect partner for Ann and an excellent negotiator-cum-matchmaker for the sixteen-year-old Grissell. It is evident that, through this very traumatic period, Coddington earned Grissell's deep affection; for in her will she wrote, *"Nathaniel Sylvester did bargaine, contract, and agree with my loving Brother in Law Mr. William Coddington of Road Island to whose care and custody I was committed by my father Mr. Thomas Brinley at my departure from him."*

However necessary, it must have been heartbreaking for Ann and Thomas to dispatch their daughters in this way. It is unlikely that they saw either of the girls again, although they probably corresponded over the years.

At the occasion of Grissell's betrothal to Nathaniel, the Brinleys already knew the Sylvester family. Her sister Mary had already married Nathaniel's brother Peter and the couple lived at Duke's Place in London. It is thought that Thomas Brinley may have become acquainted with the Sylvester family through his trips to the Netherlands where he spent time with the Dutch engineer Sir Cornelius Vermuyden, on business for the King.

The son of Giles Sylvester and Mary Arnold, Nathaniel was born in around 1620 in Amsterdam. Both parents were English, so we assume that the Sylvesters had sought refuge from the religious persecution, rife in England at the time, by settling in Amsterdam alongside other expatriates. Although it is evident the family were upstanding citizens, the Sylvester family do not appear to have been wealthy. We learn from Thomas Brinley's will, dated 1661, that Peter left Mary and their only daughter *"destitute"*. From Peter Sylvester's will, it is evident that his own beloved mother Mary owed him over a thousand pounds that he then bequeathed to his wife and daughter. Evidently the debt was never paid.

However, both Nathaniel and his brother Constant proved highly successful. Leaving England behind, they became business partners and thereafter enjoyed prosperous lives overseas. Constant married and raised his family in Barbados, while Nathaniel eventually took his new bride and settled on Shelter Island in America. After her marriage to Nathaniel, the island of Barbados would feature prominently in young Grissell's life.

Barbados was colonized in 1625 under the command of Captain John Powell who claimed the island on behalf of King James I. Soon, prominent Englishmen with good social connections were allocated lands and within a few years much of the land was deforested to make way for tobacco and cotton plantations.

During the 1630s, sugar cane became a primary export and the early plantation owners became rich and powerful. This is how Constant and Nathaniel made their money. Some time before he became engaged to Grissell, Nathaniel, together with Constant, founded a plantation in Barbados. In 1651, in partnership with Thomas Middleton and Thomas Rouse, the brothers were in need of other resources. So they purchased the 8000 acre Shelter Island, as well as Robbins Island, from the Manhanset Indians.

The Sylvesters required wood that Shelter Island could provide - at the time the island was *"covered with great white oaks"*. The Barbados plantation needed wood to make barrel staves for containers to transport goods such as wine and molasses to Europe. The estate on Shelter Island would also be used to supply foodstuffs, land in Barbados being too valuable to assign to anything but the production of marketable produce.

Shelter Island sits between the north and south forks of Long Island and the rich and fertile soil provided excellent land for growing crops. The remote location provided safe grazing for livestock such as sheep, cattle, and horses. Nathaniel Sylvester, out of the four original partners, was the only one to make his home there. It is evident from Nathaniel's will that, at some point, his brother Joshua permanently joined them on the island.

By contrast, Constant's involvement with Shelter Island would fluctuate over the years together with his finances. All of the details have not been fully explored but in 1674, when the Dutch re-established government of New York, Constant's share of the island was confiscated and sold to Nathaniel.

Back in 1652, before setting sail with his bride-to-be, Nathaniel had already built a home on the island. A second house, which still exists, called "Sylvester Manor" was erected in 1734, and stands close to the original home site. A descendent of the family still owns a 251-acre tract where the plantation once stood. Currently the University of Massachusetts is conducting an archaeological survey of the estate and its workings and thankfully, for posterity, the family still has many original documents once belonging to Grissell and Nathaniel, which have now been transcribed.

Meanwhile back in England, there was much excitement as the two couples shopped for supplies and prepared for life in the New World. Ann had lately married William Coddington and Grissell was now betrothed to Nathaniel. The joint wedding party planned to travel to their respective homes in Rhode Island and Shelter Island, after taking time to enjoy the generous hospitality of Constant Sylvester in Barbados. Indeed, it was reported that they were *"royally entertained"* by Nathaniel's brother but, no doubt, much business was done as well.

It is believed that Francis Brinley, brother of Ann and Grissell, also travelled with the party and it has been widely recorded that he was due to make his home in Barbados, but ultimately did not like the climate and moved on, eventually settling in Rhode Island. Francis is featured elsewhere in detail, however, it should be acknowledged here that, throughout their lives, Francis would remain close to his two sisters and their families. Although not converting to Quakerism like the Sylvesters or the Coddingtons, Francis is kindly treated in Nathaniels will, which demonstrates closeness between the two.

It has been speculated that the family sailed from Barbados to Rhode Island and from there, Grissell and Nathaniel set sail on their own for Shelter Island where they married. The order of events is still not conclusive. Although not himself converting to Quakerism, Francis maintained good relationships with the Coddingtons and Sylvesters. Apparently, the couple, and Francis, journeyed from Rhode Island aboard *The Swallow*, which on arrival into Shelter Island was caught in a violent storm and shipwrecked. Nearly all the passengers survived but most of their treasured possessions and heirlooms were lost. For an inexperienced sixteen year-old, so far from home, this must have been a most distressing experience!

Notwithstanding this, the Manor was soon furnished, in proper keeping with the affluent standing of its owners. The Sylvesters quickly became socially active and over the years the couple entertained a great deal, guests from places such as Boston and Rhode Island, as well as playing host to numerous Quakers from the colonies seeking refuge and solace.

The Manor house was built in a similar style to other houses in New England at the time, which was medieval late English gothic style. Many of its trappings would have been the finest in their day, such as expensive glass from Newcastle in England. Nathaniel's will tells us a great deal about the workings of the plantation; there was a mill, cider presses and orchards, as well as livestock and fowl. Also noted are twenty African slaves, all grouped into families and they were probably skilled and semi-skilled workers such as coopers, carpenters, blacksmiths, domestics, and field hands. On the island, we know there was a considerable complex that included a number of functional structures plus a barn and warehouse. Shelter Island must have been a hive of activity at its peak. The island was also multicultural. Alongside the slaves there were Native Americans, English and Dutch workers; and still in evidence are Quaker and African burial grounds.

Francis stayed with the couple for some time for, in 1654, he wrote that he had *"been on Shelter Island for a year."* That same year, the first of the Sylvester children arrived. Grissell and Nathaniel would have eleven in all and they were born as follows: Grissell in 1654; Giles in 1657; Nathaniel in 1661; Peter in 1663; Patience in 1664; Elizabeth in 1666; Mary in 1668; Anne in 1670; Constant in 1671; Mercy in 1675, and finally Benjamin, born in 1677.

In 1660, the English monarchy was restored and Grissell's beloved father reinstated to his position as King's Auditor. But he was to die a year later and it was distressing to the family that he was never able to fully restore the vast lands that the family had been granted under Charles I. A year later, in 1662, her uncle Lawrence also died.

For many years, the couple continued to work the plantation diligently, raising their family, never wavering from their adherence to devout pursuits and offering a helping hand to those in need. Three short years after their last son Benjamin was born, Nathaniel passed away and following his death in 1680, Grissell and their oldest son Giles, who was twenty-three at the time, managed the plantation between them.

Grissell's own last will and testament was drafted by Henry Fuller in Newport, Rhode Island on June 2nd 1685, and it is worth noting that, in addition to Francis, her other brother William was named as Executor, which would strongly suggest he was also there at the time.

It is a sign of the times that, even though they were deeply spiritual, the family continued to keep slaves on the plantation. Indeed, in Grissell's will, she states, *"To my daughter Elizabeth Sylvester my Bible and my Negro woman called Hope The daughter of Jacquero and Hannah his wife"* and further on in the document *"I give unto my five daughters last before mentioned my Negroes Jacquero and Hannah his wife for the use of the house."*

Grissell Sylvester died on Shelter Island on the 13th of June 1687. Her eldest son Giles inherited the property. He eventually died childless and after a contentious court case, Brinley Sylvester, Giles's nephew, gained possession of the Manor and constructed a new house that stands today.

Grissell was buried alongside her husband in the family burying ground at the northern end of the island. Many years ago, the remains of the Sylvesters were removed to the churchyard, which is situated in the middle of the island. In 1884, a descendant erected a tombstone. The inscription is opposite.

NATHANIEL SYLVESTER
FIRST RESIDENT PROPRIETOR
OF
THE MANOR OF SHELTER ISLAND
UNDER GRANT OF CHARLES II
A.D. 1666;

AN ENGLISHMAN
INTREPID,
LOYAL TO DUTY,
FAITHFUL TO FRIENDSHIP
THE SOUL OF INTEGRITY AND HONOR,
HOSPITABLE TO WORTH AND CULTURE,
SHELTER EVER THE PERSECUTED FOR
CONSCIENCE'S SAKE

THE DAUGHTERS
OF
MARY AND PHOEBE GARDINER HORSFORD,
DESCENDENTS
OF
PATIENCE, DAUGHTER OF NATHANIEL SYLVESTER
AND
WIFE OF THE HUGUENOT BENJAMIN L'HOMMEDIEU
IN REVERENCE AND AFFECTION
FOR
THE GOOD NAME OF THEIR ANCESTOR
IN 1884
SET UP THESE STONES
FOR A MEMORIAL

Daniel Putnam Brinley 1879-1963

Charles H. Brinley
1825-1907

Thomas H. Brinley who was mustered in the Civil
War in Company E, 1864-65

Joseph R. Brinley (1862-1920)
and Ellen Queen (nee Butler, 1860-1937)

Chapter 10
NEWPORT - BOSTON - ROXBURY CLANS

Thomas Brinley 1661 Abt -1693

Son of Francis Thomas Brinley and Hannah (née Carr), he was born in Newport, Rhode Island. When grown up, he moved to Boston in 1681, where he became a prominent merchant. He was a member of the Ancient and Honorable Artillery Company in 1681, and was a founder member of King's Chapel. In 1684 he went to England where he married Mary Apthorpe. In 1693, he died of smallpox in London, leaving his widow with three children - Elizabeth, Francis, and William (who also died of smallpox in 1704, aged 13). Daughter Elizabeth came to America and married William Hutchinson, with whom she had Eliakim, Shrimpton and Francis; the latter graduated at Harvard College in 1736.

William Brinley 1668 abt? -1704

He was the second son of Francis Brinley and Hannah (née Carr). He appears to have been the 'black sheep' of the family. He married *"not to his father's liking"* and forfeited his inheritance, which passed to his brother's son - Francis. He married: 1. Sarah Reape, 2. Mary Sanford. After William's death, Mary married Josiah Arnold, son of Benedict Arnold.

In 1699, William was one of the founders of Trinity Church, Newport, Rhode Island, and a stone outside the entrance commemorates his contribution.

Not much is known of his life, although he was called 'captain' for a period. Shortly before his death, he was appointed Justice of the Peace in Newport.

It is interesting to note that his father, Francis, chose to be buried at King's Chapel in Boston, rather than locally in the church founded by his son. William's name does not appear on the family plaque inside Trinity Church, Newport.

Later communications between family members refer to William's early death and him *"never having married"*. This is puzzling. One explanation might be that he was scarcely talked about and maybe they had pretty much failed to keep tabs on him. These correspondents freely admit that they are not fully aware of the facts.

His father's will, drafted in 1719, was fifteen years after William died. We will probably never know if there was a reconciliation.

Col. Francis (middle name Thomas) Brinley 1690-1766

The eldest son of Thomas and Hannah (née Carr), he was born in London and educated at Eton College. His grandfather, Francis (middle name Thomas), having lost his wife Hannah and his favourite son Thomas, wanted to make him his heir and he went to America with his widowed mother and siblings in 1710. He had a house built at Roxbury near Boston, in the style of the family home at Datchet, but smaller. He married Deborah Lyde, of Boston, on 13th April 1718. He left five sons - Thomas, Francis, Edward, Nathaniel, George, and two daughters, Deborah and Catherine.

During his younger years, Francis was by his own admission *"a sad and rakeing dog"* and, in a letter to William Bollan Esq., continues to confess that, in 1719, his grandfather placed a codicil in his will to the effect that any inheritance would be forfeited unless Francis grew to be *"solid and sober"*. Apparently, his mother Mary had kept the document for nineteen years before telling him of its existence.

Francis also admits, *"after nineteen years, several children had brought me to my thinking"*. Therefore, around 1738, he began a serious attempt to retrieve his legacy, particularly his grandfather's lands of Horton and Stanwell, in England. In his efforts to regain control of his birthright, Francis says that his efforts were not on his own behalf but "that of his family".

It is not certain what happened subsequently. However, he was hardly poor. At his death he bequeathed real estate of over 6,600 acres, valued at £9,600, including the Roxbury estate of 98 acres, a house and a barn. He held land at Watertown, Needham, Brookline, Framingham, Hopkinton, Leicester, Blanford, and in the county of Worcester.

Francis was Colonel of the Roxbury Regiment and was selected as Deputy Governor of the province. By all accounts, including his own, he was a gregarious character and was a distinguished benefactor around the town. He also had great respect for the church and was a founder of King's Chapel, Boston, where he was later buried. Francis said that his mother Mary lived with him for forty years until her death aged 92. He mixed with the highest in society of Boston and New England and built one of the earliest mansions in Roxbury, located near the Shirley-Eustice House, the one-time home of his friend, the Royal Governor William Shirley. The house may exist no longer but a sketch of it survives. Francis (full name Francis Thomas) died there on November 27th 1765, aged 75.

Although he is usually referred to officially as Francis, it looks likely that he, and the family, actually used his middle name Thomas.

In 1905, a publication called *The Town of Roxbury*, by Francis S. Drake, gives an excellent description of Brinley Place and the booklet features several tales relating to the *"Colonel"*. The following are extracts:

"Passing the new Cathedral of the Redemptionists, we come upon a fragment of what once was one of the grandest houses in Roxbury. Built about the year 1723 by Col. Francis Brinley, upon an estate of eighty acres, formerly Palsgrave Alcock's, it was styled by its owner 'Datchet House', having been modelled after the family seat of the Brinleys at Datchet, in England.

In a somewhat fanciful description of Datchet House, by Mrs Emily Pierpoint Lesdnerier, she wrote, "It was situated in the midst of a large domain of park and wooden hills and presented a picture of grandeur and stateliness not common in the new world. There were colonnades and a vestibule whose massive mahogany doors, studded with silver, opened into a wide floor, whose tessellated floors sparkled under the light of a lofty dome of painted glass. Underneath the dome two cherubs, carved in wood, extended their wings and so formed the centre from which an immense chandelier of cut glass depended. Upon the floor beneath the dome, there stood a marble column and around it ran a divan formed of cushions, covered with satin of Damascus, of glorious colouring. Large mirrors with ebony frames filled the spaces between the grand staircases at either side of the hall of entrance. All the panelling and woodwork consisted of elaborate carving done abroad, and made to fit every part of the mansion where such ornamentation was required. Exquisite combinations of painted birds and fruit and flowers abounded everywhere, in rich contrast with the delicate blue tint that prevailed upon the lofty walls.

The staterooms were covered in Persian carpets and hung with tapestries of gold and silver arranged after some graceful artistic foreign fashion. The old place has suffered many changes at the hands of its various owners who, in attempting modernizing, have destroyed almost every vestige of former magnificence.

The house also had a magnificent wine cellar and there is a story that " Col. Brinley, fancying that some of his choice wines disappeared remarkably fast, secreted himself there one evening, when his neighbour Whitney's coloured servant, Pompey, was making a visit to Sambo, the servant of the Colonel. Soon, the pair entered and Sambo, filling his goblet, preceded to take in its contents, exclaiming, " better times, Pomp!"

"Better times!" was the response, as Pompey, nothing loath, imitated his friend's example.

Just then, a new actor appeared on the scene and the enraged Colonel laid his cane in no scanty measure over the heads of the culprits. "Better times, you black rascals! Better times! Do you say, drinking wine that cost me a guinea a bottle? I'll give you better times, you infernal black scoundrels!"

And the Colonel, so runs the story, swore as terribly as they ever did in Flanders."

During the siege of Boston the Roxbury estate became Headquarters for General Ward, and it is said that George Washington hosted his Council of officers there. The Brinleys sold the property to Robert Pierpoint in 1773. Today, nothing remains. Despite exhaustive searches in trying to locate the 'family seat' in Datchet, no records can be traced to prove that the family owned a house there. We can only speculate where the Brinley family lived. All other historical houses of merit in Datchet, and their owners, are a matter of record - but no sign of the Brinleys! However, we are aware that Thomas Brinley's in-laws, the Wase family, held property in Datchet called the Manor House. Perhaps the Brinleys, in reality, were using part of the Wase's house and used a certain amount of poetic licence when claiming the house as theirs. Research has also shown that Thomas Brinley, Auditor, lived a large part of the time in London, less than a mile from his brother Lawrence. Children were baptised in Clerkenwell, London. This makes it likely in my mind that he actually spent more time in London than at Datchet. Perhaps Datchet was where his heart was!

Deborah Brinley

The first daughter of Francis Thomas Brinley and Deborah Lyde. She married Colonel John Murray and moved to Nova Scotia at the time of the Revolution. There were no children.

Catherine Brinley: 1724-1795

Second daughter of Francis Thomas and Deborah Lyde. She married the Honourable Godfrey Malbone. Died November 28th 1795, aged 71.

Thomas Brinley: 1726-1784

Eldest son of Francis Thomas Brinley and Deborah née Lyde. Born at Roxbury October 26th 1726. He attended Harvard College and lived in simple chambers in Massachusetts Hall. It was reported that he developed a reputation for skipping classes. Nevertheless, he somehow managed to graduate in the class of 1744.

On 25th January 1749, he married Elizabeth Craddock, his cousin. Her parents were

George Craddock and Mary (née Lyde). After marriage, he settled down and established a reputation for *"unobtrusive respectability and solidarity"*.

Thomas established himself as a merchant in the south end of Boston, where he ran a wharf and a distillery. For many years, he managed successfully as a general merchant and his activities included whaling. He was a regular churchgoer and served as a vestryman in King's Chapel, where he worshiped in pew 79. At the time, he resided in Harvard Street.

Thomas was a die-hard Loyalist and party Whig and we are told of him attending a political banquet at which the Stamp Act was repealed, an occasion at which he apparently celebrated by drinking fifteen toasts. In 1775, Gage listed him amongst the *"suffering Loyalists"*, and it was known that he gave refuge on his property to political refugees.

In 1776, during the evacuation, Thomas escaped from Boston to Halifax, continuing his journey to England on the 12th May the same year. Two years later, as a known supporter of the English Crown, he was proscribed under the act of 1778, and his assets were confiscated. It is believed that some of his estate was used to support his mother-in-law, Mary Craddock.

Shortly after his arrival in England,Thomas became a member of the "New England Club", which was established in London by refugee Loyalists from Massachusetts. This elite group of politicians would meet for dinner every week at The Adelphi in The Strand.

Still banished from his homeland, Thomas died in London on October 7th 1784, aged 58, and Elizabeth died in 1793. They had no children.

Francis Brinley: 1729-1816

The second son of Francis Thomas and Deborah (née Lyde), he was born in 1729. On reaching maturity, he resided on the family estate at Newport, Rhode Island. On 12th November 1754, he married Aleph, daughter of the Honourable Godfrey Malbone.

Francis's home at that time is now known as the Bellevue Hotel, located at 14 Catherine Street. The property became a hotel in 1825. Francis owned large tracts of land in and around Newport. He died there on April 23rd 1816, aged 88. Aleph died December 26th 1800, aged 72. Buried Row 11 - Stone 6 (ES) Trinity Church, Rhode Island. They had four sons and three daughters:

Francis was born October 6th 1755

He studied at Harvard and graduated in 1755. He became an understudy in medicine to his uncle, Dr William Hunter and died in Nova Scotia in 1787. He never married. Buried Row 11 - Stone 6 (ES) Trinity Church, Rhode Island.

Thomas Malbone 30. Oct. 1756 - 26. Oct. 1758, aged 2 yrs

Buried Row 1 - Stone 5 (ES) Trinity Church, Rhode Island.

Edward : 12. Nov. 1757 - 8. Sept. 1851, aged 94

Catherine: 5th Sept. 1759 - 5th Dec. 1784, in Jamaica

Deborah: 1st March 1761 - 8th Sept 1846

Elizabeth: 1st June 1763 - 19th August 1822

Thomas (2nd): 24th Nov. 1764 - 5th Nov. 1851

Edward Brinley: 1730-1809

Third son of Francis Thomas Brinley and Deborah (née Lyde). Born August 7th 1730. Married Sarah Tyler of Boston on March 2nd 1762, and died October 23rd 1809, aged 79. Buried King's Chapel Burying Ground, Boston. Sarah died December 3rd 1803, aged 66. Lies with Edward. Their children were:

Sarah: Born 12th December 1762; died 26th December 1788

She married Theodore Jones on October 27th 1785. There were no children.

William: Born May 9th 1764

Died unmarried January 30th 1836, aged 72

Edward: Born October 16th 1765; died December 20th 1823, aged 57

Never married but ran a business on the north side of the old market in Boston. His firm was Francis & Edward Brinley, Jr.

Thomas: Born June 24th 1767; died young.

Deborah; died young.

Francis: Born March 26th 1772; died March 1st 1838, aged 66

Married Elizabeth Henshaw-Harris in 1795. Both buried King's Chapel, Boston. She died March 8th 1814. They had three children who reached adulthood; Sarah, Francis, and Edward. A daughter, Catherine Putnam, died age 12, 31st May 1817, buried King's Chapel. Francis married a second time to Jerusha Cooper and had children Maria Louisa and Charles Henry.

George: Born October 24th 1774

Married Catherine, daughter of Colonel Daniel Putnam of Brooklyn, Connecticut, on 30th April 1805. Their children were Elizabeth, George, Anne, Emily Malbone, Putnam and Edward.

Nathaniel Brinley: 1733-1814

Fourth son of Francis Thomas Brinley and Deborah (née Lyde). Married his cousin Catherine Craddock and lived in South Street, Boston, where he remained during the revolutionary war. He subsequently moved from Boston and bought an estate in Tyngsborough, Middlesex. Catherine died there, aged 75, on April 3rd 1807.

Nathaniel found himself in jail in the summer of 1776 for having signed an address to General Gage two years earlier. After he posted bond to live peaceably and not aid the enemy, a court paroled him. The town committee, however, required further - that he work for John Fisk and remain at all times within twenty rods of Fisk's house. The committee admitted that these restrictions violated a resolution of the General Court encouraging parole of co-operative prisoners. In Brinley's case, the committee explained leniency was *"impractical"*, as the people *"take him for a very villain"*, and with good reason, as the committee continued, *"Brinley had a long record of behaviour, attitudes, and statements hostile to the American cause - openly predicting British victory in 1775 and ominously taking his family to the safety of Boston before the outbreak of fighting at Lexington, in April 1775."*

Nothing of his conduct or disposition suggested the least *"contrition"*, the committee explained. This failure to accuse him of actual subversion, and the attempt to explain it without endorsing the town's hostile attitude to Brinley, was underscored by the committee's inclusion, without defence, in its records that *"he says he is a gentleman and has done nothing to forfeit that character."* Nathaniel died, aged 81, February 10th 1814. They had one child, Robert.

Francis William born May 26th and died May 14th 1859

Fifth son of Francis Thomas Brinley and Deborah (née Lyde). He moved to Halifax during the Revolutionary War and was Commissary-General of the British troops in North America He married the sister of John Wentworth and had three sons and a daughter:

Thomas: A Colonel in the British Army, serving with Sir John Moore in Spain. He died while in command of his regiment in the West Indies. Unmarried.

Wentworth: A Barrister in London. Died there unmarried.

William: An officer in the British Army. Died at Halifax, leaving a wife and one daughter.

Mary: Married a Mr Moody, a merchant of London. She died in a freak carriage accident. Their daughter was the renowned authoress - Mrs Catherine Frances Gore.

Catherine Brinley: 1759-1784

Daughter of Francis Brinley and Aleph Malbone, and born in Newport, September 5 1759. Married Dr John Field, Surgeon, British Army. Died Jamaica December 5 1784. No children.

Deborah Brinley: 1761-1846

Second daughter of Francis Brinley and Aleph Malbone. She was born in Newport on March 1st 1761. She married the Reverend Daniel Fogg, an Episcopal churchman from Brooklyn, Connecticut, on December 2nd 1794; and died there on September 8th 1846, aged 85.

Elizabeth Brinley: 1763-1822

Third daughter of Francis Brinley and Aleph Malbone, she was born in Newport on June 1st 1763. On March 10th 1785, she married William Litchfield, a Captain in the US Army and aide to General Greene. She died August 19th 1822, aged 59. Their only surviving children were William Litchfield and Aleph Malbone.

Edward Brinley: 1757-1851

Third son of Francis Brinley and Aleph Malbone, he was born on November 12th 1757. Living in Perth Amboy, New Jersey, he married Janet Parker on June 17th 1792.

He went through the war on the British side until the surrender at Yorktown. After this, like so many Loyalists, he lived many years in the safety of Nova Scotia, where he took a government appointment after the war. However, after his last child, Francis William was born, he returned to America and the family estate in Newport. Edward and Janet had five children as follows:

Gertrude Aleph born May 26th 1794, and died January 17th 1845

She married the Reverend Edward Gilpin of Annapolis, Nova Scotia.

Elizabeth Parker born February 18th 1796

Married Reverend Job T. Halsey of Perth Amboy.

Maria Margaret born May 22nd 1801, and died in 1806

Catherine Sophia born March 1804

Frances William born May 26th 1798, Shelburne, Nova Scotia, died May 14th 1859.

Married Abby Maria Randolph (widow née Thorpe) and had a large family (not yet traced)

Janet died, age 37, just nine months after Catherine Sophia was born. Edward's second wife was Mary Johnson and they married on April 10th 1807. They had two children; Edward Littlefield, born on February 21st 1808, who became a merchant in Philadelphia; and Mary Gibbs, born April 27th 1814 and died at Newport on June 8th 1844.

Around 1834, Edward and his family moved back to Perth Amboy, where they settled once more. Edward served as a dedicated churchman, becoming a popular warden at St. Peter's Church. He enjoyed hearty good humour and remained a popular member of the community until the end. He died in Perth Amboy on September 8th 1851. He was aged 94.

In 1901, Katherine Johnstone Wharton published a delightful account of the life of her grandfather Edward, entitled *An Old Newport Loyalist*, for the Newport Historical Society. One particularly entertaining anecdote is as follows:

"In the spring of 1775, my grandfather, then scarcely more than a boy, went to Boston to see a brother who was at Harvard. It was a time of great excitement and a disturbance broke out among the students between the Whigs and the Tories. My grandfather and his brother tied sheets together and let themselves out of a window, escaped from Boston, both mounted on the same horse, and joined British troops who were marching on Lexington".

Katherine also tells us " He sleeps not under the skies of his beloved birthplace but on a sunny hillside far away, with his two wives (who were cousins), amid seven generations of their kindred of Scottish descent." [Edward would have been 18 at the time, and the brother referred to was Francis, who was at Harvard]

Katherine was the daughter of Edward Littlefield, and a copy of her journal can be obtained through the Library of Congress, Washington, D.C.

Francis William Brinley: 1798-1859

Son of Edward Brinley and Janet Parker, he was born in Shelburne, Nova Scotia, on May 26th 1798. He was educated at Woodstock, Connecticut, where he received a broad education, specialising in the classics. After completing his schooling, he chose the life of a merchant and joined his maternal uncle, Mr Cortland Parker, in a South American business venture. For a time, they were very prosperous but the revolutionary disorder under Bolivar brought financial disaster. Later, he went into partnership with an American named Litchfield but this was not successful.

By this time, Francis had already married Mrs Abby Maria Randolph (née Thorpe) and they had a rapidly growing family, so it became necessary to return to Perth Amboy, seeking the security of his mother's home and making it their residence. After a while, he was back in business and eventually secured a position as Surveyor-General of the State of New Jersey and Collector of Customs at the port of Perth Amboy.

Francis developed a reputation as a decent man with *"general manners and generous disposition, with a large and warm heart"*. He was well educated and took a keen interest in antiquarian and scientific studies. He was admitted for membership at the New England Historic Genealogical Society on February 8th 1858.

Francis died at Perth Amboy May 14 1859, aged 60. Two of his children were Aliph, wife of Samuel Foster of Providence, and Katherine, wife of Henry Tremaine of London, England.

Robert Brinley Esq: 1774-

Son of Nathaniel Brinley and Catherine Craddock, Robert was born at Roxbury on September 27th 1774. He married Elizabeth Pitts September 10th 1802. They lived at Tyngsborough and had one son, Nathaniel Brinley.

Thomas Brinley: 1764-1851

Following the death of two year old Thomas Malbone Brinley, this Thomas was the third surviving son of Francis Brinley and Aleph Malbone. Born in Newport, November 24 1764. Married Mary Townsend on February 26 1823. Died at Newport, November 5 1851, aged 87.

Francis Brinley: 1800-1889

Francis, known as 'Frank', was born on West Street, Boston, Massachusetts, on the 10th November 1800. His parents were Francis (1770-1814) and his mother was Elizabeth Henshaw Harris (1770-1814). He had a sister - Catherine Putnam born 21st March 1805; brother Edward was born 2nd September 1809 at Prince Street, Boston. He was baptised by his uncle, the Rev. Dr Thaddeus Mason Harris, on 7th March 1814.

Frank claimed that he was taught the rudiments of Latin by his grandfather Edward.

Franks's mother died in 1814, and his father remarried to Jerusha Cooper.

In September, Frank, aged fourteen, entered Cambridge College, Harvard, as a freshman and gained his B.A. in 1818. On leaving university he entered the office of Hon. William Sullivan as a student of Law, gaining his admittance in to the Suffolk County Bar in 1821.

In 1823 he moved to Chelmsford, Middler Village, and two years later set up his law office nearby. However, Frank was unhappy in his calling and decided he wanted to study theology. 1826 found him removed to Boston where he resided with his uncle.

In 1828, he joined the Ancient and Honorable Artillery Company of Massachusetts. His grandfather Edward had been a member in 1779, as was Thomas Brinley in 1681.

In 1829 he attained the office of Fourth Sergeant of Ancient and Honorable Artillery Company. He contributed to *Hunts, Merchants Magazine*, and *The American Jurist*. He wrote much for the newspapers and was a successful lecturer.

In 1830 he published an address made before The Franklin Debating Society of Boston.

In 1832, 1850 and 1854, he was a member of the Massachusetts House of representatives. In 1832, 1849, 1850 and 1851, he was a member of the Common Council of Boston, holding the Presidency the last two years.

On 10th May 1833, he was discharged from the Ancient & Hon. Artillery Company and on 11th June married Sarah Olcott Porter at St James Church, New York City. She became a favourite of the wider family, being known as Aunt Sarah. Her grandnephew, the artist, D. Putnam Brinley, remembered her, years later, as *"Like a beautiful Dresden figure - lace cap, lace shawl, everything so delicate, it seemed that a draft from the open window might blow her away..."*

Frank and his new wife travelled widely and, in 1836, moved to Bangor, Maine, where he associated with Charles Gilman, Esq. and later Frederick H. Allen. In 1839 he left Bangor and took an office in New York City, on William Street near Wall Street. He became active in the following year's presidential campaign. In 1841, he moved to Washington, D.C. and took up duties of Law Clerk in the office of the Solicitor of the Treasury, a position created

Three ages of Francis Brinley, 1800-1889
Below: Francis Brinley (Frank) and Sarah Brindley, 1811-1900

for him by Daniel Webster, Secretary of the State. About this time he sold his law library, an action he later regretted. He was removed from office on 29th May 1845, as he was a member of the Whig Political Party. By the end of the year he had removed to Baltimore. In 1847 he rejoined the Ancient and Honorable Artillery Company. His busy life continued and, by 1852, he was elected to the Massachusetts State Senate.

1853 saw him complete a compilation genealogy of the family that he called *The Brinley Scrapbook*. The same year saw him involved in the Convention to revise the Constitution of Masachusetts.

In 1854 he was transferred to the House of Commons and he served as chairman of various important committees. During this year he procured money from Congress toward the preservation of Cape Cod harbour. He advocated the abolishment of imprisonment for debt and the establishment of a discreet system of insolvency. He also encouraged the building of railroads, and he published an article on his Craddock family research.

In 1856, he was promoted to Lieutenant of the Ancient & Hon.Artillery Company.

In 1857 he retired from professional life to Tynsborough, Massachusetts, and the pursuit of his interest in genealogical research.

During the following Civil War Period, he pleaded the cause of the Union through lectures and writings.

In 1867 he decided to move to Newport, Rhode Island, and he resumed practicing law there. In 1870, he was elected to the General Assembly of Rhode Island and served two years. From 1873 to 1887 he was Vice President of Rhode Island Historical Society and became President of Newport Historical Society from 1882 until the year of his death, in 1889. He died on 14th June at 127, Rhode Island Avenue, at the age of eighty-nine. He had lost his eyesight in his latter years but always remained cheerful.

According to Harvard College Library Clippings, *"No truer gentleman was found among us and none more courtly and generous and this too, not from mere force of habit or social culture, but as the expression of an honest and loving heart."*

He had been always interested in everything around him and was a remarkable man.

Charles Henry Brinley: 1825-1907. An Arizona Pioneer

Charles Henry was born in Boston, Massachusetts, on October 21st, 1825. His father was Francis Brinley, born 1772, and his grandfather was Edward Brinley, 1730-1809.

After spending his early days in college and travel, including a short stint as a trading company representative in India, Brinley arrived at the port of Yerba Buena (San Francisco), California, in 1845. He had sailed round the horn from Boston on one of the Bryant & Sturgis Yankee traders then plying between Boston, California ports, the Sandwich Islands, and China. Evidently of a restless nature, he spent only a year in San Francisco before heading south, on horseback, to the pueblo of Los Angeles.

After gaining a diploma to practise law there, he formed an association with another lawyer, Abel Stearns, and became involved in trading activities with the ranching community. In the Los Angeles County California Census of 1852, Charles Brinley is listed as a ranchero, born in Massachusetts, with temporary residence in China.

The ports along the California coast serviced the large ranches of early Spanish settlers, who by the 1840s had prospered and established an elite network of extended family holdings extending from San Diego to San Francisco. A few early intruders had intermarried with daughters of the local Spanish aristocracy. They were acceptable only if they espoused the Catholic religion; most of them were Irish or Scottish immigrants. Successful entrepreneurs such as Stearns secured entry into the social and political hierarchy through such liaisons.

The rancheros raised cattle and horses on their enormous land holdings and traded skins and agricultural products. Brinley had a romantic brush with a daughter of the influential Arguello family of San Diego, whose ranch he managed, but apparently was reluctant to adopt the Catholic religion. Nevertheless, he married another Spanish woman, Loretta de Arvizu, whose family seemingly did not care about his adherence to his Episcopalian faith.

Although details of Brinley's activities during his early days in California are sketchy, records show that, after his sojourn in China, he was involved in a variety of projects. Early in the 1860s, Brinley along with his partners Jose Pico and Colonel Vineyard, a state Senator, were granted a State franchise to construct a turnpike over the San Fernando Mountain. The names of the men with whom he was associated are still land marked in city streets - Pico and Sepulveda boulevards.

Brinley was also involved in the early stirring of state politics as a founding member of the Los Angeles Bell & Everett Club, a republican group organised to support the Union. He was a delegate to their first state convention in Sacramento in 1860, along with Frank Mellus, who had arrived in Los Angeles from Boston in 1840, aboard a ship owned by his older brother Henry. Henry Mellus had come earlier to California on the brigantine Pilgrim with Richard Henry Dana, Jnr. Shortly before his death in 1860, Henry Mellus had been elected mayor of Los Angeles.

As noted in an item in the June 14, 1861 edition of the semi-weekly Southern News of Los Angeles, Brinley was also enmeshed in activities related to the Civil War in the States:

"S.H. Wilson, Esq., having resigned his commission as Captain of the "Southern Rifles", the company held a meeting on Wednesday evening last, and elected Charles H. Brinley, Esq., to the vacancy. The company will immediately procure arms, adopt a uniform, and hold themselves ready to report to any call that may be made upon them."

A later item in the same publication reflected the frustration of their isolated efforts.

"The volunteer company of this city known by the name of "Southern Rifles," have now been organised for some months, but have not as yet received arms from the State."

Eventually, Brinley was to take a more active role in the conflict. He served in the Union Navy, attached to Rear Admiral D.D. Porter's staff in the Mississippi Squadron. Before that time, however, he had already been lured to Arizona in the search for gold and had settled in Yuma, where he was associated with the Colorado Steam Navigation Company.

In 1851, George A. Johnson was given a contract to ship goods from San Francisco around the tip of Baja California and provision Fort Yuma, which had been established at the junction of the Gila and Colorado rivers. By 1852, a steamboat of his construction was plying the capricious currents of the Lower Colorado. With the discovery of gold in the central Arizona territory in the 1860s, his Colorado Steam Navigation Company became one of the main conveyances of supplies, not only to Yuma but the port cities springing up farther north along the river.

Photographs of Yuma in the 1860s show a checkerboard of squat, flat rooted, one-storied structures, monochromatic in colour, separated by broad dirt streets, wide enough in which to turn around a 20-mule team wagon. The city was built on a flat, riverbank location that for centuries had been the main crossing site for the Colorado. Brinley's sprawling adobe house faced the house of Captain Johnson, now the Century House Museum on Madison Avenue. (Then called Brinley Avenue.)

In 1868, Brinley married Loretta de Arvizu. Pre-dating the arrival of the Arguellos, Picos, and Sepulvedas in California, de Arvizus were a Spanish colonial family that had settled in Santa Fe in the mid-1600s. The name disappeared from public records there following the Indian revolt of 1680. Loretta's mother had moved to Yuma from Sonora, Mexico, where she was born, probably at the Presidio in Arizpe. A de Arvizu had been Commandant in the Royal Army in the Presidio. With his wife Loretta, Brinley raised a large family of five daughters and two sons. His correspondence reveals him to have been a man of cultivated tastes, high ethical standards, and a devoted husband and father. In public life, he held a number of government positions in the growing Arizona Territory.

He was elected as a delegate to the Arizona territorial Assembly for three terms, representing Yuma in the sixth (1871), seventh (1873), and the sixteenth (1891) legislative assemblies. In 1875, he was appointed a U.S. Deputy Collector of Customs for the treasury Department. In 1880, he was elected County Supervisor, and three years later appointed Commissioner of Prisons. On the 28th of September 1901, he was appointed a Vice Consul to Mexico in Yuma by Theodore Roosevelt, and, in turn, a Vice Consul to the United States in Yuma by Porfirio Diaz, President of Mexico, in July of the same year. Throughout his years in Arizona, Brinley was also involved in mining enterprises, ranching, and horticulture. He first introduced the commercial cultivation of citrus fruit and truck crops to southern Arizona, as was noted in the Arizona Sentinel, December 17, 1887.

"A box of magnificent oranges from Judge Brinley's garden was sent by express to New Orleans yesterday."

October 18, 1890

"Judge C.H. Brinley, of Yuma, felt very proud when the blue ribbon indicating first premium was laid on the olive and lime exhibits which he and others brought up from the citrus county of the southwest. Their display was one of the marked features of the City Hall exhibit.

Although Judge Brinley is a candidate for Legislative Assembly honors, his pleasure at the horticultural triumph of his home county made him forget for a moment his triumph at the polls next November. He feels that when our orange, lemon, fig and raisin possibilities receive the world's acknowledgement, which they are bound soon to win, every citizen will justly experience the delight of proclaiming himself to be an Arizonian."

Charles Brinley, in his waning years, served as Probate Judge for Yuma County. After his retirement, Brinley and his wife moved to Los Angeles, where he died in 1907. He was survived by his widow, four daughters, Mrs. Catalina Reynolds, Mrs. Carlotta Martinez, Mrs. Agnes Robertson, and Mrs Sarah Wiltse, and one son, Charles Brinley, Jnr. Mrs Catalina Reynolds was my grandmother.

[The above history was provided by Joseph Richards of New York]

Daniel Putnam Brinley 1879-1963

Born March 8th 1879 at Newport, Rhode Island, the son of Edward Huntington Brinley and Rebecca Maitland Porter (Bradford). He was educated at King School in Stamford, the Dwight School in New York City and the Art Student League in New York. He also studied painting in Paris for four years and also in Florence, Italy.

He was married April 19th 1904 in New York City to Katherine Gordon Sanger who was an authority on the works of Geoffrey Chaucer and lectured and read under the professional name of Gordon Brinley. His one-man show of landscapes was exhibited at the Madison Gallery, New York, in 1910. Another followed the next year at the same venue.

At first he was a landscape painter but turned to murals in 1919, following an unusual role in World War 1. He was appointed director of decoration attached to the second French Army and painted colourful murals in the foyers of centres to which soldiers returned briefly from the front to rest and write letters home. He was awarded a special medal for this work by the French Government.

He was a descendant of Gen. Israel Putnam, American Revolutionary War general, for whom he was named. He died July 30th 1963 at Norwalk, Connecticut, leaving no children. At 6ft 6inches, he appears to have been the tallest Brinley to date.

<$iOscar Brindley> - Pioneer Aviator

Oscar's family history has not yet been found. He was undoubtedly an interesting man. He gave a demonstration flight at North Beach, Corpus Christi in his Wright machine on 3rd and 4th July 1911. The machine had been shipped to North Beach and assembled on site. Brindley was Wright Brothers' manager of the field and training academy near Dayton, Ohio. It was barely eight years after Wilbur and Orville's first flight at Kitty Hawk, North Carolina. By all accounts he gave an interesting, exciting and entertaining show on both days. On one occasion he flew above 11000 feet, a record, but the judges found fault with his equipment and disallowed it.

On 27th October 1915, he set a new record for flying 544 miles along the California coast in a seaplane. Brindley died test flying around 1916. In his day, he was the fastest Brindley around.

Oscar Brindley

Mace Thomas Payne Brindley

Van Buren Brindley

Dr George Valter Brindley
1886-1970

PART III
SOUTHERN BRINDLEYS

Chapter 11
Alabama and Texas

ALABAMA

Frazier Brindley and his wife Phoebe (Riggs) were a pioneering 'first' family in Tennessee. Before long Frazier must have become restless and decided to check out Texas. He set off with his brother, never to return. Whether he got scalped by Indians or met someone else in Texas we can only guess. Anything could have happened - life was rough and tough in those days. His father was Richard Brindley who came to America from Ireland.

Mace Thomas Payne Brindley. Born 2nd October 1801, to Frazier and Phoebe Riggs, he led the way for the ox-drawn covered wagon in which his mother and siblings travelled to Blount County, Alabama. They were the first to settle in the Simcoe, Alabama, area arriving in 1832.

On 1st July 1830 he married Nancy Stuart Hanby, daughter of Gabriel Hanby, one of the original framers of the Alabama Constitution. They had eleven children, Gabriel; Phoebe; Asa Benton; John Hanby; Van Buren; Nancy Manila; Mace Thomas Payne, Jnr; George Goldthwaite; Rebecca Virginia; Portis Bethea; and Winston Yancey. Four sons served the Confederate Army in the Civil War. One, Van Buren, was seriously wounded but survived.

Mace's land holdings consisted of 1800 acres but he lost almost all of this in 1837. Not being a man to give up, he set out to recover it and eventually owned in excess of 2000 acres.

He served 12 years as the Blount County Clerk, becoming Chief Clerk and later the Probate Judge, attaining the first position at the age of 18. He also spent 2 years as State Representative and 9 years as State Senator. He was director of the State National Bank of Decatur at a time when there were only five banks in Alabama.

In 1832, Mace, accompanied by an Indian guide and one servant, forged his way sixteen miles north to a 160 acre plot of land that he homesteaded on the Old Section Line Road, $1^1/2$ miles north of present day Simcoe on State Highway 69.

He had a reputation as a philosopher and a good businessman. Testimony to the man was that a local mountain was named after him - Brindley Mountain. Died 30th August 1871.

TEXAS

George Valter Brindley, Snr. Born on a farm near Maypearl, Texas, January 8th 1886. He was one of several children of George Goldthwaite Brindley and Martha Adeline (née Hanes). He graduated as a doctor in 1911 at the University of Texas Medical branch in Galveston.

He married Martha Arabella Owens on 4th March 1913 and had three sons who all became doctors. He had an illustrious career in medicine and died on October 7th 1970 aged eighty-four. He was a direct decendent of Frazier Brindley, a founding father of Tennessee.

Brindley Reunion in 1907 at Nancy Manilia Brindley's home

George L. Brindley, son of Van Buren Brindley, seen with his wife, Nancy Ann Kyle Brindley, and their two oldest daughters, Audra and Thelma.

Chapter 12
The George Washington Papers and the 'American' <$iJames Brindley

EXTRACTS FROM THE WRITINGS OF GEORGE WASHINGTON 1745-1799
Showing references to Mr James Brindley, canal engineer, son of Joseph of Alton (ch 4).

March 1786

Rid to all my Plantations and to the fish house at the ferry where my Carpenters were at work. In the afternoon a Mr. Brindley, manager of the Susquehanna canal and Mr. Hanes manager of the James River Navigation came in and stayed all night. [James Brindley was a nephew of James Brindley 1716–1772, the talented Englishman who had initiated the dry-land canal era in England in the 1760s under the auspices of the Duke of Bridgewater].

Coming from the Susquehanna canal works Brindley and Harris took the great Falls in their way down, & both approve of the present line for our Canal," wrote GW to John Fitzgerald and George Gilpin, adding, "no person in this country has more practical knowledge than Mr. Brindley" [31 Mar. 1786, DLC:GW)]. Brindley was on his way to Richmond to consult and advise on the James River project and GW hoped he would do the same for the Potomac project on his way back to the Susquehanna.

30th March 1786

Mr Brindley and Mr. Hains or Harris, went away after breakfast.

31st March 1786. To John Fitzgerald and George Gilpin

Mount Vernon, March 31, 1786

Gentlemen: Yesterday Mr. Brindley, in company with a Mr. Harris, Manager for the James river Company (the latter having been sent for the former, by the Directors thereof) left this on their way to Richmond, from whence Mr. Brindley expects to be returned, as far as Alexandria, in seven days from the date hereof. I have engaged him to call on Colo. Gilpin on his route back. Mr. Brindley and Mr. Harris took the great Falls in their way down and both approve of the present line for our canal: the first very much; he conceives that 9/10ths of the expense of the one fifth proposed, will be saved by this cut; the work altogether as secure, and the entrance into the river by no means unfavourable. He thinks however that a good deal of attention and judgment is required in fixing Locks there; the height of which he observes is always governed by the ground; they frequently run from four to eighteen feet, and some times are as high as twenty four.

The nature and declination of the ground, according to him, is alone to direct, and where this will admit he thinks the larger the Locks are made the better, because more convenient.

With respect to this part of the business I feel, and always have confessed an entire incompetence: nor do I conceive that theoretical knowledge alone is adequate to the undertaking. Locks, upon the most judicial plan, will certainly be expensive; and if not properly constructed and judiciously placed, may be altogether useless. It is for these reasons therefore that I have frequently suggested (though no decision has been had) the propriety of employing a professional man. Whether the expense of obtaining one in, and bringing him from Europe has been thought unnecessary, or too burthensome for the advantages, which are to be expected, I know not: but as it is said no person in this country has more practical knowledge than Mr. Brindley, I submit to your consideration the propriety of engaging him to take the Falls in his way back; to examine, level and digest a plan for Locks at that place; if it shall appear good, and his reasons in support of the spots and sizes conclusive it will justify the adoption; if palpably erroneous, there is no obligation upon us to follow him; and the expense in that case [is the only evil which can result from it. This for the chance of a probable benefit, I am not only willing, but desirous of encountering; and if Colo. Gilpin has not already made the trip to that place which he proposed at our last visit, and disappointment there, it would give me great pleasure if it could be so timed as for him to accompany Mr. Brindley. This would not only give countenance to the latter, but afford him aid also; and might be a mean of preventing the little jealousies which otherwise might arise in the minds of our own managers. Taking Mr. Brindley to the works now, may, ultimately, save expence; at the same time, having a plan before us, would enable us at all convenient times, to be providing materials for its execution. I am, &c.

P.S. If my proposition is acceded to, it might be well to fix, at once what shall be given to Mr. Brindley. I will subscribe to what you two Gentlemen may agree to give him on this occasion]

[Note: From the 'Letter Book' copy in the Washington Papers. The part in brackets is from a facsimile, in Washington's writing, in the *University of California Chronicle*, October, 1925, where a note is added by Washington, April 2, explaining the delay in sending the letter]

George Washington to Henry Lee, April 5, 1786

Mount Vernon, April 5, 1786.

My Dear Sir: ....After a thorough investigation of the ground there, we have departed from Ballandine's rout for the Canal, and marked a fresh cut, which in our judgments will save ⅘th. of the labour, consequently proportionate time and expense, and in the opinion of Mr. Brindley who has just been to see it, 9/10ths.,and be equally good when effected.

George Washington to William Moultrie, May 25, 1786

Mount Vernon, May 25th, 1786.

Dr. Sir: The letter which your Excellency did me the honor to write to me, of the 7th. Ulto. Came safely to hand; and I should feel very happy if I could render the Company (who are engaged in the laudable and important design of opening a cut between the rivers Cowper and Santee) any services.

...Mr Brindley, nephew to the celebrated person of that name who conducted the work of the Duke of Bridgewater and planned many others in England, possesses, I presume, more practical knowledge of Cuts and Locks for the improvement of inland navigation, than any man among us, as he was an executive officer (he says) many years under his uncle in this particular business: but he is, I know, engaged with the Susquehannah company, who are I believe (for I saw Mr. Brindley about six weeks ago) in a critical part of their work. I have, notwithstanding, written to a gentleman of my acquaintance who is not only a member of that company, but one to whom the business is chiefly confided, and near the spot, to know if Mr. Brindley's services can be dispensed with long enough to answer the purpose mentioned in your letter: his answer shall be forwarded as soon as it comes to my hands...

Mount Vernon,
December 28, 1786

Mr. Brindley promised me by letter in Octor. That he would call upon me in his way to So. Carolina, but I have not seen or heard from him since the date of his letter. We ought undoubtedly to avail ourselves of all the aids we can derive from experimental knowledge in our search. I concur readily therefore in sentiment with you and Mr. Lee that it would be proper to see what lights Mr. Brindley can afford us in conducting the navigation thro' the little Falls, and the idea of a model for the Locks at the great Falls, I think good for the reasons you offer, the experience will be trifling and the saving may be great.

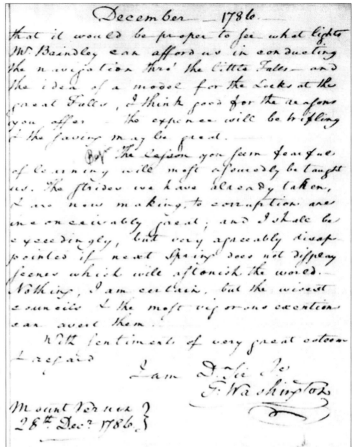

[Note: James Brindley, son or nephew of the builder of the Bridgewater Canal]

Letter to George Digges, same date.

…it would be proper to see what lights Mr. Brindley can afford us in conducting the navigation through the little Falls and the idea of a model for the Locks at the great Falls, I think good for the reasons you offer – the expense will be trifling and the saving may be great.

Wednesday January 10th 1787

…Just before dinner Mr. Brindley Manager of the Susquehanna Works and his Son in law came on their way to South Carolina.

[From 1775-1783, George Washington was Commander in Chief, American Forces. 1786-1787 he met James Brindley. 1787, he presided over Constitutional Convention. 1789 - elected President of the United States of America.]

All the above information is new to me and has not been noticed before by Brindley researchers. There were only three possible candidates for this particular James; he was either:

1. James, the son of John Brindley the potter of Burslem.
2. As an outside possibility, he might have been the son of Henry Brindley, the youngest brother of James, about whom there is very little known.
3. He might have been the James Brindley baptised on 8th May 1848 at Waterfall near Alton, to Joseph and Sarah of Alton.

Information recently proves that it was indeed James Brindley, the son of Joseph, the millwright of Alton. In uncovering the story of this James Brindley much gratitude goes to Robert Kapsch PhD, ASCE, Hon. AIA, Scholar in Historic Architecture and Historic Engineering with the US National Parks Service, and Ray Nichols, Archivist with Holy Trinity (Old Swedes) Church Foundation.

JAMES BRINDLEY: 1745-1820

Two years ago, I uncovered references to a canal builder named James Brindley, who worked on several of the earliest American canals. I did not believe at first that he had any connection with James Brindley, the renowned canal builder, but I have now discovered, through the diaries of George Washington [1786/1787] and other sources, that he was indeed his nephew and had trained under him. Few people know of the early interest of George Washington in engineering. He pioneered several canal projects and attempted to secure the services of James for the Potomac Canal in early 1786.

James's parents were Joseph and Sarah Brindley, of Alton, the brother of the famous engineer in England, who was a successful millwright himself. James's birth in 1745 pre-dated Joseph's marriage, in December 1746, to Sarah Bennitt, but he was baptised afterwards in the Brindley name. Little is known of James's early years, but the comparison of his handwriting with that of his famous uncle shows great similarity and they may have both been taught at the Quaker school in Leek, on Overton Bank.

Joseph arranged for his son to be apprenticed to his brother around the age of fourteen and the young James may have worked under his uncle's guidance for around thirteen years until the latter's death in 1772. This would explain James's claim to seniority in his uncle's business mentioned by George Washington in a letter to William Moultrie, May 25th, 1786.

The recorded trail on James really begins with his arrival in America, in *The Virginia Gazette* on July 7th 1774:

"The Jett from London is gone up the Rappahannock River. In her came John Ballendine, Esq: with about forty ingenious Mechanicks, who landed at Hampton. Mr Ballendine has made a tour of England, Scotland, Ireland, and France, in order to make himself fully acquainted with inland navigation, and has also engaged and brought with him some of the best and most experienced artists in canals, locks etc. that could be had in England; among them Mr. James Brindley and Mr. Thomas Allan, Nephews to the celebrated Engineer of that name, who were brought up with him and were well acquainted with all his works until his death."

Note: Thomas Allan's mother was Ann Brindley, sister of the famous James]

Hampton, Virginia, is situated at the mouth of the Chesapeake Bay on the Eastern Seaboard and is close to Maryland, Delaware, and Pennsylvania, where James settled. The men shared a passionate determination to progress trade through inland navigation, and John Ballendine already knew of George Washington. He and James were introduced almost immediately. They began a professional relationship that lasted many years and James stayed at George Washington's family plantation, Mount Vernon, on many occasions.

A few months later the American Revolution began. Maryland State papers show in July 1777, James writing to the Governor about the manufacture of iron wire. From *The History of Delaware* we learn that on the morning of September 11th 1777, James hosted George

Washington, just before the General, alongside the Marquis de Lafayette, led the Army in to the Battle of Brandywine. An eye-witness wrote: *"On the morning of the battle Washington took his breakfast at the mansion of James Brindley, on the Wilmington side of the river, walking the floor with deep thought ....his cup of coffee in his hand, eating little and soon hastening on to Chadd's Ford"*

We can pinpoint James's house, from surviving maps, on the west side of the Brandywine River, just inside Delaware, a few miles South of Chadd's Ford. The house no longer survives, but there is a 'mansion' of the same era close by that has been restored, and this former home of John Chadd gives an indication of what the exterior would have looked like. The Brandywine battlefield is a national monument and the area around Chadd's Ford remains reminiscent of rural England. Several original inns and taverns survive. No doubt, James would have visited taverns such as the Dilworthtown Inn, and the Chadd's Ford Inn, as they were important meeting places for the exchange of world news.

James sympathised with the Colonists, and in 1778 he subscribed to the Oath of Allegiance and Fidelity, and joined Captain John Garrett's Militia as a Private 6th Class. On October 3rd 1781, he was promoted to Second Lieutenant.

The former home
of John Chadd.

Below:
George Washington accepts
the British surrender.

On 29th April 1779, James married Elizabeth Ogle at Old Swedes [now Holy Trinity] Church in Wilmington. Shortly afterwards we find a baptism record for a Catherine Brindley born to James, with the mother identified as a woman named Rebecca Smidt. Presumably, Catherine was the result of a brief affair. She was born on November 8th 1779, seven months after his marriage to Elizabeth, and baptized at Old Swedes Church on August 14th 1780.

Elizabeth Ogle [nee Williams] had previously been married twice, and had four children with her second husband Thomas Ogle, namely Charles, Thomas, William, and Mary.

James was 34 when he married Elizabeth, and together they had three children, Sarah; Susanna baptized 1783; and James Joseph born 1783, and died 24th August 1858.

James and Elizabeth remained in the Pennsylvania/Delaware boundary area until they died. At the time, this hamlet came under the governing district of Christiana Hundred and James appears in the census records of 1790, 1800, 1810 and 1820.

The Revolutionary War ended in 1783. As life returned to normal, the focus turned again to the development of trade and industry; with it came a renewed interest in the mobility of goods and people through inland navigation. At the time, most goods would be transported to market from the interior by 'dug-out' canoes, flatboats, or 'keel-boats', and rivers often proved treacherous. Often boats could only be used one way, and were broken up and sold at the end of a journey; their owners using horses and carts to return home with supplies.

The competition for trade amongst towns such as Philadelphia, Baltimore and Boston was intense, and it became critical to make routes less hazardous and more accessible. The early American engineers faced special challenges such as the severe North East weather that froze rivers and waterfalls for several months each year. They had difficulty finding skilled men, feeding and equipping them, keeping them disease free during the summer months and warm during the winter. Such was the harshness of conditions, many workers died. Often projects relied on forced labour such as indentured English, Scottish and Irish immigrants purchased for the length of their indenture, and brought from cities such as Baltimore and Philadelphia; they were 'sentenced' to hard labour alongside slaves and free men alike. Runaway workers became so frequent a problem that managers resorted to shaving heads and eyebrows weekly, so they might be easily identified.

James was Chief Engineer on the Conewago Falls project and the undertaking was a tremendous success. Its opening was celebrated on 22nd November 1797, and in *The History of Lancaster County* we are told:

"A canal was built at a cost of one hundred and two thousand dollars ....James Brindley was chief engineer. The work was completed in November 1797. On the 27th a committee of the Legislature and Dr William Smith proceeded through the canal in flatboats to inspect the works. ......When they returned to the foot of the canal five hundred people were there to receive the Governor and rejoice with him on the successful completion of this great work. There were two locks or chambers, eighty feet long and twelve feet wide."

Note: Conewago Falls is in Pennsylvania on the Susquehanna River, 14 miles above Wrights Ferry. It was an obstacle that was deemed "a great obstruction and bar to the wealth and population of the region."

Earlier, in March 1786, Washington wrote *"In the afternoon a Mr.Brindley, manager of the Susquehanna canal and Mr. Hanes manager of the James River Navigation came in and stayed all night."* Brindley was on his way to Richmond to consult-and-advise on the James River project and GW hoped he would do the same for the Potomac project on his way back to the Susquehanna. James was said to be travelling with his 'son-in-law' and we read that this man was *"Haines or Hayes"*. The transcriber had difficulty deciphering Washington's handwriting and it may be Peter Hanson, the husband of James's stepdaughter Mary Ogle.

Although we are presently short on detail, we know that James consulted on other projects such as the Potomac Canal, Maryland; the James River Canal, Virginia; and the Santee Canal, South Carolina. The last correspondence was written the year before his death, and was a letter written to William Wright on 30th January 1819 asking the recipients to forward information to James Brindley. So at the age of 74, James was still apparently active.

In the 1800 census, we are given a glimpse into the family of James and Elizabeth, which included the Ogle children, as well as their own, and there were two slaves present. James died on November 24th 1820 and is buried in what is now Red Clay Creek Presbyterian Church, formerly McCannon's Churchyard. The family plot is in section 'S', the original and oldest part of the churchyard. The only obelisk in the section marks the plot, and seven members are buried there. Elizabeth's parents are also buried in Red Clay Creek Churchyard.

Their one son, James Joseph married Hannah Baker [baptized March 1st 1797, the daughter of Richard Baker and his wife, Rebecca née Webb, of Chester, Pennsylvania]. He also had only one son, Captain Richard Brindley, who was killed in the Civil War. There were also two daughters of the union, Rebecca Baker, named after her mother's family; and Elizabeth, who both appear to have remained unmarried, for at 76 years and 80 years, respectively, they are buried alone with their parents and grandparents.

James Joseph was commissioned to the Sixth Company of Militia in 1808, but resigned shortly afterwards. He was active in several engineering evaluations on behalf of the Governor, such as the Wilmington and Great Valley Turnpike in 1813; the Newport Bridge in 1814, the road from Wilmington on the east side of the Brandywine Bridge in 1814, and the Newcastle and French Town Turnpike the same year. In 1818, he was working on the Wilmington and Great Valley Turnpike road in connection with the erection of tollgates.

In 1832 he was a charter member of the Wilmington Savings Fund, in 1826 he was Vice President of the Agricultural Society of Newcastle County and in 1850 he was elected a Director of the Newcastle County Mutual Insurance Company. From old records, it appears that a good deal of his business was conducted at the Mermaid Tavern in Mill Creek Hundred and at the Indian Queen Tavern in Wilmington. James Joseph appears in the 1830, 1840 and 1850 censuses. In 1850, he is recorded with son Richard and daughter Rebecca Baker.

His son, Captain Richard Brindley, seems to have been born with an adventurous spirit. He was elected State Senator under the Republican presidency of Abraham Lincoln in 1860, before joining the Second Regiment of United States Infantry as Second Lieutenant, later to become Captain. He lost his life on June 27th 1862 at the Battle of Gaine's Mill, Virginia, where he was recognized for *"gallant and meritorious services"*. His commander on the day was Brigadier General Fitz John Porter, and the opposing General was Robert E. Lee. There was an estimated 91,232 troops engaged in the battle with 15,500 casualties.

In the records of Old Swedes Church one mystery remains, there is an entry for the birth of Susannah Brindley baptized on October 13th 1789 to John Brindley. No mention of the mother is made. It is not certain where the mystery John fits in, however, we know that, back in England, there was a cousin called John, the son of John the potter of Burslem and it is possible he could have joined James in America.

'The Friends Adventure' Passenger List, Liverpool, May 1682

Master - Thomas Wall

Thomas Barrett
William Beasy
John Brearly
Samuel Buckley
Luke Brindley
Thomas Buckley
John Brock
John Clows
Joseph Clows
Sarah Clows

Ralph Cowgill
Andrew Heath
Eliza Heaton
John Heycock
Job Houle
Thomas Leister
Henry Linghart
Daniel Milnot
Joseph Milnot
James Morris
Ralph Nuttall

George and Eleanor Pownall
and children: Reuben,
Elizabeth, Sarah, Rachel, and
Abigail
Martha Worrall
William and Jane Yardley and
children: Enoch, Thomas and
William
Shadrach Walley
William and Elizabeth Barrett
Venables and children: Joyce
and Frances

Luke Brindley's removal certificate and a ship like The Friends Adventure

Chapter 13
Luke Brindley

The Brindleys arrived in America from the earliest days. Brindleys were recorded from the mid 17th Century. Luke Brindley, a Quaker of Leek, Staffordshire, was well settled in Pennsylvania by 1689, having visited previously. Other Brindleys were also in the area. The children of Thomas Brinley, Auditor to Charles I and II, settled in Rhode Island from the 1660s. As previously mentioned, the pedigree of Thomas and Lawrence and their descendents is well attested.

Luke's pedigree is less well documented but he may well have been descended from the ancestors of the James Brindley Clan. One of the signatories on Luke's removal certificate, dated May 1684, was Hestor Fallowfield. She was a Brindley who married William Fallowfield 11th June 1666, and he was another signatory on Luke's certificate. She may have been Luke's sister or cousin. The location of the Quaker meeting appears to be at Wood End (probably near Basford, Cheddleton and Leek) in Joshua Dale's house.

Another interesting signatory was Henry Bowman the 2nd, whose sister Ellen Bowman had married Joseph Brindley, grandfather of the famous James, around 1683. This Henry was in Leek until 1692, when he moved to Smerril Grange, Youlgeave. It is clear that the Bowmans and Brindleys were well known to each other. Henry Bowman 1st was of Alstonfield, where many ancient Brindleys had lived.

Others who signed the document were Robert Miller, Joshua Randle, Andrea and Sarah Dale, Thomas Hammersley, John and Ellen Stretch, George Gent, John Hall, Elizabeth Misl?, Jane Rydor and Ellen Buxton. Ellen Buxton was the sister of Alice Stubbs who married Henry Bowman Snr, in 1656. This couple did not become Quakers until 1658. Ellen Stubbs married Simon Buxton, who *"suffered mightily"* for his beliefs, being imprisoned and receiving many beatings. Simon Buxton probably lived at Coal Pit Ford, Cheddleton, Leek.

So, circumstantially this company appears to contain several individuals who were well known to have close Brindley Clan connections. And Luke was almost certainly a relation of these Brindleys.

The Quaker Visitations 1662-1779 noted that the Leek Friends had, in 1668, the following individuals among their number: Randulpu Brindley, Thomas Brindley and wife, Thomas Brindley Jnr; Randulphus Brindley, Matthew and Andrea Dale.

Both Brindleys in America had family origins in or near to Leek. Probably related, they don't seem to have been aware of or in contact with each other. Yet, for their own reasons, both were settling in roughly the same geographical area of Colonial America.

Who knows what was in Luke's mind when he boarded *The Friends Adventure* in Liverpool that fine sunny day in May 1682. No doubt his head was full of hopes for life in the new land *"six hundred miles nearer the sun"* as some claimed it to be. He surely must have been apprehensive, as journeys by sea were long and perilous - two months on average. Cramped and unsanitary conditions meant a high chance of disease, sickness, or even death.

The quay was busy that day with other ships loading passengers and wares headed for the colonies, together with merchant trading ships bound for the Spice Islands and the China

Seas. Seagulls soaring above, and the salty smell of the sea were a powerful reminder of the weeks that lay ahead - to be endured, rather than enjoyed, far from the sight of land.

Leaving behind a harsh life as a stonemason in Leek was not too difficult a choice, and the *"brave experiment"* promised everything for this young man with a passion for living and a desire for adventure and freedom. A chance to really make something of his life lay ahead and he could not wait for the journey to pass.

We now know with some certainty that the journey did indeed pass quickly and without major incident. William Penn's own account states that of his twenty-three ships journeying to America, *"None miscarried; only two had the smallpox; else healthy and swift passages, generally such as have not been known; some, twenty-eight days, and few longer than six weeks."*

Although Luke's possessions were not itemized on the ships manifest, it is likely that he would have taken with him as much as he could afford in the way of practical items such as wrought iron; wool; linen; shoes; nails, and gunpowder.

All alone, but surrounded by people on the quayside, there were some familiar faces in the crowd. Luke's travelling companions included George Pownall and his wife Ellenor, of Leycock; William Venables and his wife Elizabeth, from Eccleshall Parish, Staffordshire; and William Yardley and his wife Jane from Ransclough near Leek.

All would become neighbours soon enough, and form a large part of Luke's social and working life in the community. It is probable that of these fellow travellers, Luke would have already known of William Yardley, if only by repute, for William, in attending Congleton Monthly Meeting in Cheshire, had already established a reputation for being *"a zealous Friend and avowed of his convictions with such freedom as to render him a subject of prosecution."* He was already a 'mover and shaker', as they say, and destined for leadership under the new order.

The Friends Adventure is said to have dropped anchor in the Delaware River on September 28th 1682 and was the third passenger ship to arrive that month, carrying emigrants from Staffordshire and Cheshire. Some think the ship may have arrived earlier. The original Bucks County Register of arrivals plainly gives the date as 28th September 1682; but as the Master, Thomas Wall signed The Lugger Protest of 18th September 1682, it clearly creates a conflict over the date. However, since the Register of Arrivals was not started until 1684, it is probable that the memories of the registrants were to blame.

Unlike some of his fellow travellers, young men such as John Brearley and Andrew Heath, Luke had sufficient funds to pay for his own passage, which was the princely sum of £5 12s 6d. Those not so fortunate had to commit themselves into servitude, normally for a period of four years during which time they would receive lodging, food and clothing. Once free of obligation, it is recorded that most received 50 acres of land and, in addition, some were paid 50 shillings at the end of their time.

Having landed in the Delaware Valley, Luke was now facing a future in a potentially hostile environment still occupied by Native Indian tribes such as the Susquehanock and the Iroquois. The Iroquois were sophisticated compared to other tribes and, as such, held most power in the region.

Fortunately, by the time Luke settled in Pennsylvania, relations between settlers and the local Indians were relatively friendly and colonists often looked on them as a means to wealth, especially through the fur trade. They were not thought of as savages to be feared.

Items essential for trading with the natives were sought-after goods such as blankets, guns, tobacco toungs, looking glasses, knives, flints, and flutes. It seems highly probable that Luke would have bought some of these objects with him from home, as these ways of negotiation with natives were well known to Quakers in England and Luke already had some experience of Indians from his previous experiences in America.

Yes, Luke had settled in the 'New World' once before, a few years earlier, and was registered as holding a parcel of land on the Delaware River in Burlington, New Jersey. Burlington had a local tribe, namely the Unami or Turtle Tribe, and Luke amongst others was listed as an inhabitant of Burlington on a petition written by Deputy Governor, Thomas Olive, to the Governor of York, in favour of Henry Jacobs, *"Tennant in Possession of Matinicock Island"*. This early colonial document is dated *"5th of ye 10th month 1678.*

In those days, living near to or on a waterway was not only essential for trade but also to support provincial existence in a number of ways, allowing travel to markets, churches, and to town meetings. The earliest homesteads were established in fertile creek-valleys where a flat landing and waterway ensured easy transport to nearby communities such as Philadelphia. The waterways were alive, we are told, with shad and sturgeon, beaver and otter, no doubt a welcome change in diet from local game. The rivers and creeks also carried the dead, Indian and colonist alike, with many a water-borne funeral procession to quiet creek-side cemeteries.

It is possible that Luke's first journey to America was on a ship named *The Kent*. She carried colonists into New Jersey with Gregory Marlow as Master. Sailing between March 19 and March 31 1677, the ship first boarded passengers in a northern port, probably Liverpool and then proceeded to London to complete loading. *The Kent* sailed first to New York then, after a short stay, sailed across the bay to Perth Amboy and headed south to the Delaware River. Landing first at Racoon Creek, she is said to have disembarked some 230 passengers out of 270 and the ship then moved to Chygoes Island, which is now Burlington.

Although the evidence is purely circumstantial at this point, this is a ship picking up passengers at Liverpool - the nearest port to Luke's hometown of Leek, and sailing to Burlington less than a year before Luke was registered as holding land there.

King Charles II is said to have boarded *The Kent* from his royal barge as it sailed down the Thames. Apparently, the King wished the Quaker contingent a safe voyage. However, as the King's own laws led to much of the abuse the Quakers received in England, this blessing was viewed as a polite way of telling them to go away and not return.

King Charles I and later King Charles II, were both 'masters' that Luke's forebears, Thomas Brinley and his son Francis served faithfully. It seems ironic that the actions of Charles II should mitigate against the interests of the Brindleys who served him so well.

We can only guess as to why Luke returned home to England only to return to America a few years later. Maybe he found life in the wilderness too harsh at first or simply became homesick for friends and family.

It is possible that the reason for Luke's return to America was that he became attracted by Penn's advertisements, which were aimed at the Quaker community, seeking new settlers. Enticed by some romantic vision, or just practical ambition, he might have gained renewed interest in a society promising religious freedom.

In 1681, King Charles II granted William Penn a huge tract of land in America and it was to be known as "Sylvania". The King, in his own handwriting, added "Penn" in honour of William's father, Admiral Sir William Penn. The colony thus became know as "Penn's Woods" or "Pennsylvania" as we know it today.

For Penn, this was a *"grand experiment"* and he needed the presence of a sufficient number of intelligent and capable colonists, on whom he could depend, to support and govern the province. So the new proprietor soon advertised for English settlers - *"adventurers"* he called them: farmers, day labourers, carpenters, masons, smiths, weavers, tanners, shipwrights and, in addition, merchants who understood commerce and men of administrative capacity to set the new community on its feet. Luke Brindley was one such man.

George Fox, a Leicestershire weaver's son, founded the Society of Friends (otherwise known as Quakers) in 1652. William Penn was perhaps their most passionate and influential convert and therefore it is not surprising that his *"grand plan"* would provide an escape route for many Quakers. The Quaker founders of New Jersey and Pennsylvania came largely from the North Midlands and especially from the bordering counties of Cheshire, Staffordshire Lancashire, Yorkshire, Derbyshire, and Nottinghamshire.

On the banks of the Delaware River, settlers generally distributed themselves in settlements according to their origin in Britain and Quakers from the North mainly settled in Chester and Bucks counties as the rich uplands reminded them of home. There were already many Finnish, Swedish and Dutch settlers in the area that provided a sturdy base for the coming population and a ready-made introduction into the Native Indian customs and language.

During the early migrations, for a Quaker, it was necessary to have a proper introduction into a new community by way of a Certificate of Removal. This was their way of checking that a person was not secretly married or in debt and generally was of good moral character. Luke's Certificate was dated on 1d 3m 1684 [under the old style calendar, the first month was March; which would be May today] and signed, amongst others, by William Fallowfield, and his wife Esther (née Brindley); Joshua Dale, and George Gent.

[Note: Esther, née Brunley, married William Fallowfield on the 7d 11m 1666.]

In an earlier publication, entitled *The Brinleys of Pennsylvania*, it was stated that Luke's certificate was from "Fallowfield Monthly Meeting". Initially this caused some confusion and has since been proved incorrect, as the meeting house was actually Joshua Dale's house at Wood End, Leek. We do know that William Fallowfield's signature was one of those on Luke's certificate, which is probably how the error occurred.

Although not a unique situation, there is a slight question as to why Luke's Certificate is dated two years after he left England. The wording clearly indicates that the Certificate was issued following his departure, as it states: *"he gave us knowledge of his intention for America long before he went."* William Yardley's Certificate of Removal was also issued after his departure, the wording *"the Yardley's absence is a great loss to us"* plainly shows that the family had already left England previously.

The most likely explanation is that, after two years of creating a Quaker society based on worshiping in various homes, Friends living around the Falls of Delaware decided to establish a more formal arrangement and therefore required some form of character reference to support admission. This theory is supported by the fact that on the third month [May] 2,

1683, the Friends decided to set up an official meeting place. Their decision was recorded in the following minutes:

"At a meeting at William Biles's house, the second day of the third month, 1683, then held to wait upon the Lord for his wisdom, to hear what should be offered, in order to inspect into the affairs of the church, that all things may be kept therein sweet and savoury to the Lord, and, by our care over the church, helpful in the work of God; and we, whose names are as follows, being then present, thought it fit and necessary that a Monthly Meeting be set up, both men and women, for that purpose; and that this meeting to be the first of the men's meetings after our arrival into these parts. The Friends present, William Yardley, James Harrison, Phineas Pemberton [nephew of William Yardley], William Biles, William Dark, Lyonell Brittanie, William Beaks."

The following year a quarterly meeting was established by dividing the Bucks county Friends into two monthly meetings - Falls and Neshaminy, later to be known as Middletown. Falls Monthly Meeting built a meetinghouse in the village of Fallsington in 1692. A second meetinghouse was built in 1728 and, in 1789, the present Orthodox meetinghouse was erected.

The beginning of a more organized community had a direct impact on Luke for, shortly after he joined the Falls Monthly Meeting in 1684, he was appointed Sheriff of Bucks County.

It was around this date that the county boundaries were being defined for the first time:

"In order to ye raising and collecting of taxes, public moneys, and other ways to adjust the limits of the respective Sheriffs, for performing of their power and duty; and also, that ye people might know unto what county they belong and appertain to answer their duty's and places."

This extract gives the reader some insight into what a sheriff's duties largely comprised; very mundane, it would seem, and in complete contrast to the more popular 'American Wild West' version of the job!

In 1684 Penn's surveyor, Thomas Holmes, produced a map of Lower Makefield Township and this shows that Luke was co-owner, with John Parsons, of Lot 302A; a tract of land adjoining the river north of the wood. Other passengers from *The Friends Adventure* are shown as neighbours and they include Richard Hough, John Clows, John Brock and William Yardley. We know that some land grants were negotiated directly with Penn, as in the case of John Brock of Bramhall, Cheshire, who was granted 1000 acres while they were both still in England. However, we do not know if this was true of Luke.

A solid member of the community, Luke quickly developed a reputation as a successful mediator, settling small land disputes and disagreements among neighbours from both the Falls and Neshaminy Monthly Meetings. In notes from a meeting dated 1d 2m 1685, Luke is mentioned as follows: *"As much as friends of Neshaminy have not done anything yet as to fencing off the land of Joseph Sharp, therefore this meeting doth order that Luke Brinley* (sic) *do put them in mind of it in order that it might be finished."*

Neshaminy was a district shared by Falls and Middletown Monthly Meeting. In that era there was confusion about which meeting held sway over which group of Friends. There was no specific meeting for Neshaminy - it was divided between the two groups. Bucks County Quarterly Meeting held authority over both.

The History of Bucks County states that the first court of common pleas was held on December 11th 1684, and the case was Robert Lucas against Thomas Bowman *"for withholding seven pounds wages due to the said plaintiff, in the third-month last past."* Luke

Brindley, deputy sheriff, who was also Ranger at Pennsbury, served the summons. Judgment was given in favour of the plaintiff with costs.

As the previous reference would indicate, Luke seemed to have been operating in several roles for some time, as he served on the Grand Jury in 1688, and in 1689 he was officially appointed Ranger of Pennsbury Manor, the private residence of William Penn. It is likely that he was hired by James Harrison, Penn's personal steward, as Penn himself spent little time at Pennsbury; arriving in 1682 until 1684, and then once more from 1699 until 1701. In the early days, Pennsbury and Pennsbury Manor were synonymous and the role of Ranger, amongst other things, included the same responsibility of a Forest Ranger today - making certain that all the livestock was accounted for and generally keeping everything in good order. It was a big job, as the Manor at that time consisted of 8,431 acres.

Not surprisingly, the estate is now much reduced but Pennsbury Manor still exists and is located across the Delaware River from the city of Trenton, New Jersey, some 24 miles north of Philadelphia. Today, it is hard to believe that this area was once considered a wilderness!

In 1701, a meeting of the Pennsylvania Commission refers to Luke's land in Makefield Township, Bucks County and the following reference dated 14d 10m 1703, is the last mention of Luke and it appears to suggest that he is no longer resident:

"The line between the lands of Richard Hough and Peter Worrall shall begin at a small hickory tree, standing on the northerly side of the land belonging sometime to Luke Brindlow, between the ancient road and the said Richard Hough's fence and another small forked hickory, being also marked, standing just on the outside of the said Richard Hough's fence near the land of Andrew Elliott."

It is believed that Luke sold the 90 acres to Peter Worrall on April 8 1688, and removed to the Falls area, as noted on Thomas Holmes's map.

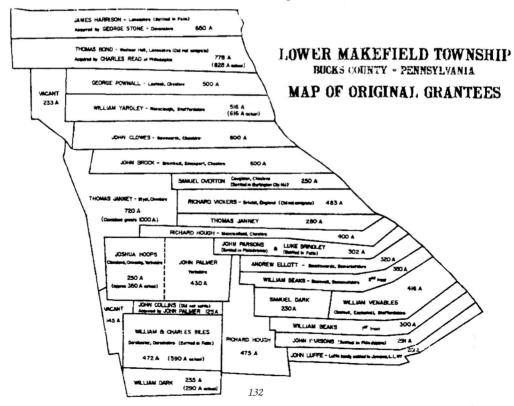

Luke has long been credited as the *"founding father"* of the Pennsylvania Brinleys. However, despite exhaustive searches in Quaker records, church records and those held by State and County archives, no evidence of Luke's marriage or confirmation that he fathered any children has been found. There is no trace of Luke's Will either.

Luke was undeniably a Friend but seems to have been a loner, keeping pretty much to himself. He was not socially involved nor did he request to be assigned or appointed to a prominent position on any Quaker committee. There is little information to go on, therefore the claim that he began the Pennsylvania 'clan' is purely circumstantial and based on the fact that he was established in the area at the right time.

However, quite apart from the Boston and Rhode Island families, there are other Brin(d)leys listed in the region around the same time. William Brinley and his family were Quakers in Pennsylvania also and Simon Brinley from Bristol, a servant to Richard Pugsly in 1661, was listed in 1685 in Piscataway, New Jersey as having administrative control over the estate of Michael Symons.

Luke's own family origins are somewhat of a mystery too. We have found several entries in original Quaker records that would strongly suggest that Luke's relatives were attending the same Monthly Meeting in Leek, alongside Joshua Dale, who signed his certificate of Removal. These Brindleys are also hot favourites to be the ancestors of the famous James, canal engineer. (Discussed elsewhere in this book)

In the Quaker Episcopal Visitations of 1668, the following are listed:

"Thoma Brindley et eius ux, Willmu Davenport et eius ux, Mathew Dale et eius ux, Randluphu Dale et eius ux, Quakers; Exom.

[Et eius ux means 'and his wife'. Exom probably means excommunicated]

Willm Gent et eius ux, Thomas Brindley, jun, Blacksmith, Thoma Finney, Johem Finney, Edrum Sailes, Andrea Dale, Joshua Dale, Ellena Adams, Sarah Adams, Randulphu Brindley, Radum Hamersely, Johem Ware, Quakers."

Leek Quaker records also show a William and Sarah Brindley, baptizing a son, Anthony, on the 27d 10m 1677.

At time of going to print the author is still trying to establish a firmer family connection!

To clarify any doubt as to how Luke signed his name, he signed deeds in 1687 and 1689 as BRINDLEY.

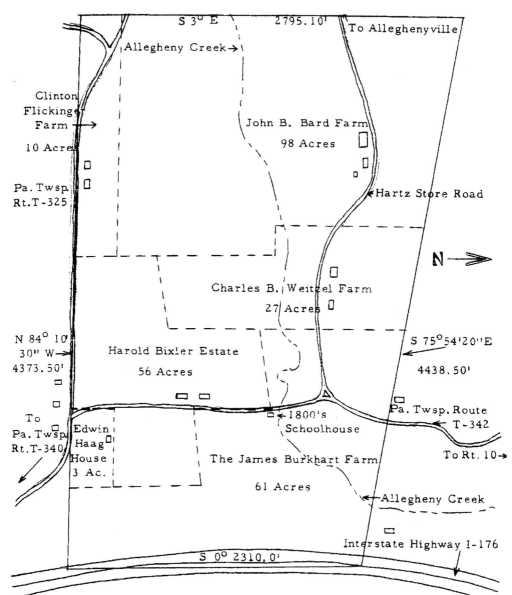

Site of the original 255 Acre Penn Warrant to Alexander Brinley in 1737.
"Alexander's Farm" today is divided among six land owners. Only a few
years ago, Interstate Highway I-176 was constructed along the easterly
border. The view from I-176 to Pa. State Highway 10 is blocked by a low
mountain range. All data compiled by Frankhouser Associates, Inc.,
Engineers and Surveyors, Reading, Pa., and Berks Title Insurance Co.,
Reading, Pa., Plan B-6-A-33 dated February, 1967. Scale 1" = 600'.

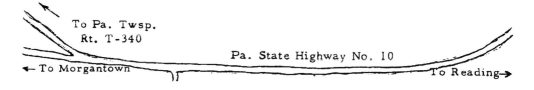

Chapter 14
The Founding of the Pennsylvanian Clan - James and Alexander Brinley

In the previous chapter it is indicated that it has not been proven whether Luke Brindley was the father of James and Alexander. No parents are named for either child and their precise dates of birth remain unclear. All we know is that James was born around the year 1688 and Alexander around 1698. We cannot even prove that they were brothers as is claimed. However, for the purposes of continuity, we will take a 'leap of faith' in maintaining this assumption. This is based purely on their surnames and their proximity to one another in location and time. What is clear is that, from Alexander, there appears to be a direct line to Brinley descendents in present day Pennsylvania.

James Brinley
Records still to be found at Christ Church, Philadelphia, show that a *"James Brendly"*, who was a hatter living in Philadelphia, married Mary Wivell on January 1st 1712.

There is nothing to indicate if James was a Quaker and no special significance should be attached to the fact that he married in an Episcopal church as, at that time in *"the City of Brotherly Love"*, churches were almost interchangeable and services conducted depending on who was available to perform a specific ceremony at a convenient time.

However, James and Mary obviously favoured Christ Church, as they baptized their first child Margaret there on 14th October 1716 and buried her there less than a year later on 23rd August 1717. Mary herself was buried close to her daughter on 9th October 1731, and five years later, on the 9th October 1736, James was buried with his wife. The graves are believed to be located on the Arch Street side of the cemetery, close to the grave of Benjamin Franklin.

Alexander Brinley
Alexander, whose wife was called Elizabeth, lived on Allegeny Creek, in Robeson Township, which was at the time situated in Lancaster County, Pennsylvania. Alexander received a warrant for land on the 25th October 1737, for a total of 255 acres, which was issued under the authority of the Penn family, William Penn having died some years before. Land records reveal that the land was known as "Alexander's Farm" from that point onwards.

Lancaster County was created in 1729 from part of Chester County and was named after Lancashire, England, and, at the time Alexander was in Robeson Township, the region was growing and fast becoming a melting pot, as there were Swedish settlements along the Schuylkill River, beginning around 1638. To arrive later were Welsh and English Quakers, then Germans, Swiss and French Huguenots. Afterwards came Jews from Eastern Europe, together with Italians, Poles, and Slovaks in the 1800s.

Alexander and Elizabeth became regular worshipers at St. Gabriel's Episcopal Church in Douglasville, PA, and they baptized their first child John there on the 2nd April 1738. A little more than a year later, James, their second son, was baptized on the 31st January 1739.

Records show that, on the 17th March 1743, the land was *"vacated by warrant"* and passed over to the Squire Boone, the father of the famous Daniel Boone. Thereafter, Alexander and his family moved on and were thought to be living somewhere close by.

The next reference to the family is when their son James appears in the 1769 tax records of Upper Merion Township, Montgomery County, where he is living with a Henry Castleberry. James lived there until 1776, when the American Revolution changed their lives.

It should be noted that Montgomery County was formed from Albany County in 1722, and at the time covered a large part of the State. The name was changed in 1784, in honour of the revolutionary war hero, General Richard Montgomery.

Records held with the National Society Daughters of the American Revolution, reveal that James married Mary Casselberry in Upper Merion Township in 1769, and eventually they had twelve children. Mary herself was born on 12th March 1750, and she proved an excellent resource, as she recorded each child's birth in her prayer book.

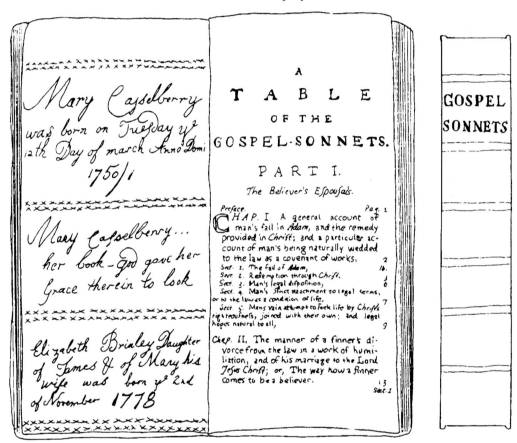

The Mary Casselberry Brinley Prayer Book of the 18th century

At the time of going to print, no record has been found as to the death of James's father, Alexander, or any further reference to his elder brother John. John does not appear to have a surviving war record either, as would have been expected if he had been living at the time. Even if John had refused to enlist, there should, in theory, have been a record.

Captain Joseph Davis of Berks County enlisted James into the Revolutionary Army as a Private receiving pay of £10.2s.6d. By nature of the fact that James was prepared to bear arms, it would indicate that he had no leanings whatsoever towards the Quaker faith, which was fundamentally pacifist. Many Quakers lived out the war as quietly as they could, even though some were right in the midst of the fighting, literally, at times, on their doorstep.

James survived the war and returned to his wife in Robeson Township. In 1779, he was listed as owning 100 acres, his livestock consisting of three horses and three cattle. The value of his estate was approximately 745 dollars.

At this time the many farmsteads of Robeson Township were scattered across the valleys; settlements had gradually developed around churches, mills and forges along the creeks. Dirt roads connected the towns and there were many taverns and inns.

By the year 1790, James and Mary had nine children between the ages of two and eighteen. Their first son, Isaac, died early, around 1780 and James himself died in 1794.

Berks County records show that Mary executed James's Will on the 18th December 1794, and confirms that they were still resident in Robeson Township at the time of his death.

In addition to household items and farm implements, the Will lists livestock as *"an old horse, five cows, two heifers, a steer, four spring calves and five sheep."* From this it is clear that, in the intervening fifteen years since the last inventory, James had not dramatically increased his livestock. Listed as *"Yeoman"* it is likely that James farmed his own land to help support his growing family.

It was James, their second son then aged 22, who assumed responsibility for the farm and the family. This is recorded in the Robeson Township Census of 1800. He remained at home until his marriage in 1809.

Money was obviously in short supply, as Mary and James took out a mortgage on March 31st 1798. Berks County records show that the property was mortgaged to Casper Wolf, who was the original owner and the amount was for £430. The mortgage was paid off in 1810.

Mary died at the age of 82 on February 13th 1828. It is not known where she or the rest of the family are buried. Many early American gravesites have long been used in other ways and most have been built over.

What follows is what we know of James and Mary's twelve children. A more detailed account of the generations that followed, up until 1967, can be found in *The Brinleys of Pennsylvania* written by Robert. M. Brinley. (Library of Congress, Washington, D.C.)

The Twelve Children of James and Mary

Isaac: Isaac was born in Upper Merion Township, Pennsylvania, on July 13th 1771. He died at the age of eleven in 1782.

James: James was born in Upper Merion Township, Pennsylvania, on August 30th 1772. On January 26th 1809 James married Rachel Bechtel of Caernarvon Township in Berks County. Rachel was the daughter of John Bechtel who was a leading member of the Harmony Methodist Episcopal Church.

As with many places between Philadelphia and Lancaster, Caernarvon Township was first settled by the hardy Welsh, around 1752. To them, the rolling hills and flowing streams reminded them of home. There is sometimes confusion as to the origin of the two separate Caernarvon townships, the other being adjacent in Lancaster County. It is thought that the townships existed as one before the county lines were drawn up.

In 1809, James purchased land in Northern Liberties, Philadelphia County, giving his occupation as *"grocer"* at the time. Census lists for 1810 shows the couple living in

Caernarvon Township. They are childless at this point and Rachel gives her age as *"under 26"*. On March 19th 1828 he was noted as a storekeeper in Kensington, having just purchased land in Northern Liberties. In 1832, James and Rachel appeared before a Notary Public in Chester County to sign their names to the release of John Bechtel's lands following his death.

Mary: Mary was born in Upper Merion Township, Pennsylvania, on March 6th 1774. Unmarried she was listed as living with her family in 1820. She was a member at the Harmony Methodist Episcopal Church Sunday School in 1822. Presumably Mary joined the church with the encouragement of her maternal grandfather who was manager at the time. She was listed as 48 years of age and still single. To-date there is no other record of her.

Ann: Ann was born in Robeson Township, Pennsylvania, on October 19th 1776. Ann married Patrick Lyons at Christ Church, Philadelphia, on July 4th 1795. To date no other record.

Elizabeth: Elizabeth was born in Robeson Township, Pennsylvania, on November 2nd 1778. In 1800 she was still listed as living with her family. To date there is no other record of her.

John: John was born in Robeson Township, Pennsylvania, on January 31st 1781. John married Mary Ann Ross, the sister of William Ross, a merchant from Morgantown, on May 29th 1806. In the 1810 Census John, Mary and two daughters are shown living in Caernarvon and his occupation is listed as carpenter. In 1815 they moved to Northern Liberties and purchased some land on June 5th.

In 1820, John and Mary moved back to Caernarvon, and settled about a mile from Morgantown. Mary, yet another family member to be involved in the same church, is listed as a member at the Harmony Methodist Episcopal Church Sunday School in 1822. Both James and Mary went on to be members of St. Thomas Episcopal Church in Morgantown.

In 1823, they lost three of their children within two weeks when an epidemic swept the town. The census of 1830 records that the other children were all alive and living at home in that year. Mary died in 1834, and in 1839 their son John Castleberry Brinley died.

The census of 1840 shows all other family members present with the exception of Ann Ross Brinley, who was to die two years later, and her brother George Ross, who by that time had married and moved away. He was listed as living in Union Township in 1837.

By 1850 the couple had lost two more children and William Ross Brinley had moved away and was living in Salisbury Township, Lancaster County. Ross Brinley was not found in any references for that year. John died on the 8th March 1855. He is buried next to his wife, Mary, in the graveyard of St. Thomas's Episcopal Church. Near to their tomb lies her brother, William Ross. Cemetery Records for St. Thomas's show the family buried there:

Name	Born	Died	Age
John	Jan 31, 1781	Mar 8, 1855	74y 1m 8d
Mary Ann [Ross]	Jun 11, 1776	Jun 9, 1834	57y 11m 29d
Ann R	Mar 20, 1807		
Elizabeth	Jun 7, 1818	Feb 23, 1843	24y 8m 16d
Isaac	Aug 11, 1820	Oct 4, 1823	
James	Apr 1, 1814	Sept 24, 1823	
John C		Jan 6, 1839	26y 5m 12d
Mary Maria	Dec 3, 1808	Sept 7, 1870	61y 9m 4d
Rebecca	Apr 1, 1822	Sept 17, 1823	
Ross	Jul 30, 1824	Jan 25, 1854	29y 5m 26d

Isaac [2nd child of the same name]: Isaac was born in Robeson Township, Pennsylvania, on the 6th November 1782. It is believed Isaac married around 1800; the 1810 Census identifies him as married and in the company of an unknown female. In the 1830 Census Isaac is listed as being with his wife and two unnamed boys born in the years 1805 and 1812, together with a female child listed as being born around 1813. Isaac was still living in Caernarvon Township in 1850, this time mysteriously living alone. A John Brinley is living nearby.

Elener: Elener was born on the 23rd September 1784. Little is known of her, except that she married Richard Threweak on the 31st March 1807. Richard was an active member of the Harmony Methodist Episcopal Church in Caernarvon.

Edith: Edith was born on the 27th September 1786. The only reference, apart from her birth, is that she was living with her family at the time of the 1800 Census.

Sarah: Sarah was born in Robeson Township 9th December 1788. As with Edith, the only other reference is that she appears in the Census for 1800.

Jehu: Jehu was born in Robeson Township on 20th November 1790. Again he appears at the family home in the 1800 Census but, in 1810, he is living with his brother John and his wife, Mary Ross Brinley. To date, there is no further record of him.

Amy: Amy was born in Robeson Township on the 13th of January 1793. Tragically, Amy was born after the death of her father the previous year. Amy appears at home in the Census of 1800 and after that there is no record of her in the area.

The heartland of Quakers, and also the Brindleys, in the late 17th century, at the time of mass migration to the colonies because of religious intolerance.

The Brindley Database>

This huge depository of genealogical data was started in 1999 and has grown to 22,000 entries. Each entry contains information on from one to five individuals. The data shows how the initial small numbers grew and spread across the country.

It was constructed systematically by combining all births, marriages and deaths available from the Civil Registration Indexes between 1837 and 1940. To that was added all Brindleys from the 1881 census of England and Wales, plus selected locations from the 1841/1851/1861/1871/1891 censuses. Welsh records are systematically being checked and added. Scottish Brindleys are also being gathered in.

In addition, I added Brindleys found in my searches of parish registers in Derbyshire, Cheshire and Staffordshire. Many Brindleys and non-Brindleys with a Brindley interest have freely sent their gleanings to be incorporated. There are also many entries from other sources, such as internet sites, will depositories, newspapers and so on.

Many researchers have been helped from this ever-growing source and anyone is welcome to submit information. Here is a summary of some places, dates and people covered:

<u>Alstonefield, Elkstone, Warslow, Hartington:</u> This beautiful and apparently isolated area of high moorland has spawned more Brindleys than you would believe possible. The first resident recorded was John of Owsley, who lived at Elkstone in 1489. He was a son of Christopher of Wyldegoose House, Bradnop. John was 9th generation from Brundelegh de Brindley. The 792nd entry is Ann Brindley, 1982.

<u>Alton:</u> The first entry is dated 1687, for the marriage of John Brindley to Ann Johnson, 406 entries later and the last entry is dated 2001. This was the location where Joseph Brindley, brother of James, settled and prospered. Most of the Brindleys here are his descendents from then to the present day. New information is still coming in for this area.

<u>Ashbourne, Derbyshire:</u> Located near the Staffordshire border and close to Alstonfield, many folk went to town for baptisms and marriages. Anyone interested in the Alstonfield area should not overlook this place. First entry is 1540 and last in 2002.

<u>Aston:</u> First entry 1679 and 153 items later it finishes in 1924.

Audley   Astbury   Acton   Ashton under Lyne   Ashton on Mersey   Anglesey   Aylesbury. Ashby de la Zouch   Arizona, USA   Alabama, USA

Barnsley, Yorks   Basford, Staffs   Bedwellty   Belper   Biddulph   Birmingham   Bournmouth   Bradford, Yorks   Bradley in the Moors   Burslem   Bollington, Cheshire   Brighton   Bristol Burton on Trent   Bury, Lancs   Buxton

Cauldon, Staffs   Caistor, Norfolk   Cambridge   Cheadle, Staffs   Chapel En Le Frith, Derbys   Checkley   Cheddleton   Chelmsford   Chester   Chorlton (Manchester)   Christchurch   Congleton   Cotton   Crewe

Derby   Darlaston   Dudley   Durham   Dukinfield   Doveridge   Datchet   Danebridge   Devonport

Eccles, Lancs   Eccleshall   Evesham   Exeter   Elkstone

Fairfield, Derbys   Foley   Fenton

Grindon   Gloucester   Glossop   Gnosall

Hanley   Hartington   Hereford   Hollington   Holmes Chapel   Holmes-next-the-Sea

Ipstones   Ireland   Isle of Man   Ilkeston

Jersey

Kinver   Kent

Leek: Entries start in 1450 with Christopher, a Brundelegh de Brindley descendant and finish, 920 entries later, with a 2001 entry. The list is by no means complete but is already extremely useful. It also contains some early Quaker information. From this data, much new information about early Brindleys has been collated. My prime and current goal is to concentrate on completing the records for this area to as full an extent as possible.

Lapley   Liverpool   Leeds   Lancaster   Longton   Lincoln

London: The first Brindley presence recorded was Lawrence, who served on Oliver Cromwell's Commonwealth Committee. His son Lawrence was born in London in 1622. The Brindley presence remained and grew. By the late 17th century there were many Brindleys engaged in trade. There was a James Brindley taking on apprentices for the Broderers' Company for several years from around 1696. Today, Greater London has one of the largest Brindley populations outside Staffordshire but they are more scattered.

Macclesfield: This town is effectively the twin of Leek. The closeness of the two places has meant mutual benefits over a couple of hundred years. The earliest records of Brindleys in the Macclesfield area show they arrived around 1770. From then on, their numbers quickly increased and by the mid-19th century they were almost as numerous as in the Leek area

Manchester   Mansfield   Marple   Marston Montgomery   Maidstone   Meerbrook

Nantwich   Newcastle on Tyne   Newcastle Under Lyme   New Mills   Norbury   North Rode Norton in the Moors   North Rode   Norwich   Nottingham   Nuneaton

Norfolk: Brindleys have always been thin on the ground here. Earliest entries occur in the 16th century. Modern Brindleys are mostly around the Norwich area.

Oxford   Oldham

Parwich   Preston   Penkridge

Rocester   Rushton Spencer   Rochdale   Roston   Rudyard

Rhode Island, USA   Many entries

Sefton, Lancs: This has the earliest Brinley reference: the marriage of Adam de Molyneux to Letitia/Lettuce de Brinley in 1189. Was she from Brinley/Brunley in Cheshire?

Stoke-on-Trent: Together with the towns of Longton, Burslem, Fenton, and Hanley, Stoke forms a large conurbation. Newcastle under Lyme is effectively part of the area. Brindleys abound in this area.

Sheen   Stalybridge   Sefton   Sheffield   Stramshall   Sutton, Cheshire   Southend   Stockport   Stone, Staffs   Swansea   Sutton Coldfield

Scotland   Only a few gathered in so far.

Tean, Staffs   Tipton   Tutbury   Tunstead   Tunstall

Uttoxeter: Ancient Roman town. Brindleys here from 1500s.

Warslow   Whalley Bridge   Warwick   Wells-next-the-Sea   Wincle   Winstanton   Wistaston   Wirksworth   Wokingham   Wolstanton   Wooton   Worcester   Wormhill   Wrexham

Wolverhampton: There are over 800 Wolverhampton related records including Willenhall and surrounding areas. The first entry is for William, born 1579 at Wolverhampton and a William married 1678 at Willenhall; final entry at the moment is for Phoebe Brindley, married in 1947.

Yarmouth   Yoxall   York   Youlgreave

Other countries with Brindleys include Australia, Canada, France, Italy, New Zealand, South Africa, Tasmania, USA, Wales.

SUMMARY

We have discovered much new information. We have discovered a likely link for Luke Brindley, the emigrating Quaker, with the James Brindley Clan. We have found Quaker Brindleys in Leek, who were almost certainly of the clan but need to be pinned-down further, who might be the 'missing link' between the James Brindley Clan and the founding family.

We have discovered Keith, a living male, direct descendent of the original Brundelegh de Brindley, whose DNA may serve as a bench mark for validating Brindleys.

We have discovered that there *are* living male descendents of John Bennett, the alleged love child of James Brindley. If willing, their DNA will show if John was James's son.

In George Washington's papers lay the tantalising clues that led to new James Brindley Clan information, proving that James Brindley, the Engineer's nephew successfully built the Conewago Canal, and that he had a grandson Richard who was known to Abraham Lincoln.

A group of German 'Brindleys' in the United States had the surname bestowed on them by English speaking officials. It is believed that their original name was probably Hildebrand. On entering the English-speaking world, embarking on a British ship for onward transportation to the new world, their Germanic name would be rendered as Brendl, Brindel, or Brendeley. In no time at all it transmuted to Brindley. Modern American Brindley researchers should be aware of this fact. These Brindleys are believed to have settled mostly in the South in the 18th century.

We have discovered that Brindleys and Stokes are parallel descendents, having common ancestry. And we know that the story started about 820 AD in an area near the Norwegian-Swedish border, where mining took place.

Today, the most exciting prospect for anyone wanting to research their ancestry, is the innovation of DNA profiling. It is now possible, and a relatively simple matter, to have one's mother's line traced back to a female ancestor who lived many thousands of years ago. Everyone, male or female, inherits mitochondrial DNA from their mother. The results take about a month. Mine was profiled by Oxford Ancestors (www.oxfordancestors.com) and revealed a maternal ancestory going back to 'Jasmine', a woman who lived some 10,000 years ago in the land now known as Iraq. Her descendents are particularly numerous in the west of Britain. Through parish records I have only been able to trace my mother's maternal line back four generations and her father's line back 200 years. So DNA has enabled me to bridge an insuperable gap here.

My male, Y-line DNA, has also been profiled. Every male inherits this chromosome from his father and it allows men to compare their male ancestoral code with that of other men. This will increasingly prove true male descent, as opposed to what we believe from records and 'inherited' surnames that, as we have discussed earlier, can be unreliable. Male Brindleys can have their Y-line DNA compared to mine, and that of Keith - the only known living male descendent from the founding father of Brindleys. By this means, in a very short time we should be able to re-unite the disparate Brindley strands worldwide.

THE END

Appendix 1
Some Wartime Brindley Deaths in Service of their Country

<u>Extracts from the Commonwealth War Graves Commission website</u>

Arthur Brindley, Private, Royal Army Medical Corps, died 29th September 1915.

Adam Brindley, Private, Royal Fusilliers, died 14th March 1916.

Albert Brindley, Corporal, Sherwood Foresters (Notts & Derby), died 21st March 1916.

Albert Brindley, Private, Herefordshire Regiment, died 26th March 1918.

Alfred Brindley, Stoker 2nd Class, Royal Navy, died 18th January 1918.

A. Brindley, Private, Royal Berkshire Regiment, died 8th April 1918.

A. Brindley, Lance Corporal, North Staffordshire Regiment, died 4th November 1918.

Albert Brindley, Gunner, Royal Defence Corps, died 2nd October 1919.

Alfred Brindley, Flight Lieutenant, RAF, died 15th October 1942.

Albert Edward Brindley, Driver, Royal Field Artillery, died 23rd March 1918.

Anthony Harley Brindley, Flying Officer, RAF Volunteer Reserve, died 19th September 1944.

Anthony Leonard Brindley, Lance Corporal, Royal Corps of Signals, died 18th August 1946.

Charles Brindley, Sgt, Rifle Brigade, died 31st July 1917.

C. Brindley, Private, Royal Warwickshire Regiment, died 10th April 1918.

Cyril Arthur Brindley, Trooper, 24th Lancers, R.A.C. Died 9th June 1944.

Charles Leonard BRINDLEY, Private, South Staffordshire Regiment. Died 18th June 1917. Buried at Lijssenthoek Military Cemetery, Popeeringe, West Vlaanderen.

Charles S. Brindley, 2nd Lieutenant, Royal Scots Fusiliers, died 23rd April 1916.

C. William Brindley, Private, York & Lancs Regiment, died 14th March 1917.

David Brindley, Private, East Yorkshire Regiment, died 5th August 1916.

David Brindley, Private, Durham Light Infantry, died 26th April 1918.

David Brindley, Private, Duke of Wellington's (West Riding Reg.) died 29th Oct. 1944 in Belgium.

Eric James Brindley-Nicolson, V.C. DFC. Died 2nd May 1945; *Nicolson's Story* 1993 pub. Lisek On 16th August 1940 near Southampton, England, Flight Lieutenant Nicolson's Hurricane was fired on by a Messerschmitt 110, injuring the pilot in one eye and one foot. His engine was also damaged and the petrol tank set alight. As he struggled to leave the blazing machine he saw another Messerschmitt, and managing to get back into the bucket seat, pressed the firing button and continued firing until the enemy plane dived away to destruction. Not until then did he bale out, and when he landed in a field, he was unable to release his parachute owing to his badly burned hands. He was killed in action, Bay of Bengal 2nd May 1945. He was also awarded a DFC.

He was the only Battle of Britain VC and the only RAF fighter pilot to gain the award during the Second World War. Later, he achieved the rank of Wing Commander.

Presumably Brindley is his maternal name. His father was Christopher Charles Nicolson-Church.

E. Brindley, Private, North Staffs Regiment, died 5th October 1916.

Ernest Brindley, Private, Coldstream Guards, 30th November 1917.

Edward Brindley, Corporal, RAF\Volunteer Reserve, died 2nd July 1944.

Ernest Henry Brindley, Gunner, Dorsetshire Regiment, died 15th September1944.

F. Brindley, Rifleman, King's Royal Rifle Corps, died 30th June 1915.

Francis Bernard Brindley, Flight Sgt RAF Volunteer Reserve, died 25th July 1945.

Frank Ewart Brindley, 2nd Lieutenant, North Staffs Regiment, died 4th October 1918.

G. Brindley, Gunner, Royal Field Artillery, died 24th August 1914.

G. Brindley, Rifleman, West Yorks reg.(Prince of Wales Own), died 28th Nov 1917.

G. Brindley, Private, Gloucestershire Regiment, died 9th October 1918.

George Abraham Brindley, Marine, Royal Marines, died 18th February 1944.

G.F.W. Brindley, Lance Corporal, London Regiment, died 2nd October 1915.

George Harold Brindley, Private, Cheshire Regiment, died 3rd October 1915.

G.H.J. Brindley, Private, Essex Regiment, died 29th May 1918.

George William Brindley, Private, Grenadier Guards, died 15th October 1915.

Harold Brindley, Private, North Staffs regiment, died 28th April 1916.

H. Brindley, Sgt, The Queen's (Royal West Surrey Reg.) died 15th September 1916.

H. Brindley, Private, Sherwood Foresters (Notts & Derby), died 16th March 1918.

Henry Brindley, Gunner, Royal Garrison Artillery, died 28th October 1918.

H. Brindley, Company Sergeant Major, Manchester Regiment, died 22nd March 1918.

Harold Brindley, Private, Borders Regiment, died 29th March 1944.

H.J. Brindley, Signaller, Royal Garrison Artillery, died 16th November 1918.

John Brindley, Rifleman, King's Royal Rifle Corps, died 23rd May 1916.

John Brindley, Private, Northumberland Fusilliers, died 15th February 1916.

James Brindley, Private, Manchester Regiment, died 23rd April 1917.

J. Brindley, Lance Corporal, Royal Scots, died 28th April 1917.

J. Brindley, Engineman, Royal Navy Reserve, died 2nd May 1945.

Joseph Brindley, Private, Cheshire Regiment, died 31st May 1915.

John Brindley, Private, South Staffs Regiment, died 8th December 1917.

J. Brindley, Private, Sherwood Foresters (Notts and Derby Regiment), died 13th October 1915.

J. Brindley, Stoker 1st Class, Royal Navy, died 5th June 1915.

J. Brindley, Boatswaine's mate, Merchant Navy, died 2nd July 1940.

James Alfred Brindley, Civilian. Died 27th June 1944

James Bernard Brindley, Gunner, Royal Artillery, died 26th April 1943.

John Henry Brindley, Private, North Staffs regiment, died 21st March 1918.

John Lewis Brindley, Company Sergeant Major, North Staffs regiment, died 13th October 1915.

John Thomas Brindley, Corporal, Rifle Brigade. Died 23rd May 1916.

J.W. Brindley, Private, Royal Warwickshire Regiment, died 18th July 1916.

Joseph William Brindley, Private, Royal Marine Light Infantry, died 5th September 1918.

Kenneth Lindon Brindley, Sgt, 103 Squadron, Vol. Reserve, aged 20; son of Frank and May Brindley of Newcastle under Lyme, Staffs. [RAF memorial, Runnymede] died 18th October 1943.

L. Brindley, Rifleman, King's Royal Rifle Corps. Died 19th January 1944.

Martin Brindley, Private, Royal Irish Regiment, died 14th February 1916

Norman Brindley, Lance Corporal, London Regiment (Post Office), died 28th April 1918

N.F. Brindley, Corporal, RAF, died 17th April 1944

Philip Bernard Brindley, Aircraftman 1st Class, died 9th June 1940, body not found.

P. Brindley, Private, North Staffs Regiment, died 26 July 1915.

Roy Brindley, Private, Royal Army Ordnance Corps, died 13th June 1947

Ralph Brindley, Private, South Staffordshire Regiment, died 1st December 1914.

R. Brindley, Gunner, Royal Field Artillery, died 3rd June 1917.

Robert Brindley, Private, Sherwood Foresters, died 26th September 1917.

Roland Brindley, Corporal, Royal Engineers, died 28th April 1916.

Roy Hollick Brindley, Gunner, Royal Artillery, died 9th March 1944.

S. Brindley, Private, Oxford & Bucks Light Infantry, died 30th September 1917.

Thomas Brindley, Private, Leicestershire Regiment, died 6th October 1916.

Thomas Brindley, Corporal, Royal Warwickshire Regiment, died 9th October 1917.

Thomas Brindley, Corporal, Cheshire Regiment, died 9th August 1917.

Thomas Brindley, Private, South Lancs regiment, died 10th April 1918.

T. Brindley, Private, Royal Army Service Corps (Canteens), died 13th November 1920.

Thomas Brindley, Private, Gloucestershire Regiment, died 30th July 1944.

Thomas Francis Brindley, Private, Royal Welsh Fusilliers, died 20th July 1916.

T.F. Brindley, Armourer, Quartermaster Sgt. Sherwood Foresters, died 21st July 1919.

Thomas Henry Brindley, Gunner, Royal Field Artillery, died 20th September 1917.

Thomas Leslie St John Brindley, Private. Coldstream Guards, died 1st February 1915.

T.W. Brindley, Lance Corporal, The King's (Liverpool Reg), died 22nd June 1917.

Victor George Brindley, 2nd Lieutenant, RAF, died 30th August 1918

William Brindley, Lance Corporal, Sherwood Foresters, died 19th August 1917.

William Brindley, Private, Machine Gun Corps (Inft), died 2nd December 1917.

William Brindley, Private, South Wales Borderers, died 17th April 1916.

William Brindley, Private, Lancahire Fusiliers, died 2nd November 1918.

William Brindley, Fusilier, Royal Fusiliers (City of London Reg.) died 21st May 1944.

W. F. Brindley, Corporal, Machine Gun Corps (Inft), died 3rd August 1917.

William Henry Brindley, Gunner, Royal Field Artillery, died 30th October 1917.

William J. Brindley, Gunner, Royal Field Artillery, died 31st July 1917.

W.N. Brindley, Sgt, RAF Volunteer Reserve, died 3rd April 1941.

William Percy Brindley, Private, North Staffs regiment, died 26th September 1917.

William Victor Brindley, Rifleman, Rifle Brigade, died 22nd February 1941.

Extracts from the Avenue of Honour, Trees & Soldiers, Hotspur, Victoria, Australia. 1918 Memorial

Hugh McD. Brindley, 37th Batt, died on service. Tree No 12 planted by Mrs H. Hiscock.

James Gordon Brindley, 39th Battalion. Tree No. 13 planted by Mrs F. Fidler.

William Brindley, of A.I.F. Tree No. 29 planted by Miss C. Hiscock & Master Con. Brindley.

Thomas Brindley, 37th Batt. Tree No. 31 planted by Mrs R. Jeffries & Miss A.Jeffries.

John Herbert Brindley, AIF. died on service. Tree No. 33 planted by Mr C.S. Hiscock.

The planting took place Wednesday 2nd June 1918 at 2pm.

Appendix 2
Coats of Arms

There have been few Brindleys who aspired to Coats of Arms. The earliest one was used by Thomas Brinley, the Auditor, and his forebears. It was said to have been used by Lawrence of Willenhall in the 1500s. He inherited the right from the earlier Brindleys. An undated 17th century volume records the Crest of Brindley (A) as being: *A Lion's head erased Azure (Blue) ducally crowned Or (Gold)*. A marginal note records the Arms of Brindley to be: *Per Pale Sable (Black) and Or (Gold), a Chevron between three Escallops countercharged.*

Per Pale means shield divided by a vertical line. The scallop is the badge of a pilgrim often associated with pilgrimage to the Holy Land or perhaps participation in a crusade. It is also a symbol of St. James the Great, who is generally drawn in the garb of a pilgrim. As it is found in ancient heraldry as early as Henry III's time, it was probably suggested by the eastern pilgrimages. The Romans used the scallop as a fertility symbol. The chevron usually indicates participation in a battle. It is symbolically a broken lance.

The next Coat of Arms was granted on 11th August 1828 to Thomas John Brindley (B) of Chell House, Wolstanton. He was a grandson of John Brindley, the Potter of Burslem. The inclusion of the three scallop shells would appear to indicate that the Heralds accepted that his lineage was connected to the earliest Brindley line from Brindley in Cheshire. The grant also conferred the right to display the arms on his father James, as well as on Thomas John, and the other male descendents of his father. There were few male descendents after the next generation, and John Pargeter Brindley was the last qualifying male. He died in 1859, unmarried.

This next crest is unattributed and unauthorised but is mentioned in a 1920 book on Family Crests. It shows a Wyvern with a hand in its mouth. It is sometimes said to be associated with a red shield on which is a Silver Lion Rampant. (Probably the Arms of the Beaumonts (C))

Crest of Brindley (A)

Thomas John Brindley (B)

Arms of the Beaumonts (C)

Burke's General Amory (1884) has the following entry: The Arms of Brindley are given as: *Gules (red) a Griffin sergeant Argent (Silver). The Crest being: On a wreath of the Colours A Wyvern holding in the beak a Hand proper.* Some think there may be a link to Northern Ireland and the 'hand' of Ulster.

A lozenge was granted to a Susan Brindley (D) (William Salt Library, Stafford, date unknown). These were typically allowed to the widow of an entitled male, to be displayed at the funeral of her husband. Women are normally excluded from the right to bear or display arms.

Susan Brindley (D)

This next shield is quite complex and is that of Brindley of Wistaston (E), Cheshire. John Brindley (Generation 3) was born about 1325, and married Beatrice Brescy. Thomas Brindley, born about 1350, married Alice de Crewe. It seems logical to believe that this coat of arms was created for Thomas or his heir. Thomas's son was William of Wistaston and he married Margery Bulkeley. The probability is that the arms were for Thomas, since there is no heraldic reference in the shield to 'Bulkeley'.

It is officially described as follows: *ARMS - Quarterly 1 and 4. Per pale Or and Sable a chevron between three escallops countercharged [Brindley]   2. Quarterly, per fess indented Sable and Argant, is the first quarter a mallard of the second. [Bressy]. 3. Azure, a lion rampant Argent [Crewe].*   Seen in Randall Holme's collection 1424, fo 33. Harl. 1505, for 31 & Ormerod's.

Brindley of Wistaston (E)

The Brindley quarters are at 1 and 4 showing the three scallops and single chevron.

The last escutcheon (shield) was used by Grissell Sylvester (F) (née Brinley) for display at her husband Nathaniel Sylvester's funeral. Its provenance was not apparently 'approved', or authorised by the 'authorities', but as a daughter of Thomas Brinley, Auditor, she obviously assumed she was entitled to use it, and did so.

Grissell Sylvester (F)

Appendix 3
The 'Brindley Pedigree'

This was compiled by John Beavis Brindley, revised and improved by Harold Hulme Brindley. 21st century additions and pre-Brindleys are added by myself. This is necessarily a sample version, with many brothers, sisters and others left off. A complete tree would be too difficult to produce here - two full direct line pedigrees are shown. Some of the pre-Brindley data was from 1958 research undertaken by American Stokes families and deposited in the Library at Lenox, Massachusetts.

The Jarl of More near Mora and Koppabergsland, near the Norwegian/Swedish border, had several sons, the youngest of whom was Hrolf/Rollo the Viking. Rollo, with his followers, took by conquest what is now known as Normandy. After many clashes he made peace with the King of France in 911 and kept his land gains, becoming the Duke of Normandy. Ranuph de la Haye was one of his followers and from him came the following:

I would point out that 1) I have not established if William Beavis Brindley had children and 2) It can be seen that Keith and his son Thomas are the only proven male descendents of Brundelegh de Brindley from genealogical records

The Brindleys are a directly descending parallel line of the Stoke family who likewise take and share their descent from the De Praers common ancestor Ranulphus/Rani/Randle, Lord of Stoke, Cheshire, near Nantwich and Crewe, Cheshire. But whereas the Brindley' line (out of the Stoke line) was slow to get going, the Stoke' lines were spread all over the Country from the earliest times. They seemed to like putting the 'Stoke' name into various localities and properties. Hence we have Stokesay Castle erected by Picot de Say (Shay or Haye), a descendent from Ranulphus de Stoke, Stokes Castle in Shropshire, North and South Stoke near Bath. Stoke Haul (hall?) at Seend, near Calne, Wiltshire, and Stokesley in Yorkshire. There are more than fifty place names in England that include the 'Stoke' component. Most can be linked to this famous and ubiquitous family.

The modern spread of
Brindleys in 2001.

Geoffrey Lord of Rie, Normandy
|
|
Eudes of Normandy =
|
Hubert de Rie, Normandy = Albareda de Preaux
near Bayeux.

Ranulph/Rani de Praers = (1)dau of William de la Ferte (Feritate)1087M   Eudo
1038 B. Lord of Stoke   (2) Alicia Newhall de Chester 1100M

Gilbert de Stoke = Isolda Brereton   Richard. Matthias. Roger. William.
| 1084 B   1086B
Brundelegh de Brindley   =   Geoffren
| |
Piers Brindley of Brindley =   Chief Justice
| Under Henry I.
John Brindley of Brindley = Beatrix Brescy   dau of John
Born 1325 abt
|
Thomas Brindley of Wistaston = Alice de Crewe dau of David
Born 1350 abt

Hugh 1370B   William Brindley = Margery Bulkeley of   John = Alice Wythers
              1375 born abt   Wolstanwood   1377B
              of Wistaston   about.
|
Thomas Brindley of Wistaston = Katherine Venables of Kinderton, dau of Piers
Born 1400
|
John Brindley of Wistaston   = Margery   2nd John = Elizabeth Crewe
Born 1425 abt

Thomas 1450B   Christopher of Bradnop   Marjorie   Joane
=   =
Margaret Holford   Elizabeth Palmer

James 1487 born   Stephen, Wyldegoose Hse, 1484 born
=   =
Cycylie Morris   Katherine
|
John 1520 born of Eaves Kingsley
=   Lawrence 1522B
Alice Wythers   Of Wilenhall
| =
Richard 1548 born of Kingsley   Alice Flecher
=
Alice
|

|

John 1580 born Eaves, Kingsley

=

Elizabeth

|

John 1615 born Eaves, Kingsley

=

Mary Whywall

|

John 1640 born abt Died Alton 1716

=

Edith Hollins 1672M at Leek

|

John 1684C 16.10 at Kingsley

=

Ann Heath 1714M 29.10 at Dilhorne

|

John 1721B 16.09 at Kingsley

=

Jane Whitehurst

|

Whitehurst 1758 born of Hanchurch

=

Mary Stoke/Stake 1784M 2.12 Trentham

James 1803 born of Newcastle U L	Francis Hicken 1795B 7.2 Trentham
=	=
Mary Beavis	Elizabeth PHIPPS
John Beavis 1827 born Middlesex. 1st Recorder of Hanley	THOMAS 1831B Birkenhead
	=
=	Jane KELLY 1852M
Mary Brough	
	Francis 1858B
	=
Harold Hulme 1865 born	Hannah Mary COLLEY 1882M
=	
1. Roberta Froggatt Brindley	Thomas Frederick 1829B
	=
	Violet Scott 1923M
Beavis William 1901 - 1941 and Dorothy M.	
	Frank 1923B
	=
= 2. Maud A. Haviland	June M. Stansfield
Avice Haviland	Pauline Frances Keith D.

Mary   Thomas   Martha

Appendix 4
Further Brindley Pedigrees and Photographs

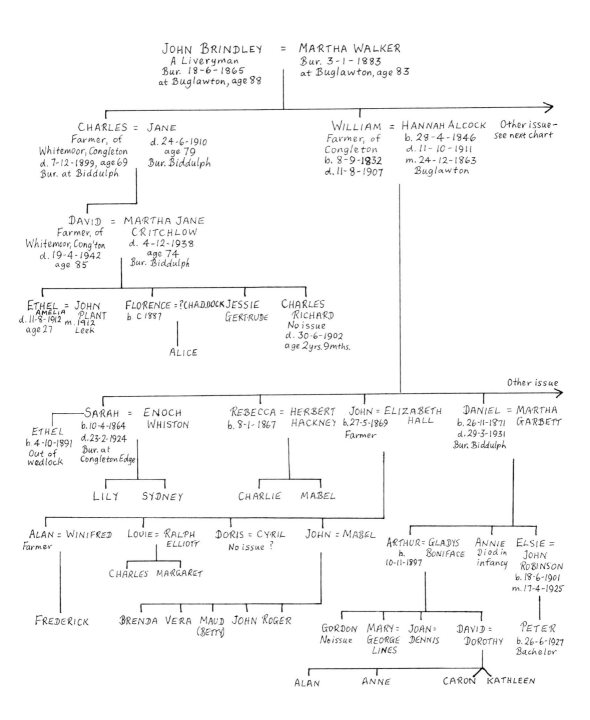

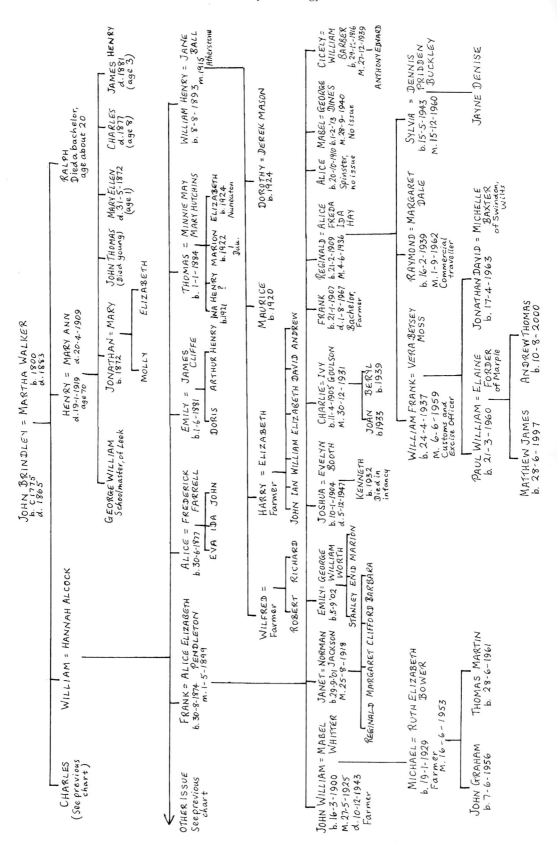

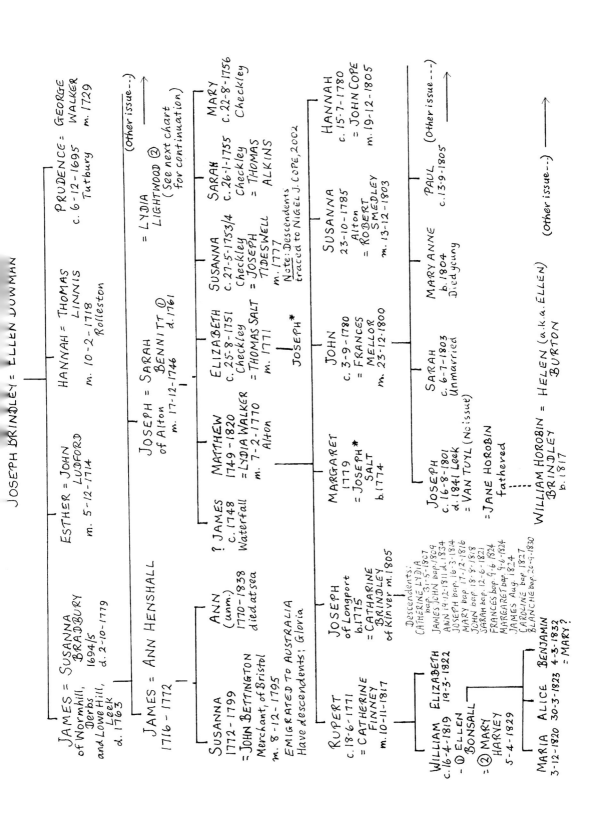

JOSEPH BRINDLEY = ELLEN DOWMAN

JAMES = SUSANNA
of Wormhill,   BRADBURY
Derbs   1694/5
and Lowe Hill, d. 2-10-1779
Leek
d. 1763

ESTHER = JOHN
          LUDFORD
       m. 5-12-1714

HANNAH = THOMAS
          LINNIS
       m. 10-2-1718
          Rolleston

PRUDENCE = GEORGE
c. 6-12-1695   WALKER
Tutbury   m. 1729

(Other issue---)

JAMES = ANN HENSHALL
1716 - 1772

JOSEPH = SARAH   BENNITT ①
of Alton   d. 1761
m. 17-12-1746

= LYDIA
  LIGHTWOOD ②
  (See next chart
  for continuation)

SUSANNA
1772-1799
= JOHN BETTINGTON
Merchant, of Bristol
m. 8-12-1795
EMIGRATED TO AUSTRALIA
Have descendents; Gloria

ANN
(unm.)
1770-1838
died at sea

?JAMES
c. 1748
Waterfall

MATTHEW
1749 - 1820
= LYDIA WALKER
m. 7-2-1770
Alton

ELIZABETH
c. 25-8-1751
Checkley
= THOMAS SALT
m. 1771

JOSEPH *

SUSANNA
c. 27-5-1753/4
Checkley
= JOSEPH
  TIDESWELL
m. 1777
Note: Descendents
traced to NIGEL J. COPE, 2002

SARAH
c. 26-1-1755
Checkley
= THOMAS
  ALKINS

MARY
c. 22-8-1756
Checkley

JOHN
c. 3-9-1780
= FRANCES
  MELLOR
m. 23-12-1800

SUSANNA
23-10-1785
Alton
= ROBERT
  SMEDLEY
m. 13-12-1803

HANNAH
c. 15-7-1780
= JOHN COPE
m. 19-12-1805

MARGARET
1779
= JOSEPH*
  SALT
b. 1774

JOSEPH
of Longport
b. 1775
= CATHARINE
  BRINDLEY
of Kinver m. 1805

JOSEPH
c. 16-8-1801
d. 1841 Leek
= VAN TUYL (No issue)

= JANE HOROBIN
fathered

SARAH
c. 6-7-1803
Unmarried

MARY ANNE
b. 1804
Died young

PAUL   (Other issue---)
c. 13-9-1805

(other issue---)

WILLIAM HOROBIN = HELEN (a.k.a. ELLEN)
BRINDLEY   BURTON
b. 1817

RUPERT
c. 18-6-1771
= CATHERINE
  FINNEY
m. 10-11-1817

Descendents:
CATHERINE LYDIA
  bap. 31-5-1807
JAMES JOHN bap. 1809
ANN 19-12-1811 d. 1834
JOSEPH bap. 16-3-1814
MARY bap. 17-12-1816
JOHN bap. 18-8-1819
SARAH bap. 12-6-1821
FRANCES bap. 9-6-1924
MARGARET bap. 9-6-1924
JAMES Aug. 1824
CAROLINE bap. 1827
BLANCHE bap. 26-9-1830

WILLIAM   ELIZABETH
c. 16-4-1819 14-3-1822

- ① ELLEN
    BONSALL

= ② MARY
    HARVEY
  5-4-1829

MARIA   ALICE   BENJAMIN
3-12-1820 30-3-1823 4-5-1832
                     = MARY?

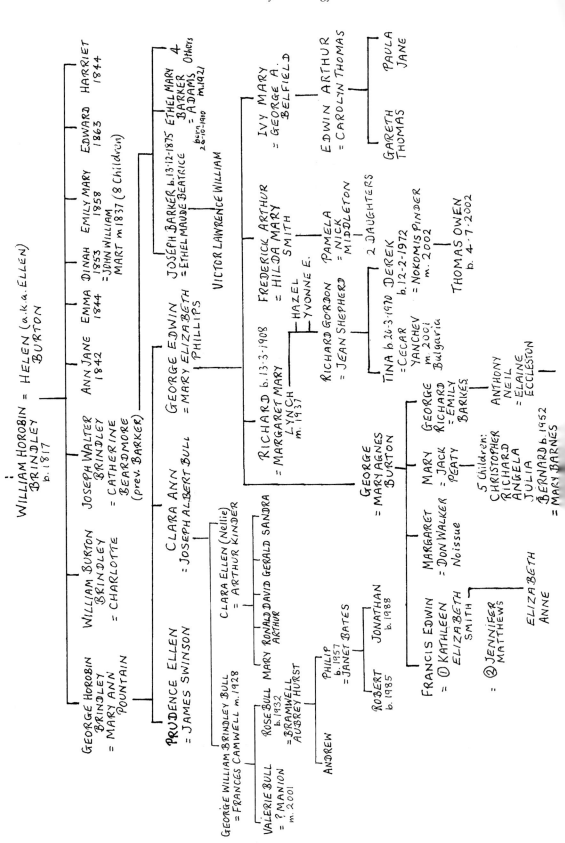

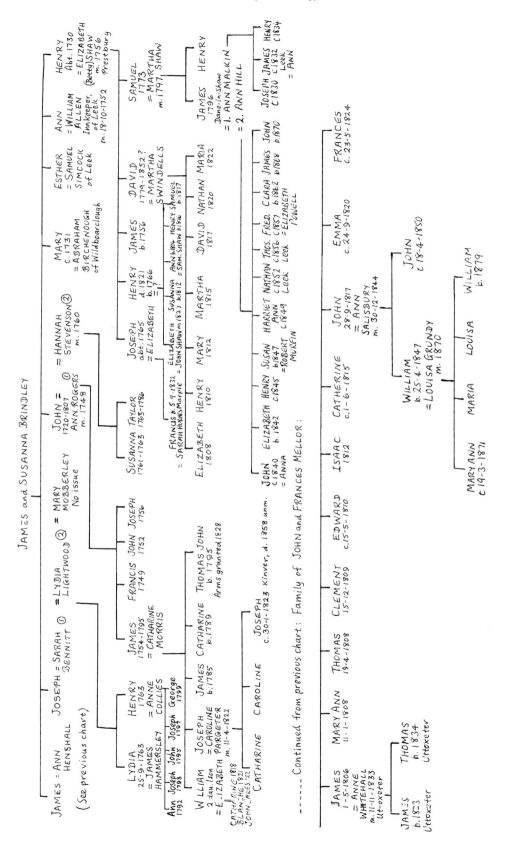

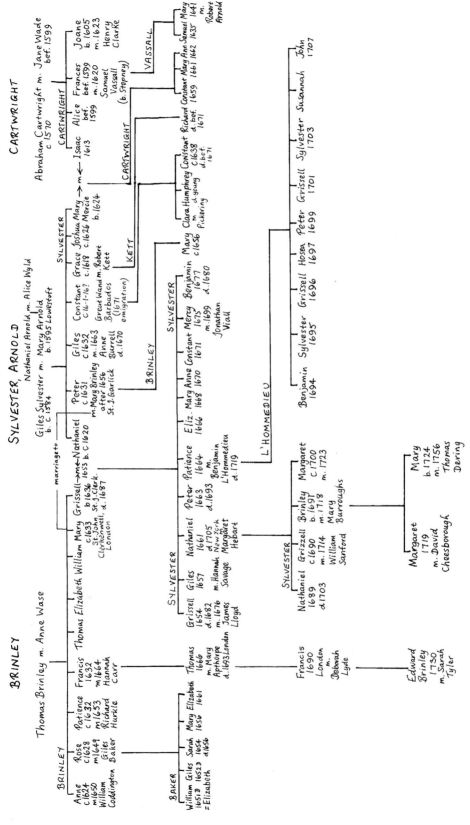

DESCENDANTS OF ANN BRINDLEY

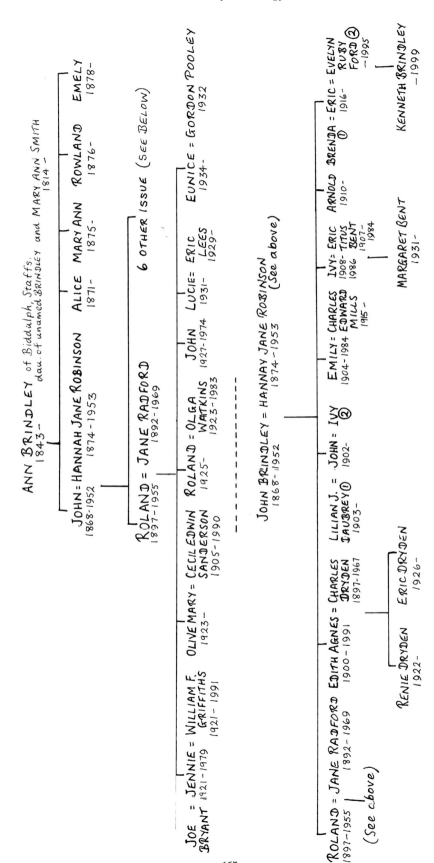

ANN BRINDLEY of Biddulph, Staffs,
1843 – dau. of unnamed BRINDLEY and MARY ANN SMITH
1814 –

JOHN = HANNAH JANE ROBINSON   ALICE   MARY ANN   ROWLAND   EMELY
1868-1952   1874-1953   1871–   1875–   1876–   1878–

6 OTHER ISSUE (See BELOW)

ROLAND = JANE RADFORD
1897-1955   1892-1969

ROLAND = OLGA WATKINS   JOHN   LUCIE = ERIC LEES   EUNICE = GORDON POOLEY
1925–   1923-1983   1927-1974   1931–   1929–   1934–   1932

JOE = JENNIE = WILLIAM F.   OLIVE MARY = CECIL EDWIN SANDERSON
BRYANT   1921-1979   GRIFFITHS   1923–   1905-1990
1921 – 1991

JOHN BRINDLEY = HANNAY JANE ROBINSON
1868-1952   1874-1953   (See above)

EMILY = CHARLES EDWARD MILLS   IVY = ERIC TITUS BENT   ARNOLD   BRENDA = ERIC = EVELYN
1904-1984   1915 –   1908-1986   1907-1984   1910–   ①   1916–   RUBY FORD ②   –1995

KENNETH BRINDLEY
–1999

MARGARET BENT
1931–

LILIAN J. = JOHN = IVY
TAUBREY①   1902–   ②
1903–

ROLAND = JANE RADFORD   EDITH AGNES = CHARLES DRYDEN
1897-1955   1892-1969   1900-1991   1897-1967
(See above)

RENIE DRYDEN   ERIC DRYDEN
1922–   1926–

157

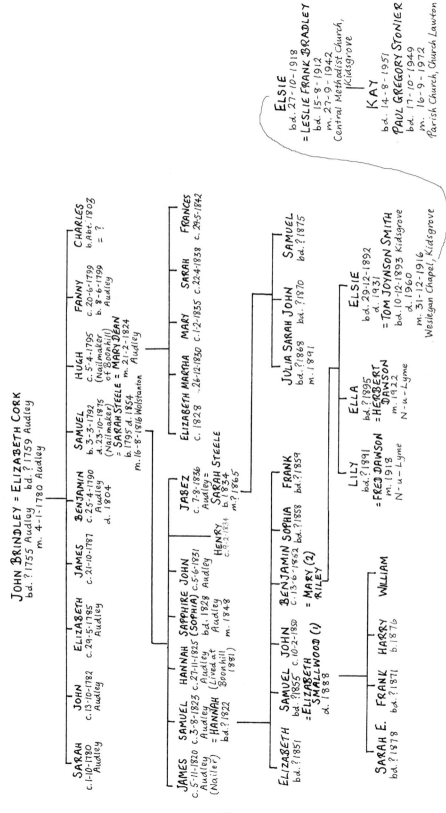

INDEX

Thomas Owen Brindley b. 2001